Skewed

I'M NOT BIPOLAR, I'M AN ASTRAL TRAVELER

A Memoir

Kris Rock

Copyright © 2022 by Kris Rock.

ISBN: 978-1-957009-31-5 (sc)
ISBN: 978-1-957009-32-2 (e)

Library of Congress Control Number: 2022902917

All rights reserved. No part of this book may be reproduced, stored, or transmitted by any means—whether auditory, graphic, mechanical, or electronic—without written permission of both publisher and author, except in the case of brief excerpts used in critical articles and reviews. Unauthorized reproduction of any part of this work is illegal and is punishable by law.

Contents

Preface 1
Introduction 9
Diagnosis 15
Acceptance 17
Compliance 21
Pseudonyms 27
Bipolar at Birth? 31
A Childhood Illness 33
Meditation and the Aliens 37
A Horrid Child 39
An Imaginary Friend 41
Naked in the Corn Field 45
The Wicked Witch and Her Mate 49
Lonely and Aware 53
Many Homes 55
I See Star Street 57
Pink Pills 61
Shots 63
Summer Vacation 67
Crimson Beaver 71
Dance Class 75
Adventures in the Civil War Ruins 77
A Normal Family Life 81
Beginnings of Skewedness 83
Twitterpated 87

Seventeen	93
Summer Nights	97
Leaving Home	101
My First Real Friend	103
Easing in to Breaking In	107
I Fall in Love Again	109
The First Time	113
Repressed Memory	121
Sex, Drugs, and Rock-'n'-Roll	123
Garden of Eden	127
Group Hallucination?	131
Movin' On	133
Chicago and Independence	135
Revolution	143
On My Own and Looking For a Job	145
Life at Freddie's	149
South Side	161
Back to School	167
Meds--Yes or No?	169
The Dig	173
Wedding	191
The Outlaws	201
Beautiful Baby	205
Kassie	211
Blue Baby	219
Donne	225
Postpartum Blues	229
Let's Move Again	231
House Hunting	235

Swap 237
Walden Pond 243
Escape and Help from Friends and Family 251
Stormy Weather 255
Getting Fit 261
Charlie 263
Blue Collar Work 265
The Refinery 267
Blue-eyed Jim 273
Off to School 275
Do You Drive Trains? 277
A New Way of Thinking 281
I Betray My Sister 285
Disconnected 293
Crash and Burn 295
You're Sick! 307
Recovery, Sort of 313
Starting Over, Again 317
Head-Butting Dad 321
Menotony, MI 323
Down Then Up 329
A Great Job and a Married Boyfriend 331
Problems 339
Office Politics 343
Sexy Babe 345
House by the Tracks 349
Business Trip 365
Hard at Work 367
The Morning After 379

Sex at the Thunderbird 383
Test Results 387
Easter and Abortions 389
Pregnant and Happy 391
Playing with Matches 395
Cheating 401
NASA Langley Research Center 407
How Could Work Possibly Be More Boring? 409
Super-Conducting Supercollider 413
Kris in the Valley 417
Moving Back Home 425
Sex, Drugs, and Rock-'n-Roll, Again 429
Psychiatrists—Bah! 431
Cornucopia 435
S. Divinorum 439
Little Yellow House 443
Coming Down 445
An Aluminum-Head's Journey to Ozzfest 2007 451
Feeling Better and Back on Meds 457

Preface

As a Bipolar Type 1 person, I have spent most of my life in a manic blur, working and playing as fast and hard as my body would allow. Type 1 is the version of bipolar disorder that is characterized by moods that are mostly high. If I ever found myself depressed, which wasn't often, I usually took on a new and fascinating course of study to distract me from my sadness and lethargy. In grade school, I read voraciously. In high school, I worked to get good grades and win contests. In college, I took courses as diverse as anthropology, mechanical engineering, math, business, German, Russian, English literature, journalism, physics, and nursing. I took so many courses that I would be hard-pressed to remember anything I learned in any of them. I earned nearly 500 college credits and attended 13 different universities. I was the epitome of the perpetual student. I kept depression at bay by fleeing away from it as fast as I could both mentally and physically.

I was a tomboy in every way possible. I played every sport that was going on in the neighborhood: football, baseball, and basketball were the most popular in our town. If nothing was going on, I organized games for the hordes of kids always hanging around our house. We walked, ran, and rode our bikes for miles around. In high school, I played intramural sports and danced in the popular annual talent show. When I wasn't busy or reading, I was studying. I never just "hung around" friends or family, and I rarely watched TV.

About the only time my mania wore down was when I picked up some disease or other, like an earache, bronchitis, or once, mumps. Of course, I probably got sick because I had worn down my immunity by abusing my body pushing myself too hard. In any case, when my mania wore me down to the point where I couldn't go on any more, my body would run out of energy to continue on its frenetic pace, and I would crash bigtime. Because of the crashes, I have rarely finished any course of study. I used mania and hypomania to get me going on a goal, and when my mood cycled down and I wore out, I would have to drop out of what I was doing because I couldn't get out of bed anymore, and my mind was too cloudy to understand what I was thinking.

Fortunately, I have been able to accomplish some things along the way, namely raising three terrific children, who all turned out fine. That was mostly because my parents were so generous with their time, energy, and resources and helped me out when I was not functioning. I did work for most of 30 years as a technical writer, and I enjoyed the first ten of those. The last ten were mostly drudgery and I performed them just barely and only for the paycheck needed to support my little single-parent family. I tried to switch careers after that, but the results were nothing less than a total disaster, and I retired at the age of 58 and went on social security disability due to my illness. When I was hard-pressed to support myself on $1150/mo, I moved back in with my father, who was lonely, physically failing, and couldn't drive anymore.

For five long years, my meds didn't seem to work very well. I mostly slept, read, and smoked. I must have done something else. I put my first book together. I took care of my dad. I tried to take on a few easy jobs that I was fired from. I'd love to tell you what else I did, but I don't really remember. I felt low on creativity, spontaneity, and overall happiness. I was content, but not really living. I was like a racehorse let out to pasture after the racing days were done. I wasn't unhappy, but I wasn't satisfied either. I played a lot of Scrabble on the computer.

Then one day I finally asked my doctor to try me out on a new medication. I was sleeping until 2 p.m. every day and staying awake until 6 in the morning. I was missing out on life, and suddenly, I wanted to be back in the swing of things again.

We decided to try me on Geodon, an atypical antipsychotic. The problem was that it wasn't covered on my insurance plan except in the liquid form. I'd either have to pay $800 a month for the tablets or learn to inject the liquid into a deep muscle myself twice a day.

To my own wonder and surprise I chose the injections. Up until then I had fainted at the sight of needles coming near my body. But I've always enjoyed a good challenge. This was to be more of a challenge than I realized, though.

The injection method wasn't all that straightforward. You had to go through a terrific rigamarole just to mix up the solution and get it into the little bottle. Then you had to transfer the liquid to the syringe, just so. I couldn't inject myself in the arm or the buttocks, so my only choice was to slam the needle nearly as hard as I could into the meat of my thigh. It hurt like hell. You had to get it straight in, too, or it hurt even worse. This was not a pleasant experience. I'll tell you what, though. My brother's wife watched me do it the first time, and from then on, she and my brother were finally convinced that I was serious in my efforts to get better. When they saw me go through that painful routine, they knew I meant to be well. It was particularly important for them to know, because during my last manic episode I had viciously attacked my brother's wife and had screamed obscenities at her, all for a very minor reason. She had accused my father of being incompetent with his money matters and had wanted to take over his finances. For some reason, that had infuriated me. I didn't like to think of my father as incompetent, so I attacked her. The family never really accepted that I was bipolar until that incident.

Anyhow, I bore with the Geodon injections twice a day for ten days. They cost me all of $6.00. Unfortunately, I couldn't inject enough of it to keep me from getting manic. I felt terrific. In fact, I felt more than terrific. I was manic as hell. I went shopping every day using my father's credit cards. I cleaned every closet in the house and the whole basement. I replaced all the sheets, towels, pillows, curtains, bedspreads, and throw rugs. I bought a new used car. The house was sparkling. I was having a blast. I edited my book four times and prepared it for publication. I moved the furniture around. I invited people over a bridge party. I probably even cooked nice dinners. I bought some clothes and new shoes. It was clearly time to find a new medication, even though I couldn't have felt better.

I had tried another medication in the atypical antipsychotic group once before called Abilify. At ten milligrams it caused me to pace endlessly. I had paced back and forth, forward and backwards, to and fro, all day and all night long. My mind had raced. I couldn't settle down. It seemed a strange reaction to a drug, but I wasn't manic exactly. I just couldn't calm down. I stopped the drug after two weeks of constant pacing. My new doctor suggested something brilliant that I can't believe my previous doctor hadn't tried: he simply cut the dose in half. It worked like a charm. The first week after being on 5 milligrams of Abilify I was sleeping 6 hours a night from 12 at night to 6 in the morning and taking an hour nap in the afternoon from 2 to 3. This schedule has almost never wavered for the last five years. Abilify was like a magic drug for me from the very first day I took it. When the manufacturer stopped making it for a brief time this spring I stopped sleeping again. As soon as I was able to get the generic form I started sleeping again and am back on schedule.

After going on Abilify, my moods have absolutely stabilized to the point that I no longer feel I have a mood disease anymore. I also take an antidepressant, Cymbalta, which reduces my arthritis pain. I also don't feel any side effects from any of the drugs that I am aware of. I don't feel that dampening of moods that I did with the Seroquel, lamictal, lithium, Zyprexa, and several others. I am finally in that nirvana state of being successfully treated for a mental illness with drugs that do not have bad side effects for me. I am one lucky mother!!Fk!R!!

It took me a long time to figure out what medications were good for me and to know when it was time to change them. I never allowed the doctors to perform electroshock therapy (EST) on me because most of my life I worked full-time and supported children, and I couldn't afford to destroy even a few of my brain cells. One doctor assured me that the after-effects of EST would be very mild and that I might be "cured" after one series of treatments. I'm glad I did not take him up on his offer to shock me into normality. I like both my long- and short-term memories.

After the 40 years since my diagnosis, I finally feel like I have some tools to survive this disease. I can only take it on faith that I will able to keep on feeling the renewal of my creativity, happiness, and productivity in light of the previous dampening effects of mood-leveling medications. As of now, it's all coming back slowly, but piece by piece, more and more each day. I'm finally awake again. I can turn my radio up full volume. I just don't know if I'm ready to hear it yet!

I have taken up duplicate bridge playing, begun swimming almost daily, and started an editing/ghostwriting business to keep my mind and body occupied. Best of all, I am writing for myself again, gloriously, naturally, creatively writing. I feel like I've come alive again after a long spell of unconsciousness. In these books I hope to show some of the ways I have defeated my manias and depressions and stayed alive, unlike many of those who have chosen nothingness over pain. My disease is not gone, but I have come close to controlling it by following a strict medication regime and maintaining eternal vigilance for signs that portend either up or down episodes on the way. I feel like I am ready to face the past and, in doing so, attempt the control of my future.

A diagnosis of bipolar disorder does not have to mean a life sentence in a mental jail.

I have divided my experiences into three volumes, which delineate three different aspects of my illness: mania, depression, and recovery. I tell the story of me as an energetic and adventuresome child who begins to experience mania and depression after a concussion I sustained in a high school gym accident. The moods, mostly mania, get worse and worse until the age of 33, when I was diagnosed in a psychotic manic state after staying up for a month straight while attending engineering school in 1983. Next, I talk about my midlife crisis, where I experienced my worst depressions and my unhappiness with the treatments available for bipolar disorder, which seemed to steal all my creativity and strong feelings from me. Finally, I describe how I come back to life after discovering an effective medication regime that has a minimum of side effects and few or no obvious dampening effects on my natural moods and feelings. Whether you are suffering from the disease yourself or you have loved ones with the illness, I recommend that you read this book to see how I overcame the obstacles I faced. No one could have been more stubborn and hard-headed than I was when I first heard I was bipolar. If I can overcome this illness and take meds to treat it, you can, too.

Introduction

By the time I was 50 I had been committed to psychiatric wards four times, attempted suicide several times, divorced twice, roved from job to job and home to home, subjected myself to analysis by dozens of therapists and psychiatrists, used sex and drugs freely as needed to control my moods, took dozens of psychotropic medications, slept with 100 men and women, and spent several fortunes. To top the whole thing off, I had been labeled with all of the following at one time or another: psychotic, paranoid schizophrenic, ADHD, obsessive-compulsive, bipolar, depressed, alcoholic, addict, and just plain fucked up. I also managed to have three children whom I took care of by myself. Sounds impossible? Well, it was. I learned to put on a good face in most social situations. People who didn't know me well thought I was a normal person. Underneath my friendly exterior I was a dragon lady, a monster, a criminal, an addict, or a slug. Which character I played depended on where I was on my mood-swing spectrum.

Was I just a spoiled, well-off girl trying to get attention? That is what my family thought when they heard my diagnosis. They could believe anything except that I might really be mentally ill.

I've been writing this book for years. Writing has been my best therapy in spite of the thousands of dollars I've spent on mental health care. I started keeping journals back when I was about 24 and newly separated from my first husband. By now, after all these years of frenetic activity and struggles to keep myself and my children alive, I'm happy and carefree most days; but I often wonder if a life that is merely happy is enough. A heroin addict is perfectly happy every day, as long as the drugs keep coming. For years after I quit uppers and downers on top of all sorts of other psychotropic drugs I was broke, out of work, owned very little except books and movies, drove twenty-year-old cars, was unmarried, had no close friends, and was facing the empty nest syndrome.

So now that I am stable for the time being, what do I have left to look forward to? No one talks about mentally ill people once they are stable. Stability is great, but what happens to thrills and excitement, monstrous ups and downs, and the adventures that come with a skewed mind set? The hardest adjustment for any bipolar person who is now "cured" is finding meaning in a "lesser" kind of life and satisfaction in the smaller details of living. A bipolar person, more than other people, needs a substantial goal to work towards, something attainable yet complex. Without a goal, I feel scattered and aimless even while feeling mostly happy and content. It's a conundrum.

There is hope for me, as I see it. I can finish this book. I can watch my kids grow up. I can see my father into a ripe old age.

I never thought about how I would feel when the weight of the world and its responsibilities was off my drooping shoulders. I never realized that my worst struggles in old age would be fending off boredom and lethargy every day. Many days I feel like I'm swimming through mud. I feel that I must find something exciting to do or I will drown in the sucking depths of this psychic pool of quicksand.

Is it normal for a stable bipolar person to feel that without the manic moods life is going to always seem somehow depressing? I keep thinking some great inspiration is going to be revealed to me that will add something important to the world. That hasn't happened so far. I'm realistic enough to realize that probably only two or three people will read this book. Yet I go on for my own benefit.

With the kids gone, I'm getting used to life alone. No six meals a day to prepare, no constant picking up of random items strewn about the house, no chauffeuring duties, no heart-to-heart talks about who has a crush on whom, and most of all, no telephone calls at irregular intervals throughout the day and night. No fighting over who gets the car, no anxious vigils waiting for the sound of the tires crunching in the driveway. No buying ice cream flavors I don't like. What did I ever do before I had children? I feel guilty because I'm not busy all the time.

What shall I do with all these free hours? I find ideas muddling around in my brain like oatmeal boiling in a big black pot. I still think about UFO's. According to Whitley Strieber in *Communion* and his other "non-fiction" books, I ought to be a prime candidate for visitation from the little gray creatures. I hallucinated as a little kid, had an imaginary evil twin, saw a huge giraffe-like creature chasing me down the street every time I rode in a car, and had some pretty convincing paranormal experiences such as making small objects move. Large blocks of time have disappeared from my conscious mind. All these events happen to people who are visited or abducted by aliens, according to Strieber. So where are the little creatures, anyway? Of course, these experiences are also shared by many of those people kindly termed the mentally challenged, or more coarsely, the loonies of the world (of whom I'm really not one).

I have to admit, I wouldn't mind being hostess to alien visitors. I'd serve them beer and lasagna for dinner. Don't they know where I am? So I've moved fifty times since I was born. Don't they have mail forwarding or at least e-mail?

At this point of my life I'm searching for something more than just thrills. I'm not into No More Nukes, Save the Animals, or Down with Capitalism. The psychiatrists continue to label me with long, ominous-sounding names. I accept that I must take pills every day for the rest of my life, but often I suspect that these meds and potions are giving me an excuse to be a failure. I am not going to let that happen. Even though I am stable, boring, uninspired, and un-manic, I have work yet to do.

Forgive me, dear family. I hope you won't kick me out on my ear after I spill the beans on all the family skeletons. I think the truth is going to emerge at last whether you like it or not. I would love to have your approval and enjoyment of what I have written, but I suspect you will be somewhat horrified instead. It's my turn to fly freely again like my own personal totem the butterfly, creating a haze of purple and pink and blue in the airy sunlight. My story is ready to burst from its sheltered home, and perhaps I will escape, erratic and flighty, but genetically blessed with a strong and accurate homing instinct. My real home is not geographic in any way, but rather a quiet place in my mind, or perhaps in the "collective" mind. Perhaps there I'll meet the aliens.

When I jokingly mentioned these thoughts to my latest therapist, she came up with my favorite diagnosis of all, "You're not bipolar; you're an astral traveler." Makes a helluva lot of sense to me!

Diagnosis

I was diagnosed with bipolar disorder in 1983 in the middle of a horrible semester in engineering school at the University of Minnesota. When I received the diagnosis I was stunned, horrified, and dazed. I felt as though someone had hit me over the head with a baseball bat.

If you have been diagnosed with a major mental illness you know what I am talking about. First you feel disbelief followed rapidly by denial, anger, shame, and finally depression. Particularly if you are high functioning, as many bipolar people are, you think the doctor must have made a tragic mistake. Then you begin to look back on the events of your life and finally you realize that yes, perhaps you have experienced more dramatic mood swings and have gotten in more trouble in more drastic ways than almost anyone you know. You haven't functioned well for large periods of time. Finally, you were so miserable that you were forced to seek a doctor's care or you were involuntarily committed to a hospital or jail. At that point you are told that you are sick and that you will have to take meds for the rest of your life.

"Are you kidding me?" was my response, and I'm sure it was yours, too. There's nothing all that wrong with me. Still, I breathed a sigh of relief that perhaps there was help for me out there after all for my "minor" mood problems.

In an ideal world no one would be labeled as mentally ill. After all, no one would ever say "I am a cancer" or "I am a heart disease." However, in the mental health groups I have attended you are encouraged to fess up to your disease as though that's all you are, as in I am alcoholic, schizophrenic, or bipolar. It's demeaning and depressing to think that way. I denied my illness for many years because of the way mentally ill people are treated in our society. Ultimately, though, I have come to accept my illness through years of therapy, medications, and support from friends and family. It's not easy to do.

Acceptance

Compared to many people with mental disorders I haven't had such a bad life. Along the way I experienced long periods of lucidity. I read thousands of books. I supported and counseled many mentally ill people who were in trouble. I am happy now most of the time, and I take my meds as prescribed. I can almost say that extreme mood swings are in my past.

On the other hand, at times I behaved in ways intolerable to conventional society. If I wanted to buy a gun I wouldn't be able to do it legally. If I was on trial for murder I could be declared not guilty by reason of insanity. At one time I was deemed an unfit mother, and my child taken was away. I was incarcerated in a mental institution against my will. I spent long periods addled by drugs of many kinds, and I took drugs with teenagers. I slept with mates of my family members, married bosses and numerous random people. I squandered several small fortunes and gave away my earthly possessions any time I owned any. I attempted suicide in ways that I never should have survived.

In some societies bipolar people have been called shamans or visionaries. But mostly we are more likely to be labeled with derogatory terms. No one expects a mentally ill person to be responsible or capable of doing anything worthwhile, unless you happen to be a gifted artist, musician, painter, or writer. In that case, you are expected to have a disastrous and lonely life that will most likely end in suicide even though you might produce a few dazzling works of art along the way.

In today's world the term "mentally ill" brings with it a sense of shame and failure. I have a strong sense of lacking the tools for a functioning life without handfuls of pills that I must take daily and at regular intervals. I always feel on the edge of disaster even when I've been stable for a long time. I have to watch myself closely and ask whether what I am doing is appropriate or whether I'm making choices that will send me over the edge, again. I voraciously read autobiographies of other mentally ill people so that I can find new ways of dealing with my disease. One of the reasons I decided to write this book is so that other bipolar people can learn from my mistakes.

If you have been newly diagnosed with a mental illness you are probably feeling worthless, depressed, and angry. At this point you have some soul searching to do. You might not want to take meds though everyone around you will want you to take them. The best thing you can do is to work with a doctor to find meds that work for you. Remember, the meds are supposed to make you feel better, not worse. Many medication side effects will disappear after a week or two. If they don't, you will have to weigh the benefits versus the results. It's not easy to commit to taking meds for the rest of your life, but you do want to have a life, don't you?

If you are a long-time pro at being bipolar chances are you are on meds. If not, your chances for survival are not that great.

Compliance

Almost no bipolar person truly believes that she needs meds all the time. Many of us experience long stretches of normality. By normal, I mean we function. Otherwise, we might be at either extreme of normal; exceedingly bright, charming and successful, or on the other end dazzlingly criminal and bad-tempered. Whatever we do, we do it intensely. Let's say we experience a time of stability and we are convinced we are finally cured or at least well controlled on meds. Then one day an exciting new lover comes along or the robbery that is going to set us up for life. The thrill of our venture motivates us to dream of a glorious future. We think about how ecstatic we will be when our ship finally comes in and we are ultimately happy forever at last and won't need meds anymore.

We are so thrilled we can't sleep, and our new plans have excited us so much we throw ourselves into more adventures. The world is suddenly coming together for us, all our previous questions suddenly appear to us with answers, and lights are going off in our minds by the second. We have just gained forty points on our IQs. No subject of study is too hard for us. No creation is beyond our ability. We are the very best at what we do.

People want to be around us, and our social life improves. We make new friends. But mostly we set our eyes on our thrilling new goals. We are so organized and focused that people around us label us geniuses, sure to succeed, and deserving of that fabulous new job with benefits. We create brilliant poems, novels, symphonies, songs, companies, paintings, essays, operas, and scientific breakthroughs; in fact, most of the best things in the world come from the minds of the hypomanic person.

Of course all the worst things come from them, too: war, murder, rape, theft, manipulation, pedophilia, and all kinds of mental and physical destruction of other people and things. I don't really know, but a subtle imbalance in the brain chemicals determines whether we are going to be "good or evil." Since it's pretty hard to "make" a person bipolar, I have to believe that this illness is set in the genes.

If we have access to cocaine or amphetamines, we ingest, snort, inject as much as we can tolerate and still appear for work in the morning. To sleep we might drink massive amounts of alcohol that really don't seem to have much effect on us. We take sleeping pills but they don't work. We turn to painkillers and those work but we need more and more of them until to get enough we have to obtain them illegally. When we do sleep it is hell waking up. Where is the Adderall or cocaine? And then where is the Klonopin?

Our sex lives improve to the point where everyone seems like a new conquest. Since we are so sparkling and attractive, finding sex partners is no trouble at all. Friends of our spouses, our siblings' spouses, or our bosses; in fact, no one is really off-limits. We can't help it if they fall in love with us.

Even our parents and psychiatrists might not be immune to this seductive sexuality.

We jump from normal to hypomanic in a subtle manner so that even we don't know what's happening. Some people can function in this hypomanic mood for weeks, months, or years.

Then comes a time when we haven't gotten enough sleep or eaten enough of the right foods; have taken too many drugs or drunk too much alcohol; have smoked too many cigarettes and too much pot; have spent all our savings and maxed out the credit cards; when everyone has found out who we were sleeping with that we shouldn't have been; when all the members of the opposite sex around us are either terrified because we have propositioned them or sneak out with us illicitly; and when we have gotten involved in some slightly or maybe not so slightly illegal activities.

Suddenly we don't feel so well any more. Our heads are pounding with pain. Our stomachs are bleeding. We have diarrhea or else don't eliminate for weeks. We are always sick with something or other. We realize we are in trouble but deny it second by second as we continue the downward spiral. We are so tired we fall asleep at the wheel or just fall over.

Then people around us are no longer helpful but simply annoying. In fact, we can't stand for anyone to be around us to interrupt our creativity and brilliant thinking. We yell at them derisively to straighten up their acts, and we tell them exactly what we think they should be doing. In fact, they are all a bunch of idiots.

They don't like this, and they don't react well. They don't want to be around us anymore; in fact they will cross the street to avoid seeing us. At our work we begin making big mistakes and our bosses confront us. We belligerently tell them it is someone else's fault or that they are being unreasonable. We get fired.

As we begin to get more and more irritated, all of the smooth successes and good messages from the universe switch to frustration and a feeling that things are not going to work out right. We try to force good outcomes but suddenly our thinking isn't very clear. We can no longer do our jobs or be good parents or finish that novel or song. In fact, nothing we do is right. We forget what seemed so clear earlier, even things that we have done for years. In fact, we have forgotten all the studying, preparation, and organization that have brought us so far. We are discouraged that our high goals are getting further and further away.

Now we are not only irritable but also angry and depressed that things haven't worked out again. We drink more, take all sorts of drugs to make us feel better, smoke fiendishly, and seek sleazy entertainments. We can't stand being around normal, happy people. They just don't understand our genius, our uniqueness. No one understands us. We have what one friend calls "terminal uniqueness."

Our doctors are quacks and thieves. We can't trust anyone. Our old friends are so flawed we don't see them or talk to them anymore. We hit or lash out at people who try to help or indicate criticism in any way. Our grand projects are piled up randomly on our desks or in a box. We stink because it is too much trouble to take a shower. We revel in our illness. Nothing we do brings us back to those moments of ecstasy that we remember so well. We can't get to sleep, and when we are awake we feel like the living dead.

In fact, by now even sex brings nothing but numbness. If there were a chocolate sundae or a naked lover across the room we would not get up. We can't read more than a few minutes before we find ourselves rereading the same paragraph again and again. Stupid annoying songs like "Jesus Loves Me" or "You Light up My Life" play constantly in our heads, and we can't shut them off. Our thoughts change subject by the second, and we can't concentrate on any one of them at a time. Finally, the only thing that feels good is a dead-out, extended period of sleep. If sleep doesn't come easily we take downers. All the downers we can get our hands on. We sleep 16, 18, or 20 hours a day. We are totally isolated. People leave us alone because of how mean we have been to them in the past. We either gain or lose a hundred pounds. When we are awake we write depressing poems or very sad songs. Occasionally something brilliant even comes out of this mood.

At this point we think, "Should I stay or should I go now?" Those who can't take it anymore generally choose a dramatic exit. The others of us sleep until the sun comes out and the chemicals change ever so slightly in our brains.

And it begins again. Like the movie *Groundhog Day* only without the happy ending.

When I am tempted to call myself misdiagnosed and I decide that psychotropic meds are not for me, I remind myself of some of the bumps in the road. I decide to take my meds faithfully.

Naming Myself

My maiden name is Kristina Kay Estebo, and I've always disliked that name. When I met, lived with, and married Eugene Frederick Rock, the choice was clear: my new name would be just Kris Rock. Not only is it a very cool name, but now I have the same name as the world's funniest comedian, though he spells his Chris Rock. Thank you for making my name memorable, if nothing else!

In real life, I'm Brunhilde with a huge bosom, spreading hips, a stern furrowed brow, and a jutting chin that I lead with during arguments. I used to be a lovely, slender, natural blond. My combination German-Norwegian heritage has made me more a survivor of disasters than a seducer of men; I am a combination Viking, prairie-settler woman. Definitely manic-depression fits in with the seasonal work schedule of early Midwest farmers, and maybe I inherited that tendency from my farmer ancestors. You can see why I might wish to be imagined as other than I am in light of society's current love for the thin and wispy and beautiful.

Most of the things I have written herein are true; I have used fictional names as I don't wish to hurt or offend the characters I have included. If I had my choice I would use the name Maya Angelou, the most beautiful name in the world, but it was already taken.

Sometimes I feel like Palaniuk's unique and delicate snowflake with a short attention span, one that has been whirled up from the midst of a raging blizzard and never lights down before being blown on to the next destination. Unlike that snowflake, though, I intend to survive the storm and imprint my identity on these pages.

Every time I sit down to write a book I end up completing a catchy new beginning then halt, feeling as if I have really accomplished something. I have written half a dozen good introductions just waiting for the rest of the book to follow. Unfortunately, my concentration is such that what usually follows is a small part of the middle without an end in sight. I've never finished a book yet, and I don't have much hope for finishing this one. However, I seem to have found a medication that works well for me, and I have been stable for almost fifteen years now. Maybe I will be able to pull everything together today or soon and slay this monster. In any case, the act of writing it all down is soothing and perhaps even self-healing.

This story is about a woman who attempts to find stability, productivity, and love in her life. She isn't very successful, but there are hints that everything will turn out right in the end.

I dedicate this book to my friend Henri, the person who ruined me for conformity. After him, I could only have chosen a path towards an artistic life. For a long time I blamed him for setting me on this bipolar path.

It's not really his fault, I know; it would have happened anyway. But it started with him. I'll make sure he reads this book sooner or later. I know he will be looking for the juicy passages, and I hope he won't be disappointed.

Bipolar at Birth?

I was an unmanageable toddler. I walked and talked early and could eat a whole steak by the time I was one. I was the kid who jumped into the deep end of the swimming pool when mother's back was turned, who ran into the street in traffic, who climbed out of her crib before she could walk, and who basically could drive a nervous mother into debilitating asthma attacks with her behavior.

There is a lot of discussion these days about when bipolar disorder begins and how it manifests itself in children. Danielle Steele has written eloquently about how early her son began to display signs of a mood disorder in her book *His Bright Light*. Much as I hate labeling children, I started out in the womb being hyperactive and mood-challenged. If your mother says that even in the womb you were restless, hyperactive, and didn't let her sleep, the reason could be that you were bipolar at birth. Of course, I am not a doctor, and I only know what I have observed and experienced. If you have been diagnosed bipolar it might be worth looking back on your childhood for early signs of the illness. If we could diagnose bipolar children early, we might be able to save a lot of heartache and damage to families by starting treatment early. That does not necessarily mean drugging children, but employing behavioral therapies that might work even better.

A Childhood Illness

My mother was a California girl and did not relish the prospect of life in the land of ice and snow. For love she followed her husband to the UP of Michigan where he had gotten a job as a plant engineer for a large paper company. She worked part-time as a clerk while they saved up money for furniture, a refrigerator, and a new car.

I was born when my parents were in their mid-twenties. When my mother found out she was pregnant she bought a bizarre little Pekingese puppy to celebrate. All my baby pictures show both me and Dinky dog.

One winter day in 1952 my daddy took me sleigh riding in the deep snow of a Michigan winter. I had a bad cold, but that didn't prevent us from staying outside for several hours and sliding, sliding, sliding. My first memory comes from what happened afterwards.

I was in a cavernous white room dimly lit and full of distorted shadows. A loud speaker squawked in the distance. A dozen cribs were aligned in neat rows; I was aware of the acrid smell of fresh urine. All around me were toddlers and screaming infants incarcerated in the barred baby beds. Mother was nowhere to be found.

My black-haired co-patient Maria lay in the crib across from mine. Maria was allowed out of her bed to sit in the small rocking chair at the end of the room. It wasn't fair. I was able to crawl out of my crib at home to play but the bars were too high here. They wouldn't let me rock in the blue and white chair, and that made me mad.

I was alone for a long time, and then a big fat nurse wearing a black and white dress came to change my diaper and give me a shot. I thought of myself as a Big Girl—I had been potty trained for over a year. Still, the doctors wouldn't let me out of the crib, and I was forced to wear diapers, which seemed all wrong. I couldn't get out to pee or even play. I screamed when the nurse stuck me with the needle. I was alternately burning up and freezing, and my throat felt like burned toast. I couldn't breathe right, and I coughed all the time.

The nurse came back again and again. She would wipe a spot on my bottom with a cloth that smelled funny, like daddy's mouth after he drank those "martunies." She stabbed me there with the long needle, and I howled in pain like Dinky dog when somebody stepped on his tail.

When mother was there she held me down for the shots. I hated her for that; I wanted her to take me home to my own bed. I screamed and cried and kicked the nurses, but even more people came to keep me still. I wanted to rock in the chair and get out of that horrible place and away from the mean people who were hurting me and holding me down and making me stay in a baby bed. Though I didn't have a rocking chair at home, I wanted to be home with my Dinky-dog and my Billy baby, and I wanted to go sleigh riding some more with my daddy.

One day Maria wasn't there anymore, and I got to rock in the chair. It felt so good to be out of bed, and I rocked like crazy and ran around the room. After I knocked over the chair, the nasty nurse put me back in the crib.

"Let me out," I screamed, but no one came to take me away.

. . .

I was resilient, and I pulled through the double pneumonia seemingly without lasting damage. It is no mystery why I have always been deathly afraid of needles. During my recovery, I remember looking out through the bars of my crib and feeling that life was strange and unpleasant, hardly to be borne. One of the more destructive people I foolishly allowed into my adult life suggested to me that the 107-degree fever I suffered from the illness might have caused permanent damage to my young brain, because brain cells don't regenerate, you know. Some people look for any reason to cut you down, and I've had a few of those in my life.

I always think I can keep these vampiric people out of my life, but sometimes attack comes from unexpected directions. My father believed that I was never quite normal after the high fever, that though I didn't die some damage might have been done. Otherwise, I would have been his perfect golden girl, which I really wasn't in the long run.

Meditation and the Aliens

Plenty of perfectly normal people believe in aliens these days. They say you don't have to be particularly special in any way to receive a visit from them. Some people think they visit you when you are very young and perform tests on you or give you special powers.

I'm not a genius, an artist, or a mover and shaker of any kind so I don't see any reason why the alien bosses would have sought me out. I do have an exceptional imagination, though. Maybe my early bout with pneumonia shaped my brain in some unusual way. The fever might have actually enhanced rather than hampered my powers of creativity.

Maybe after my illness I had a meeting with the Higher Ones who gave my mind a little push. I have often wondered if the little people took me for a while. Perhaps they are hovering nearby, waiting for the right opportunity to take me back. Or are they somehow a part of me and we will be integrated for the rest of my life here on earth? Do I have a hereafter with them?

If I did meet those Higher Ones I have certainly forgotten about them long ago. But I do remember one morning when...

I was three. I had the measles and was shut up in a darkened room so as not to damage my eyes, as mother said. A wedge of morning light streamed through a crack in the Venetian blinds. I was bored to death.

I concentrated on watching the sunlight and found that if I closed my eyes halfway and looked through my eyelashes, strange little objects began to dance across my field of vision.

The objects were round or oblate, shimmering white, and clearly outlined with a black ring. They looked amazingly like small, glowing fleets of UFOs. The groups would dart quickly past my eyes and keep on coming as long as I had the patience to watch them. Later in life, I would decide that I had been seeing dust motes floating in the sun-drenched air or possibly neuron transmissions in my brain. My optometrist says they are called floaters and are actual physical manifestations in the eyes. Everyone has them, but I think I might be the only three-year-old who ever noticed.

It didn't matter to me at the time what they were. Watching these funny little dots racing past my line of vision served as a hypnotic method for allowing me to enter a deeper part of my mind; in other words, to perform a rudimentary kind of meditation.

A Horrid Child

"No daddy, no. Don't sing that song. NO, NO, NO. I hate that song; I hate it (Daddy laughs)."

> There was a little girl
> Who had a little curl
> Right in the middle of her forehead.

"No, don't sing that! I hate it when you sing that. And don't tickle me!"

> And when she was good
> She was very, very good;

"I'm good, I am. I'm so good!"

> And when she was bad
> SHE WAS HORRID.

I knew what horrid was. Horrid was when you threw mom's new hat in the toilet. Horrid was when you pinched the baby. Horrid was when you opened a Christmas present early. Horrid was when you pulled Dinky's tail. Horrid was when you lay down in the middle of the street and played dead. Horrid was when you ran away to the park with Jeff. Horrid was when you took your clothes off and played in the corn field naked with the other kids. Horrid was when you tied Derek to a sheep.

I knew I was horrid. "YOU DON'T HAVE TO REMIND ME!! IT'S NOT FUNNY!"

I wanted to go hide in the woods.

Being horrid was why the giraffe man came; to remind me how very bad I was. I felt that my parents didn't like me very much most of the time. They seemed to be always mad at me.

An Imaginary Friend

After I learned to meditate but before I went to school, I developed a fear of getting into cars, especially back seats. My parents bought a new gray Chevy sedan in 1952 to celebrate Dad's first promotion at the paper mill. Mom was busy taking care of a new baby and adjusting to a new town. Every morning she would drive dad to work so she could keep the car during the day. After the baby was strapped into the front seat, I was free to roam the back.

Off we'd go! The back seat was a huge territory, with a house full of room. I could stretch out on the floor for a nap or I could use the seat as a trampoline. Mom was far, far away, on a different planet almost, as though we were in a taxi with a clear but impenetrable barrier separating front from back. On one of these drives the giraffe man first appeared to me. It was a hot golden day in August 1952. My hair was stuck to my face and my hands were sticky with pink bubblegum sugar.

I was napping comfortably on the back seat floor. The floor smelled of cinnamon candy and smog. Suddenly I heard the sound of sharp, loud hoof beats on the pavement a block or so in front of the car. I could see the heat waves rising from the cars. What's... a horse doing in the road?" I thought dreamily.

The sounds got louder. I shouted for mother's help, but she didn't seem to hear me. How could she not hear those thundering sounds?

Against all my better instincts I peeked up over the back seat and watched the horse weave in and out of traffic towards our car. How odd. I quickly ducked back down and hoped he would go away. Then his beaming face was at my window, and he looked down at me.

He wasn't a horse at all but a towering yellow furry giraffe with large purple blotches and a long neck that leaned over the car. He had the legs, hooves, and body of a horse, which explained the clip-clopping noises. His face was long and rectangular with a high forehead and curly gray-brown hair brushed straight back. He was a part-human, part-giraffe anomaly. His bright white teeth were like the artificial choppers that snap at you in toothpaste ads. He wore big square black glasses and a fake smile like he was trying to get on my good side.

I tried to scream but the only noise to come out of my mouth was a little mousy squeak that didn't attract mother's attention in the least.

I shivered in spite of the morning heat, and my hands were shaking. I sensed that no matter where I went the giraffe man would somehow find me. He was as real to me as trees and flowers and in no way seemed imaginary. I was wide-awake and acutely aware of everything around me. I could suddenly see everything so clearly it was like looking through binoculars. I squinted at the monster and forgot about everything else in the world. The traffic noises quieted and then faded out entirely.

Out of the light the giraffe man stuck his head through my open window and looked directly into my eyes. "Hello, Kristy," he said, and smiled. "I've come to fix your teeth."

"What's wrong with my teeth?" I questioned indignantly. "They're white and straight, and I brush them most days."

The subject of my teeth was a sensitive one. Mother told me that if I didn't stop sucking my thumb, my teeth would all come in crooked and my chin would stick out, like the wicked witch's in *The Wizard of Oz*.

I knew I would never be able to stop sucking my thumb. Maybe this monster was a mixed blessing. If I could control my fear, in turn he would straighten out my teeth. Seemed like a fair trade.

Gathering all the courage of my three years, I addressed my new buddy, the giraffe man. He asked me to come closer to the window. "Open your mouth, Kristy," he demanded. I closed my eyes and opened my mouth. Maybe he'd give me ice cream or a piece of chocolate. He stuck his foot? arm? hoof? through the rolled-down window and shoved it in my mouth. I felt no pain or sensation other than a heaviness pressing down on my jaw.

Then he was gone. I was left with a funny bitter taste in my mouth and a sour stomach. His rhythmic clip clops receded from the car, and when I looked back he was nowhere to be seen. I named him the Ajax Man after the bald cleaning man in the TV commercials.

The Ajax Man visited me every time I rode alone in the back seat of the car. Sometimes I tried to hide from him; sometimes I resigned myself to his inevitable visit. I checked my teeth frequently in the mirror for subtle changes in alignment, but I did not stop sucking my thumb.

After a while I started throwing up in the car on our trips around town, and I developed throbbing migraines. I didn't drive much until I was twenty-five, after my first divorce. Later in life, my chin grew very long indeed, in the classic Norwegian way. I must not have fulfilled my end of the bargain with the Ajax Man. I didn't remember him until my freshman year in college when I was sleeping alone in the candle room of a church.

Maybe the Ajax Man was an alien, sent by the exalted leaders to analyze me and compare my body functions to their own biological processes.

. . .

Lots of kids have imaginary playmates, so I can't say that my hallucination of a yellow and purple giraffe was a red flag for early bipolar disorder. I can't say that it isn't, though. I wasn't a bad tempered kid like many bipolar kids, but I was stubborn as all hell. Normally, I refused to do anything I didn't want to. As I look back on my childhood I can see that many of my experiences are common to other children who have grown up to be bipolar.

Naked in the Corn Field

The first time my mother went to the hospital in Massachusetts was to have the baby who was to become Janie. She was a fussy, noisy, irritating baby. She almost never slept; the household was always in an uproar when she was awake.

Instead of playing with this imperfect, whiny creature, I played with my Billy doll, the only doll I could ever tolerate. Billy was a quiet, cooperative boy who had a porcelain face and wore a long white gown. He went with me everywhere.

One day Billy baby disappeared. I suspect that mother finally threw him away when he got old and unsightly. My friend was gone, the household was in chaos because of the new baby, and I needed an escape.

Although I don't remember, my mother says I developed another imaginary friend at this time: an evil twin called Bad Kristy who lived deep in the woods and only showed herself at opportune times. Bad Kristy was responsible for all my naughty behavior. She would sneak into the house, perpetrate a crime, and then slink back out to her home in the forest, leaving me with the blame for her misbehavior. Fortunately for my family, she went away after I made a real friend, Jeff, who lived up the street.

Jeff introduced me to my first manic feelings. He had older brothers who picked on him, so he was meaner and more streetwise than I was. He had ideas for having fun that I would never have imagined but that I embraced wholeheartedly.

Jeff knew a secret place where we could go to avoid siblings, parents, and other fearsome or annoying adults. The secret place was in the cornfield. We felt safe in our hideaway. The corn stalks towered over us and formed a thick barrier from the rest of the world. We thought that no adults could find us there.

One warm summer afternoon I took my special path to the secret place and found Jeff and several friends already there. They were all naked and were examining each other's bodies, peering closely at one area then touching and probing another. They told me to join them, so of course I did. What they were doing looked very interesting. We formed a human ring, each child looking and poking at the buttocks of the person in front. All the other children were boys, but I never got to see the parts on the front. Maybe I just didn't notice anything unusual.

Our play was suddenly and rudely interrupted. We heard the crackling and tearing sounds of crushed cornstalks. Jeff's mother had found our hideout. Her mouth twisted with disgust and horror as she pushed her way into our private clearing. None of us could figure out why she was so mad. We hadn't done anything wrong; we were just investigating a very interesting subject: our clean, unblemished bodies.

She screamed, "Get your clothes on right now." She jerked my arm and turned me around for a stinging swat on the butt, then ordered me to get my clothes on and go home immediately. As I hastily pulled on my underpants, shorts and top, she gave the final and worst injunction, "You may not play with Jeff anymore." I was confused and ashamed, of what I didn't know. I had lost my best playmate and only human friend.

One morning Jeff sneaked over to my house and invited me to set off for a real adventure. We decided to run away together. Several miles from the neighborhood was a wonderful park with a beach, sailing ships, and best of all, a roller coaster and other carnival rides. Jeff knew how to get there, and we set off. Unfortunately, Jeff could run much faster than I could, and he quickly outpaced me. I cried for him to slow down, but I think he needed to run away more than I did. After all, look at how mean his mother was. He ran as fast as he could. I had lost him by the time I got to the park. Without my friend to share the excitement, the fun was gone. I wandered around miserably, trying not to cry.

I saw an old ship pulled up on the beach. Where could I go on that boat? Across the ocean? I looked at the roller coaster and realized I was too scared to ride it. It was time to go back home without Jeff. I didn't know the way exactly, but we hadn't made any turns off the main road. I started running and when I got home I went straight to my room to be alone again.

The Wicked Witch and Her Mate

I never realized how beautiful my mother was until I watched the 1949 movie *A Letter to Three Wives* and saw that my mother in her mid-twenties looked exactly like the actress Linda Darnell. My mother's eyes were closer together but she had the same tall, stately, and curvy body as Darnell's and lovely brunette hair arranged in rolls that swept back from her face, emphasizing her jade eyes. My father was jauntily good looking too, in that tall blond Norwegian way, with lazy blue eyes and a strong jaw.

Together they made a very handsome couple.

I can't recall either of my parents ever asking me how I felt about anything. I was encouraged to think but never to show any actual emotions except for happiness and good cheer. It didn't take me long to figure out that bad feelings were embarrassing and best kept under cover. What a cruel twist of fate and how ultimately disappointing it was to them that I turned out to be bipolar, with a range of moods and emotions they never seemed capable of and certainly never showed us. I almost feel as though I created the disease in myself as my way of rebelling against a mode of living that was repressive and stifling.

I also never realized how my mother's asthma affected her until a few years ago when I came down with pneumonia and suddenly and unexpectedly I couldn't breathe. I wanted to bring her back from the grave and tell her how sorry I was that I could never understand how frightening life is when you have to struggle for every breath. I know now why she took Prednisone for fifty years: it was the only way she could live without feeling like she was drowning.

My father lived to 89, and he was never full-blown crazy, exactly. More like he was hypomanic for his whole life. Whatever he did he did obsessively and with huge amounts of energy.

Being around someone that cheerful all the time was like being in a room with a flock of chirping birds. It was not unpleasant but more distracting than anything. The last thing I want to hear when I'm trying to write, watch a movie, or just be alone is someone raving about the hummingbirds at the bird feeder, how huge and tasty his garden tomatoes are, how it's sure to rain tomorrow, how well he did at bowling, or how adorable his dog is.

When he came out of his room in the morning, with his fly unzipped and his hearing aids out and that goofy happy grin on his face, sometimes I wanted to leave the room immediately before he turned the TV on full blast and get the hell away from the hurricane of his cheer. On days when I was feeling good, I just grinned back and said, "What's up for today?"

I always wanted my mother to be like Glinda, the Good Witch of the North. I wanted her to sing, "Come out, come out, wherever you are," the way Glinda sang in the city of Oz. I wanted to dance around her, shouting and laughing with the cheery munchkins. I wanted her to have good magic that she would use to make the world a better place. She would do away with monsters, big winds, thunderstorms, snow drifts, undertow, and especially dark and scary nights.

To me it seemed as though I had gotten instead the Wicked Witch of the West, Glinda's evil sister, even if mom was beautiful and did not have a long chin. My mother was the wolf dressed up as grandma. My mother's home was the oven disguised as a gingerbread house. My mother sold poison apples on the side for spending money. My mother sent me out to buy food with a shriveled bean.

She couldn't really have been all that bad. Exaggeration is second nature to me. Still, I didn't think of her the way other kids seemed to think of their mothers.

Lonely and Aware

In 1955 I started school. The teacher was old and had short white hair. There was nothing great about school. The teacher kept putting my pencil in the wrong hand. I learned to read, slowly. I got to be the Virgin Mary in the school play, but when I was up on the stage I forgot my lines, and the teacher was yelling in a loud whisper for me to pick up the baby Jesus and say my part. I looked out over the stage and saw a sea of laughing faces. I felt hot and ashamed. Suddenly everything went black, and I couldn't see the stage or the people anymore. The laughs were silent. What a relief to have escaped from that horrible embarrassment.

Many Homes

My father was an executive at a large paper company, and in the '50s in America, getting promoted usually meant moving around the country often. We were on our third move when I went to second grade.

Then grandma and Uncle Daniel came for a visit, and my arm was in a cast. I know, because grandma took a picture of me, and I was so proud; it was my first day of second grade, and mother had bought me a book bag. My arm was in a cast, because I tripped on a rock and fell on broken glass. I had tried to hold the skin together, but the blood gushed all over my clothes. We had to go to the doctor and have him sew up the cut. I got 20 stitches.

I hated my mother, but I decided she was right about sucking my thumb. I finally stopped in the middle of second grade. After that I bit my nails, picked scabs, squeezed zits, and ritualistically destroyed other convenient parts of my body. I didn't stop these nervous tics until much later, when I discovered drugs that calmed me down.

My younger brother and sisters were great targets for my aggression, especially my brother Derek. I often pounded on him unmercifully and scratched bloody streaks down his back with my jagged, bitten fingernails. I had to watch out for my two sisters, though, because Janie was a hellcat when she was mad (most of the time), and Belle was sneaky enough to throw hot water on you when you were asleep.

I See Star Street

By 1955 my younger siblings and I loved to do two things in the car: singing and yelling. We recognized the street we lived on and had a contest over who could see our street first. Whoever saw it first had to shout out, "I see Star Street," and keep screaming it at top volume until we reached the driveway. We sang the songs we knew as loudly as we could: "God Bless America", "My Country 'tis of Thee," and "Jesus Loves Me." Later we sang "Leavin' Ole Texas" and "The Autumn Leaves." These harmless activities might have driven dad to early deafness, but they did foster family spirit and also made me forget how scared I was to ride in the car. We needed extra family spirit in those days, because mother was in the hospital, and we had to go to somebody else's house for a while in the daytime.

When the world got to be too much for me, I opted for escape. I could always find somewhere exciting and frightening to run away to. When I ran away I got lots of attention. Once I lay down in the middle of the street and pretended I was taking a nap. The lady who found me asleep in the street thought I was dead. Wasn't she surprised when I woke up and winked at her? After a while, I didn't need to run away to get attention anymore. All I had to do was hide behind a chair and wait for mother to notice I wasn't around.

Mother nearly died in the hospital the year I was four, but a new drug invented that year at the Mayo Clinic in Minnesota saved her life. The drug was Prednisone, and it was used to treat her asthma. No one knew about its horrible side effects then. Mother took the drug for almost fifty years, even though her condition progressively worsened. Prednisone is as addicting as heroin in its own nasty way. Its side effects are almost too numerous to mention, but they include mood swings and violent behavior, brittle bones, paper-thin skin, destruction of the body's immune system, a tendency to cause diabetes and heart disease, easy bruising, cataracts, and a myriad of other symptoms. Sooner or later, my mother suffered from all of them.

Through the years mother also experienced a lot of what anyone outside the family would call psychotic episodes. She experienced the same problems as her daddy that led him to the Washington State Mental Hospital. The bottom line is that the Prednisone kept mother alive all those years, even though it turned her into a monster some of the time. She might have been called bipolar but she would have died before going to a psychiatrist.

The drug didn't prevent occasional bouts of severe asthma that threatened to take her life. Talk about attention-getting devices. No wonder I learned to hide and play dead in the street. We kids learned that we had a certain amount of power over mom when she was sick, and we could even make her sick by being bad and getting her upset. She was still the boss, though, even when she didn't feel well, and we learned to avoid her as much as possible.

Pink Pills

During mother's long recoveries from her asthma attacks, dad tried to help out by taking us fishing on the weekends. The first time he took all of the kids, Janie and Derek were fighting over who got to bait the hook with the squiggly worms. Janie swung at Derek with her little bunched-up fist, missed, and flew off the dock into the ten-foot-deep freezing water. Of course she wasn't wearing her life jacket. Dad had to jump in the lake with all his clothes on to rescue her. He was pretty mad, but he kept on taking us fishing. The fishing trips usually lasted all day long. Our fishing spot was near the carnival, where I ran away with Jeff.

When mother came back from the hospital, she brought home some small round pinkish-orange pills. She stored the pills in the same cabinet as the one where she kept the candy treats for us. My favorite candies were the little colored buttons you peel off a strip of shiny white paper. The candies were different colors: pink, blue, green, and yellow. The pink candy buttons looked exactly like mom's pills. One day we were playing doctor. I got a chair and took all the pink candies from the long paper strip in the cabinet and then carried them into our "sickroom." I told Janie that she was very ill, and I gave her some of the candy "pills" to cure her. We also had a stash of other candy, and Janie happily ate every last piece of it. I went off to check my other "patients."

Then mother was yelling for me, screaming in that voice which warned me to get out of her way, quickly. I ran to the refuge of the woods and dug in behind a bush for a while. The woods felt so empty, though, and I was getting hungry. I kept thinking about all the candy Janie had eaten, and I wanted some, too. I walked nonchalantly back into the house. Mother grabbed me and dragged me into the bathroom, where Janie was crying in the bathtub. Mother had been washing vomit out of her long, fine hair.

"Look what you did to her! You've killed her," my mother shrieked at me. Janie didn't look dead to me, but maybe I was missing some important clue. I asked what was wrong with her. Now mother was sobbing. "You fed her all those pills. You've poisoned her. She's sick as a dog."

Mother had confused pink-pill with pink-candy vomitus. You couldn't really blame her. I tried to explain that I hadn't touched her pills, and that I knew the difference between candy and medicine. I didn't want to admit that I had taken the candy. That was breaking the rules and an equally bad breach of conduct in my mind as poisoning my sister. When mother got mad, who knew what might happen? So I didn't bother to straighten her out about the candy, and Janie didn't die after all, because candy is rarely fatal. I was banished to my room, a place I was coming to hate with a passion. I fought my loneliness by becoming a voracious reader. Reading is still my best escape.

Shots

I got my first booster shots at school in second grade. All the kids were forced to wait in a long line for their turn to get poked in the arm. The doctor had set up a small area in the hallway, and the kids were herded through the line like calves to the slaughter. I didn't think much about what it would be like to get a shot, but I had a feeling of dread about it. I didn't consciously remember the hundreds of vicious shots I had gotten when I was a two-year-old with pneumonia in the hospital.

Our class was at the very end of the line. A girl who had gotten her shot walked by us looking wounded. "It wasn't so bad," she said to me bravely. I could tell she was lying.

My hands started to shake, and then suddenly my mind was no longer in control of my body, which attempted to flee from the scene. One of the more perceptive teachers intercepted me and led me to the front of the line. The nurse gave me the shot; it hurt like heck. The kind teacher led me back to my classroom, but I couldn't see because everything had gone dark. I woke up with my head on the desk and my whole body shaking violently. I couldn't even write my own name.

As I got older, my fear of needles only got worse. By fifth grade, I was 5'4" tall and I towered over my diminutive pediatrician. When I fainted the doctor neatly folded me over his shoulder and carried me to an examining table. I rested while the adults hovered over my prone body.

Fainting was a wonderful and effective response to my fear of sharp, intrusive objects. Just before passing out I would be totally transported from the present threatening situation to a wonderful dream world. Unconsciousness came as a blessed relief. I would remain in this fantasy world until consciousness returned, usually only a few minutes later, but seeming like an eternity. The side effects of waking up from a fainting spell were not quite so pleasant: nausea, dizziness, and disorientation. Nonetheless, escaping to the dream world was like taking Valium and was the only thing that made getting a shot a bearable experience.

The next time I fainted was at home. I was a seventh grader by then. I had a deep splinter in my hand from a thorn bush in the yard. A round, ulcerous area had formed around the penetration point in the soft pad at the tip of my finger. Mother got out a long sewing needle and began jabbing away at the small infection. I started to feel the familiar dizziness, ringing in my ears, nausea, diarrhea, and the sense of being in a dark tunnel while receding speedily from the room. A sharp, Band-Aid, adhesive smell assaulted my nose, and I felt myself floating to the floor. Only I didn't really float; I fell straight forward and hit the floor hard, forehead first.

I woke up with a headache and a large rug burn on my face. My family teased me unmercifully about fainting from being stuck by a tiny darning needle. They kept at me until I cried, and even my younger sisters seemed to enjoy my discomfort to no end. I didn't see what was so hilarious.

Later in life when I fainted from shots, I learned to transport my mind to quiet, peaceful places just before I blacked out. I might find myself on top of a snowy mountain or on a warm, tropical beach. I later conquered this fear in a most ingenious way--by taking a phlebotomy class. Now I take injections like a pro and can even give them to myself.

Summer Vacation

In spite of having to put up with my paternal grandmother Mary Elizabeth, my siblings and I looked forward to our annual summer trips to St. Paul, Minnesota. We went to Minnesota every year from when I was very young up until I went away to college. The weather was usually cool and sunny, and if we were lucky, we didn't hit the mosquito season. My grandmother was a large woman. She always wore a dress, usually frilly and floral, and high-heeled shoes that made her ankles turn in when she walked. It was a miracle that her feet could support her large frame. She was apple-shaped and easily outweighed all the men in the family.

My grandmother talked too much. With what I know now I would have called her hypomanic; that is, just short of full-blown manic. She talked as though words were being pushed up from her stomach and out through her mouth. No one could get a word in while she talked, and even if you did, she was clearly uninterested in what you had to say.

Grandma loved to show us her trick elbow, which she could twist around in almost a 360-degree circle. She told us all about Uncle Daniel's polio and Donny's rickets. She never told us how grandpa lost the farm, a key event in the lives of the family.

We kids loved to watch grandma sit down. Her legs were so large that she couldn't pull them together when she set her bulk into a chair. We could see her stockings and garters, her slip, and her underwear. I couldn't imagine how she could squeeze herself into a girdle but apparently she did.

Grandma ate the way we kids were told not to; that is, she literally shoveled food into her mouth, and she wasn't very careful about shutting it when she chewed. She ate pie before meals and pie after meals. Who gave her permission to eat sweets before dinner?

Grandma Estebo was a highly liberated woman for her time, as were two of her three sisters. She worked as a business instructor at a local school for wayward young women. She taught them typing and shorthand from a book she wrote herself, and she also taught them how to behave in the business world. You could say that this school was a combination charm, secretarial, and life skills (meaning how to be a single parent) institution. It was run by the local Catholic charities association.

My father has nothing good to say about his mother. When pressed, he infers sexual misconduct on her part. It's true that she was pregnant when she got married. I remember her telling us that she used to make her husband walk the streets when she was ovulating. But was she a mother who fondled her sons to make them calm down? My father hints that this is so and that it is "a cultural thing, like incest in certain cultures." Those things are not in my culture! I wondered what sort of sexual awakening he must have experienced on a Norwegian farm in the early twenties.

My father adored his dad but all I remember of grandpa was beer and smoke. My dad glorifies him, though emotionally he was as affectionate as a rock as far as I could tell.

In that family you always knew how all the women were feeling but you didn't have a clue about the men's emotions. They fished and smoked and drank beer. There was never a whisper from either sex about family or personal problems. Everyone was over-the-top great all the time. It wasn't a very natural place for a lonely little girl who did little else but read all day.

My parents seemed satisfied to let their family members take up the slack of emotions they never showed to us. My mother didn't kiss me goodnight nor did she ever initiate a hug until she was fast approaching her death. Dad wrestled and brought us treats and took us fishing, but like mom he was not a kisser or hugger or a "How you doing sweetie?" until he got old. My parents weren't deliberately cold or unfeeling. They just had habits that didn't include having an emotional life with their kids. Both of them had family members who showered attention on them. I think they were used to being on the receiving and not on the giving end of open emotions.

In pictures of us (of which there are hundreds) in Minnesota we look like one of the world's most idyllic families if you don't look too closely. Mother and dad are beaming (as long as grandma isn't around), grandma is happily cradling her bad arm, grandpa is smoking with one hand and drinking with the other, and Uncle Daniel is looking away, like he is trying to avoid having his image captured. I look goofy, spacey, and carefree; Derek is smirking because he gets to be one of the men; Belle looks cute; and to tell the truth, Janie looks very pissed off.

Crimson Beaver

Childhood passed, we moved many more times, and we fished with Dad. Mom cooked, drove us to lessons and games, and got sick every so often. I didn't practice meditation again until I was 13 years old when I was in 8th grade.

My period came that summer, and I didn't like it at all. I whined and groaned, hoping that the cramps, bleeding, and queasiness would go away. During these times I would seek out mother in the kitchen, enter the room clutching my stomach dramatically, and moan. I resented the force that brought this pain to me; it was out of my control, and I wanted my mother to take over her job and do something about it. I was a tomboy. I played football, baseball, and basketball, and I swam in quarries. This female occurrence did not belong to me. I knew I should have been born a boy. How could god let this happen to me? It didn't occur to me that all the other girls were suffering from it, too, since no one ever talked about it. Menstruation always brought out the worst moods in me. If I was manic I would be an irritated manic during my periods. If I was depressed I would become suicidal. My bipolar symptoms eased off somewhat after I had a hysterectomy.

Mother had no sympathy. See would snap at me impatiently and go on with what she was doing. So when I entered Robert E. Lee Middle School, it was obvious that

I was not going to be able to handle what was happening to me, namely that I was turning into a girl.

I vowed to make eighth grade a good year. Seventh grade had been the worst year of my life. Acne defaced my previously clear complexion. I was forced to wear that binding item of clothing, the bra. Mother had cut off all my beautiful, long blond hair and frizzed the rest. No one would sit with me at lunch. I was the smartest person in class (then, as now, having brains was a terrible stigma), and no one invited me to parties. Worst of all, Teddy Bergman no longer had a crush on me.

Because of my denial about my feminine body, overwhelming shame came to me twice that year. The first time was one day after English class. Someone ran up to me in the hall and told me to go to the office. What had I done? In those days, I was the perfect student, just like I thought I should be. In the office the school nurse tossed me a sanitary napkin and told me to go put it to use. The boy who sat at my place for the next hour had found the seat smeared with menstrual blood. He had announced to the class, "Some girl's bloodin'." I never would have realized that I was bleeding until it started dripping down my legs; that's how oblivious to my body functions I was in those days. I cleaned myself up as best I could and pinned on the Kotex pad, which wasn't very helpful with my heavy periods. I didn't discover Tampons for another three years, unfortunately. I was lucky that time that the blood didn't smear my dress.

I'm Not Bipolar, I'm an Astral Traveler

The second time of unbearable shame happened one morning in science class. We were studying plants. By now, the teachers in my classes didn't see my habit of meditating all day as a particularly constructive thing: they called it daydreaming. Why pay attention in class when you could study all the material in the book later at home and get an A on the test every time?

A few of the boys across from me started to snicker. I figured they were laughing at Mr. Berenson, the science teacher, and I continued to dream. Then a few more boys guffawed, louder this time. I looked at my friend Danny, who had his hands stuffed in his mouth, as if trying to stifle a particularly loud chortle.

Mr. Berenson droned on, oblivious to his students, as usual. What was going on? All the boys were laughing outright, choking with giggles. I looked at the girls sitting alongside of the room at a 90-degree angle between me and the hysterical boys. They looked horrified. Jenny North looked the most embarrassed, so I caught her eye. She looked back at me, and trying to be subtle, spread her hands out slowly in front of her, then slowly closed them back together. Of course, the boys saw her and that was the final straw for them. Several actually fell to the floor in hysteria.

Mr. Berenson said, "What's going on here?" When no one volunteered any information he resumed his lecture on plants.

I finally got the picture and shut my knees together. When I got to a bathroom, I realized what had happened.

My profuse bleeding had leaked out all over the edge of the pad I was wearing and had stained my plain white cotton panties. I had given the class a crimson beaver. It seemed to give the boys quite a thrill. Is it any wonder I couldn't get enthusiastic about being a girl? I meditated on what it was like to be born feminine in what seemed to me to be a predominantly male-dominated world.

Dance Class

I needed outlets from the tensions of growing up a damn Yankee in the South and being a girl who didn't know how to keep her legs together when seated. There were girl outlets and boy outlets; I had one of each that year, being not quite a total girl yet.

My girl outlet happened once a week when I went to ballet class. I was the only student, which was supposed to be like having a private lesson. Every Thursday afternoon after school, I met with Clark Williamson in the huge, echoing Y gym. I found that I loved to dance. In eighth grade I was en pointe and loved the soft clopping of the blocks in my toe shoes on the wooden floor. Best of all I loved to spin and leap. Clark Williamson was a much better dancer than anyone at Floyd Ward School of Dance and if I had stuck with him I would have turned into a good dancer. I didn't figure out until later that he was homosexual (his partner was my piano teacher) and an alcoholic. Being gay in the fifties and early sixties was nowhere near as acceptable as it is now.

Because I loved to dance, I happily agreed to play the part of the scarecrow in the Y version of the Wizard of Oz along with all the other klutzy girls. After the main performance I got to do a solo to "Theme from the Apartment." For my costume, Clark gussied up a plain white leotard with flowing colored scarves. I won a trophy for best dancer of the year, and I got my picture in the paper.

Clark Williamson committed suicide 10 years later. I wish I had been a more cooperative and enthusiastic student for him, instead of the sullen, self-conscious adolescent I was. I would have quit worrying about how I looked in a leotard and about whether blood was smearing the crotch of my tights. I would have excused the pungent gin-smell on his breath and appreciated him for his talents, encouragement, and patience. I missed a great opportunity, not for the first or last time, to become a better person through the mentoring of a perceptive but eccentric adult.

Like most kids I feared eccentricity in grownups; I suppose I knew I was going to end up that way, and at the time all I wanted to do was to fit in with the other kids, somehow, anyhow.

Adventures in the Civil War Ruins

As a child I was braver and more reckless than most other kids. I know that being bipolar early affected my judgment. My parents had no idea what I was doing, and if they had known I suspect I would have been relegated to my room more often. The word used to describe me then was "tomboy."

My tomboy side emerged when I could sneak out of the house unaccounted for and race on my sturdy blue Huffy to nearby Riverside Park. I didn't realize it at the time, but we lived in the Piedmont section of the Blue Ridge Mountains, and there was a portion of the Appalachian Trail just down the hill from our house. I waited with trembling excitement for the times when I could escape from civilization with fifty cents in my pocket and a few friends or siblings in tow.

On Saturday afternoons the neighborhood kids and I converged at the same point on the street. We didn't discuss where were going; we just jumped on our bikes and flew off. We rode fast on the assumption that the less time spent on the road the less our chances were for getting caught.

Our play place was in the back of the Riverside Park near the James River. We'd stop at the scenic view first and mess around throwing rocks and dirt at each other, and then we'd head over toward the railroad tracks.

We followed these tracks for miles and did all the things kids do around trains. We lay pennies on the tracks, pressed our ears on the rails to listen for the vibrations of the oncoming trains, and waved for the conductors to blow the horn.

Only my very bravest friends would go anywhere near the old Civil War train tunnel. It was a solid stone structure high enough to accommodate a big train. It was wide enough for two sets of tracks and a muddy ditch next to the wall on the right-hand side. The trains ran on the new tracks next to the ditch, but the old Civil War track on the left-hand side was intact though the ties were rotting and spongy. One day my best friend Clark Wingfield dared me to walk all the way through the tunnel alone. He ran in ahead of me and said he'd see me at the other end. He quickly disappeared into the darkness.

The tunnel wall comprised dripping cold stones held together by moldy, crumbling gray mortar. If a train came by I would have to throw myself pronto into the ditch. I put my ear to the rails and listened carefully. No vibrations, no sounds of whistles in the distance. I stood up and entered the gaping hole.

The light from the tunnel entrance began to dim after I had walked inside fifty feet or so. Suddenly the tunnel curved noticeably to the left, and then the light blinked out entirely. I couldn't see a thing and could only hear the pounding of my heart in my ears, like the noise from a monstrous seashell. The cool, moldy breeze flowing through the long, narrow space revived me somewhat and kept me from hyperventilating.

Then I heard a train whistle. The whistle blew again, and chuffing train sounds were clearly audible. I stumbled down a short incline and splashed into the ditch that materialized at my feet. I groped for the stone wall that I knew was next to the ditch and suddenly felt a gap in the wall. The space suggested what seemed to be a human sized indentation. I was able to fit into the hole by standing up with my face forward into the cold stone. I smelled rotting moss and imagined spider webs draped across my cold shoulders. I merged with the chilly surface and willed my mind to become blank.

The train came. I felt like a bug on a wall. The tunnel was all sound and vibration. My body hummed in tune with the screeching sounds of wheels resisting track as the train slowed around the curve. If I had been older or at least more aware of my body, I might have felt a perverse sexual thrill. The walls throbbed with sound. The train roared past, and I sensed its sides bulging out to scrape me from my cozy hiding place. But I was safe, homogeneous with the tunnel wall. Soon enough the train passed through and left me cold, alone, and covered with black soot.

The next year our family moved, and I never saw the park again except in memory. I remembered the years in Virginia as some of the best of my life. I got to do exactly what I wanted and paid no price for my risky behavior. I got used to having my way, and I continued to expect that into my high school years. I was a very happy manic child almost all the time.

A Normal Family Life

To my knowledge I was not raped, abused, molested, or even bullied much as a child except to be called a damn Yankee for a few years. True, my family moved a lot, and there was always a time of adjustment until new friends were made and new schedules were established.

When I was born and throughout my childhood, my father had excellent professional, though modest, jobs and we never lacked basic survival needs. My mother was a stay-at-home-mom, though she was a terrible cook. We lived on the good side of the tracks, and our neighbors were friendly and helpful. I never saw a drug dealer, a child molester, or a murderer that I ever knew of. I saw the occasional gun, but it was used for shooting birds. There was no TV until we were in grade school.

I was beautiful, smart, and funny as a young child. I had no disabilities that were obvious to anyone. I did well in school, and as I got older I became assertive and self-assured. I experienced true joy while playing football, baseball, and basketball with the boys in the neighborhood and riding my bike to kingdom come, wherever I desired. I felt happy and free. Even though I had these boyish tendencies, I discovered an early love of dancing, and was never happier than when clopping across a wooden floor practicing dance routines on toe shoes.

My parents were a golden couple of the '50s. Both of them attended not only good colleges, but you might even say the best colleges, due to a combination of natural intelligence, support from home, a natural willingness to work hard, and the G.I. Bill. Mother grew up as a spoiled princess but my father was raised by hard-working farmers and teachers.

My dad (who has no tact) often mentions to us kids that we should have turned out better, given our advantages of good genes and at least an adequate upbringing. I have no good answer for him. On closer inspection of the family tree, I see that there were plenty of alcoholics, depressives, and manic depressives, though predominantly the family members were smart and successful. I must have gotten some of the recessive genes for craziness.

Beginnings of Skewedness

I started high school in the fall of 1962. I had butterflies, crickets, and ants in my stomach whenever I thought about going to high school. I was so excited I was a little bit manic, which wasn't surprising. When the long-awaited first day came, I was confused by the new routine of changing classes, different teachers for each subject, and a dizzying array of new classes unlike any I had taken before. Journalism! Geometry! World history! English literature! Latin! There would some old faces there but mostly the kids would be fresh and new to me. Possibly I would make a friend this year.

I felt like I was floating above myself as I looked down at the crowded halls. Most of all I hoped that no one would call me a damn Yankee like my history teacher and most of my classmates did in eighth grade. I hoped I could find someone to eat lunch with.

The name for this book comes from a term I learned in geometry class: skewed. I realize that skewed is as good a word as any to describe my place in the world. Everyone else's life seems to move along straight lines in a linear progression and an ordered matrix. I am more a series of lines in different planes going off into space randomly and in different directions. Skewed lines never run into each other. I'm like those lines: I don't connect with normal people and I'm generally living on a different plane than everyone else.

After a few weeks in my new school I began to have paranoid thoughts that someone was following me. I thought I recognized her as the sister of one of my classmates. She had thin, mousy brown hair, and a pasty complexion. She wore large black-framed glasses and old, unstylish clothing. Nowadays she would have been called a geek or a nerd.

I saw this girl everywhere. She was outside the door when I came out of class and in the back seat of the bus I rode. I could always pick out her face in crowded hallways. I began dreaming about her. Then one day she confronted me as I was getting on my bus, and she started to curse me in words I had never heard before. I didn't know what they meant but because of the vitriol she was spewing at me I realized they must be bad. It seemed as though she was speaking a foreign language. One thing was clear: she hated me for some reason I couldn't imagine, and I was afraid she was going to attack me right there on the steps of the bus. Instead of confronting her and finding out why she was so mad at me, my mind flew away from my body, and I was off on a skewed line again. As I watched her, she became more and more transparent, and soon I could see right through her. I blinked, and she was gone. I didn't see her again after that.

Aside from being visited by frightening apparitions, I was a happy airhead who lived in a world of books and barely noticed the people around me. My parents had sheltered me well from street life and unpleasantness of most kinds. If I was faced with something that was disturbing or that I couldn't handle, my mind protected me by transporting me to a different place where the real world faded away.

Occasionally I would have to face my mother's raging mood swings, but when she was at her worst I simply locked myself in the bathroom for hours until she went away. I really didn't see her very much.

By the time I had adjusted to high school life it was time for us to move again. My father had gotten promoted, and we would be moving to Cincinnati, Ohio in the middle of the school year. I didn't have any close friends, but I had a lot of friendly acquaintances. I liked Virginia better than any other place we had lived. My grades were excellent: I was sixth in my class of 500. My teachers all loved me. This was not going to be a good move for me.

Somehow in the transition between schools I missed huge chunks of material in many of my new classes. I was most behind in my senior-level geometry class. I didn't have a clue what was going on. My teacher took me aside one morning and made me cry when he told me I just wasn't getting the material, and I would have to try harder.

The truth was that I had missed out on the Pythagorean Theorem. No wonder I was failing the class. I was skewed again; I had been learning completely different things in my Virginia school. I took my geometry book home and began at the very beginning. I spent hours catching up on the material. As soon as I figured out that $C^2 = A^2 + B^2$ I was fine. I had been humiliated by a math teacher instead of rewarded for my advanced skills. For the first time in my life I did not enjoy going to school. I got my first B's ever.

Somehow I finished out the year in a daze. Sophomore year was more of the same. I took physics, which I was desperately unprepared for, and I got my first C. I improved as the year went on, but my overconfidence in schoolwork was undermined. The smart kids in my grade were taking easier courses and making better grades. It wasn't fair. I was no longer the smartest girl in the class. Even so, because I was a year or two ahead of everyone I got a certain amount of respect from the other students. They didn't know I was only getting average grades in the harder classes.

Then my world exploded. I discovered sex, and I was never the same.

Twitterpated

I probably learned a lot of useful things in high school, but the two I valued most were how to write and how to make out. The writing I learned from Mrs. Perry, who stomped her feet, cried, and yelled at us until we could write a passable thesis sentence. We studied literature filled with sex and violence, the most interesting kind according to Elizabeth Perry. We read stories, we acted, we memorized Shakespeare, but mostly we wrote. A major theme paper was due every Monday. I always turned in my assignments at least a week late.

I was not the best writer in class; that honor belonged to Charlie Goodman, but I was undoubtedly the most prolific. I produced 69 pages for my senior term paper on *Tom Jones*. My creative work consisted of pages and pages of off-the-wall, surrealistic ramblings. I didn't understand the physical workings of sex, so I created all sorts of strange images to substitute for the reality of it. My fictional characters were repressed and fatalistic.

I learned to love written expression. Talking I didn't learn until later but I've always been a great listener. I made friends with some of the quiet, sensitive kids in the class, the ones who had been overlooked by popularity and high school success. I learned making out with one such person, Bob, and lost him to another, Judy.

Judy Price, for a while, was my best and only friend. I met her on the bus we both rode to and from school.

Judy was someone you could really be jealous of. She had won a national writing contest her freshman year, played the piano like a pro, and was the best math student in her class. Most incredible of all, she looked like an Egyptian princess.

My friendship with Judy broke up towards the end of my junior year when she asked my boyfriend Bob to a party he had already promised to attend with me. He must have felt wonderful to be wanted by both of us. So wonderful, in fact, that he accepted both of our invitations. The event was a hayride, and early in the evening he and I indulged in some heavy making out under blankets in the sweet-smelling hay. I was high on hormones when we entered a warm cabin for cider and donuts. I was having a great time until Judy's brother John grabbed my arm and shoved me into the center of the room, which was ringed with my friends and acquaintances. He started yelling at me and finally spit out, "You whore." Other than my fictional ghost from high school and Mrs. Perry, who had once called me a brazen hussy in English class for wearing a tight sweater, no one had ever cursed at me before.

Considering that I had been dating Bob all year, I couldn't imagine that my best friend would ask my boyfriend out. The experience disoriented me, and once again my mind skewed. I rushed over to where Judy and Bob were talking together and screamed in their faces. Neither one apologized or tried to explain. Bob wouldn't look at me. I went into my inner dream world, and I can't remember how I got home.

From then on my relationships with girls in high school were either superficial or downright hostile. I kept dating Bob but I watched him very closely for signs of unfaithfulness. At that time I didn't understand the meaning of going out with more than one person at a time. He must have felt trapped and resentful, but I clung to him even more tightly after the incident with Judy.

On Monday of the week before the Junior Prom there was a pep rally. Bob and I were entering the gym at the same time, and in his typical Bob fashion, he said, "You'll go the prom with me, won't you?"

I couldn't believe he was asking me the same week as the event without giving me more notice. I had accepted an invitation from Mark, a popular athlete, since Bob hadn't asked me to go. I told him I was sorry, but I had another date.

I thought I was in love with Bob and so without telling him I followed my heart and called Mark back that night to break our date. I realized he wouldn't have much chance to find someone else to go with before the weekend, but I did it anyway. He called me a fucking bitch, my second cussing out in a few months. I hung up on him. He was right, but I still felt relieved not have to go with him. Now I could call Bob back and tell him I was available after all.

When I called Bob, he couldn't believe I had broken my date with Mark. We started arguing. Soon our fight escalated into a major screaming match. He told me to forget about going to the prom after all. He wouldn't go with me even if I paid him.

It had been one of the worst weeks of my life.

On Tuesday I prepared as usual for gym class. Our sport for the day was floor hockey, a pointless and mindless game during which two teams tried to kick a ball into a goal at either end of the gym. It's like indoor soccer on a hardwood floor, only the ball has to stay on the ground. I was competitive at games and usually scored most of the goals for my team. On this day I was hyper and disconnected. I dashed madly back and forth trying to get my feet on the ball. There was no score in the game when I ran aggressively toward the biggest member of the opposition, Fay, who outweighed me by 80 pounds.

I ran straight at her generous middle as hard and fast as I could. We reached the ball together, and our feet tangled. I fell over backwards from the momentum of her angry rush toward me. The back of my skull cracked resoundingly throughout the gym as it hit the wooden floor. The next thing I remember was sitting in the gym office with bloody towels wrapped around my head and the gym teacher shouting, "Somebody clean up that mess on the floor."

I was blank until the next day when the doctor was waving fingers in front of my face and asking me who the president was. What a dumb question, I thought, until I realized I had no idea. Was it Eisenhower? Mom and dad taught me to say "I like Ike" when I was younger. Finally, a fuzzy picture presented itself to my barely functioning brain. Was it Kennedy? No, he was dead somehow. Yes, Jindon Lonson, that was his name, no London Jinsen. Slowly I oriented myself to conscious life.

Several days passed before I remembered any of the events of the previous week. I conveniently forgot that I had no date to the prom, and no one else knew that Bob and I had fought and that he had disavowed me. He relented in the wake of my injury and gallantly took me after all. We had a terrific time. I wore a sexy yellow dress my mother had altered for me and had my hair rolled into a French twist to hide the bald spot where my head had been shaved in the hospital.

My detractors would later claim that my cracked skull might have resulted in further brain damage that affected my mental health in later years. I found out later that the doctors had drilled a hole in my head to relieve the swelling of my brain.

I don't think bipolar disorder can be caused by a concussion but I don't think any studies have been done to either prove or disprove it.

Seventeen

In the spring of 1967 I was a senior in high school and bursting with passion. I had come out of my shell. I had gotten rid of Bob and was dating a shy boy named Karl, who adored me. I would have forgotten all about how I felt then except that recently I found a copy of a letter I had written to Karl and a sonnet I foolishly submitted to my English teacher as part of an assignment. I was out of my teenage mind with love and hormones. I wrote in Karl's yearbook:

Karl (Slinky, Snarl, but mostly just you),

Since you made this year the most wonderful of my life thus far, I dedicate this poem to you--composed during one of my typical emotional and most twitterpated moods!!

Seductive Spring

Swirl free, impulsive passion, lose restraint!
Inflame desire intense, caress moonlight;
Torment puffed, radiant clouds, oh fleeting saints--
Excite and kindle love, ecstatic night!!

My soul, incensed as flame within a bloom
Before its perking, flickering, tumbling glow
Bursts forth profusely from empetaled womb;

Cascading scents to liquid skyline flow--
Our shivered kisses, sweeping feverish breeze
O'er ruffled, leafy sentinels illumed
By glowing moon. Seductive spring, thus tease
Emotions fierce--submissive lovers doomed.

Though reckless dreams for restless love will yearn,
Springs nights and you inspire spring love to burn.

Really--you have changed my whole inexperienced life by being truly, absolutely the greatest, best person I have ever met. I doubt if any of it rubbed off on me, but you've at least put me on the right road (or tried to--I hope I'm not too hard-headed to follow your examples). I'll just never forget your sweet, tender consideration (Teddy bearness) and how huggable you are in cranberry Bermuda shorts--I love you for all these things. How can I ever swim after hours, watch the sun rise, or bite anyone else's ear--with that shivery tingle again? I cry when I think about all the unforgettable times we have had together from the first kiss to walking around the circle to three-hour phone calls, kissing during the three minutes between classes, and prom weekend. It's just unbelievable how you understand my typical confusion and twitterpatedness this year and how you gave me every reason to be more enthusiastic than humanly possible and then tried to calm me down and keep me out of trouble. Well, I can't express properly the way I feel about you--I hope you keep everything locked up in that crazy head of yours. I know I'll never forget you. By the mere shadow of your smile you have made me happier than I can ever hope to be again.

> *Keep buttoned up and...*
> *No matter what happens in years to come*
> *Your angel forever,*
>
> *Kristy*

Karl's response to the poem was, "I consider it an exaggeration." My English teacher said only: "I'd love to read this poem to the class but I fear it is too personal." When she said that, I knew she was referring to my poem, and with a bright red face I hoped to god she would make good on her word.

One night I told Karl I could die from the happiness I felt when I was with him. He thought that was rather a strange statement. If only we could have preserved our precious innocence.

We both applied to the same college and were accepted. I chose Purdue over Northwestern, at least partly because Karl wanted to study engineering, and I didn't really know what I wanted to study, so what did it matter where I went? At the last minute his parents made him stay home and attend the University of Cincinnati. I was particularly furious with his father, who said that Purdue was too expensive. Before long I realized that the true reason he was forbidden to leave town was because his parents didn't want him anywhere near me. His mother made the pointed comment to me that summer that "Your sister Belle is so sweet." I knew she was really telling me, "And you're a dirty whore." By that time I knew what a whore was.

After a painful summer, I said goodbye to Karl and blithely went off alone to Purdue, my second choice of colleges. In light of later events, I never really forgave Karl for not standing up to his father and coming with me. I was as innocent as a lamb and just as vulnerable. I needed protection, but I didn't know that until the world conspired to snuff out my pretty thoughts and naive passions.

I date my bipolar illness as truly starting when I was sixteen, after I suffered that serious head injury in the gym accident. I had probably always been bipolar but I didn't notice debilitating moods until I was off on my own and free to be the self I thought I always wanted to be. If I had known then the way life was going to unfold for me, I might have consummated the blissful death I imagined while rolling in the leaves with Karl, feeling high as the sky thanks to my unique brain chemistry and a sexy boyfriend.

A friendly medium told me a few weeks ago that my children would surpass me. I can only thank the seven divine guardians for that.

Summer Nights

By the end of high school I had a strong urge to leave town and escape from my parent's grasp. My bedroom was in a separate wing from the rest of the house and had a door which led to the side yard and ultimately to the street. After midnight I would leave the house on foot and meet Karl in the quiet night. It was three-and-a-half miles to town, and I thought nothing of jogging through the woods, across the tracks, and up Shawnee Run hill to the Madeira town square. I would throw rocks at Karl's window to let him know I was there. Most bipolar people like to play throughout the night.

I loved the freedom of the night and lived for those expeditions. One night I went into town to get Karl, taking my brother and sister with me. I threw rocks at Karl's window and soon saw a palm displayed in the window pane. I figured he'd be right out for a walk and some making out. We all waited behind a full fir tree.

Soon my siblings got tired of waiting and ran off towards home, leaving me alone behind the tree. I saw two dark figures come out the front door. One of them had a gun in his hand. Karl and his dad thought I was a prowler. It was too late to declare myself and too late to run. They walked over to my tree and began to circle it towards me. I decided that flight was better than fight, so I ran as fast and as hard as I could out of the yard.

I imagined a bullet chasing me and plunging into my back. I was so worried about getting shot that I failed to see a large stone wall directly in front of me. I smashed into it head-on and bounced backwards a good six feet onto my butt. Blood poured from a three-inch gash on my knee down into my shoe. When I got home the other kids were waiting outside for me. Every light in the house was on, and every main door in the house was locked. It was 5 a.m.

We found a small shop window downstairs that was unlocked, and we crept in. Janie and I hid under the stairs where we could hear mom getting hysterical and dad soothing her quietly. Derek went into his room downstairs and jumped into bed. I was way too excited to sleep. After a while dad came down and checked Derek's bed. When he felt the body in it, he dragged Derek up the stairs, all the while swatting him (thwap, thwap) with his belt. Janie and I began to feel guilty that Derek was getting whipped, and we weren't. Besides, we had to come out sometime. We climbed the stairs slowly.

Mother screamed at me that I was too immature to go to college, and I would have to stay home the next year. We were all grounded for the rest of summer. From then on Karl came to my room every night and joined me on the small daybed which served as my sleeping place.

We never consummated our relationship that summer. Even so, I gave myself orgasms by just rubbing up against him. I don't know why we were so chaste. Just dumb, I guess, and filled with guilt about something neither of us understood fully.

Mom finally relented, and I was allowed to go off to college. That would be my last summer of innocent fun. I was about to bloom into a flower child.

Leaving Home

It was great to be away from home. I kissed mom and Karl goodbye at the dorm, and they both cried. I didn't. However, I wasn't prepared for a dorm with stricter rules than the ones I was used to at home. First of all, we had to wear skirts to dinner, and the hems had to fall below the knee. Worst of all, there were actually "hours," or evening curfew restrictions. This schedule didn't fit in with my internal clock. I would have to figure out how to get out at night without getting caught.

A solution presented itself right away. Another rule at Purdue was "mandatory" church attendance on Sunday nights. I made some friends at the local Presbyterian Church about a mile from the dorm. This group planned "religious" retreats every weekend at a cabin on an island in the middle of the Tippecanoe River. It took a little rowboat to get over the river to the camp. I could tolerate some religious training if it involved camping out all weekend.

I found out an even more intriguing fact: the church saved four or five live-in rooms for needy Presbyterian students to live in while they attended college. In return for the free room, these students were supposed to clean the church, cut the grass, and perform other menial tasks. Actually, I never saw any of them lift a finger doing anything.

There was one room no one ever went into as far as I could see. I called it the candle room, because it was filled with white votive candles used in church services. The candle room was furnished with only a rusty metal table and a musty, damp, single bed used for God knows what. A window led out to a ledge on the roof. "What a perfect hideout," I thought to myself, "It's the college version of the secret place." I could study here, sleep, or entertain a friend. There were still a few details to be worked out like how to lock the door. I felt certain that something would work out.

In the meantime I went on retreats every other weekend, where I met boys I made out with and girls I chatted with. School was like a big party so far. I had registered for general liberal arts courses that were not a challenge to me nor were they very interesting. It's not very exciting to go to a class with 300 other people and no professor, just TV's at the end of the aisles.

My First Real Friend

I noticed another student in the dorm, a beautiful girl-woman who worked in the dorm kitchen. She always smiled as though she knew a particularly wonderful secret that none of the rest of us knew. She was 20 pounds overweight at the time, but her size took nothing away from how gorgeous she was. She had high, Polish cheekbones and a flawless peaches-and-cream complexion. At that time, before amphetamine usage and weight lifting, she was pear-shaped, with most of her weight in her hips and thighs. Her clothes were stunning and tailored to her as though they were hand-made, which it turned out they were. She was a talented seamstress, and she had made most of the clothes she brought with her to college. When elections came around, she and I were elected President and Vice-President of our dorm. This girl was Julia. She became my best friend, and she is a long-distance friend to this day.

Julia and I talked about boys and complained about our roommates. Julia was enrolled in a science curriculum and was outnumbered by males 100 to 1 in her classes. Many of these boys would nose around her like puppy dogs and beg for dates. She didn't meet even one she considered worthy of her attention. I, on the other hand, met Henri, an extraordinary guy (at 18 are they boys or men?) in my church group. He was dazzlingly good-looking and a piano prodigy. He was also a brilliant science and math student. Julia and I valued intelligence above all other qualities in men at that time, and Henri fit all our qualifications. Julia encouraged me to develop my relationship with Henri. She thought I should have sex with him as soon as possible.

Julia's mom had educated her fully in all the details of a normal human sex life. Her mom was so unlike my own: young-looking, pretty as a china doll, and possessed of an impish sense of humor. My mother was almost masculine in her way of viewing the world, and she never laughed. Julia's mom allowed her daughter to be an equal not just a vassal. She was more friend than mother to her daughter. I had never met a mother like this, one that her kids actually liked. She and Julia talked about sex the way I talked to my parents about what was for dinner. All I knew about sex was what a side view of a limp penis looked like and that fallopian tubes were like snaky ropes dangling down somewhere inside the lower half of my body. I had no idea how to insert a tampon, and I had not discovered masturbation except by rubbing against Karl while we made out. When Karl got a hard-on I never noticed. In seventh grade the other kids had started telling dirty jokes that I didn't understand.

With no solid information to go on, I decided that a girl could get pregnant by just being touched by a boy. My favorite fantasy was that if a boy really liked a girl, he would take a pair of her panties and wear them stuffed under a baseball cap on his head. Then if she wanted to get pregnant, she would put the panties on. As much as I loved touching, hitting, and wrestling with boys, every contact had a terrific potential for possible impregnation. As high school went on, I came to realize that perhaps I had overreacted. But that emotional fear of pregnancy remained.

Karl was a naturally sweet and considerate person, so he never confronted me with my ignorance until later on in the summer, nor did he force me to do anything I didn't want to do.

Finally, one night even his patience wore thin. We were on our way down to the neighborhood swimming pool when he suddenly grabbed my hand and stuck it into his pants. I felt a hard penis and was amazed, but I still didn't get the picture. "Don't you see?" he said. I had on a brief bikini and nothing else (Cincinnati is steamy in the summer). We lay down on a picnic table and he started to take off my bikini bottoms. I was confused more than anything, and I looked at him with incomprehension. He burst into tears saying, "I can't do this." Apparently the other guys had been goading him to nail his chick. He ran away from me, crying, and I didn't see him for several days.

That was the extent of my sexual experience before I went off to college. I needed a knowledgeable friend like Julia to educate me. She had never actually performed the sex act herself, but she lusted after the experience.

Being a virgin in those days was not at all cool. Things were changing. Prim and proper was out; free and easy was in. The truth was that Julia was about formal a person as I had ever met. She even wanted to be in a sorority. I was more laid back, but I had grown up thinking you could get pregnant by being breathed on. Now I had to deal with the reality of a gorgeous, thinking, feeling man who very soon wanted to have sex, the real kind. Julia desperately wanted me to have this experience so I could tell her about it and she could experience it vicariously without taking any of the risks.

Easing in to Breaking In

My life in 1968 became a whirlwind of college activities and cramming for tests at the last minute. I was the fresh-faced golden girl at last. I was fine until I decided to have sex with Henri. Looking back, I blame him for causing my second big depression, the first one being the time I got turned down for a date at the prom. My depressions have always lasted so much longer than the manias.

My adventures with Henri started at "mandatory" Sunday night church.

I Fall in Love Again

Henri spent a lot of time at the Purdue Presbyterian Church. He earned money playing the organ for Sunday services, and he was allowed to use the grand piano in the sitting room for practice. He also gave piano lessons there. He was accustomed to practicing six to eight hours a day and was depressed over the lack of time to maintain that schedule and get passing grades as well.

Our first weekend together was at a "church retreat." We spent the night in a single sleeping bag on the bank of the Tippecanoe River. Psychologically, I was still hanging onto my puerile views about sex. I had maintained an ignorant bliss on the subject for more than ten years. It was not so easy for me to face it square-on now. Besides I didn't want to get pregnant. What would everyone think? What would I do with a baby? Pregnancy was as incomprehensible as sex was to me. However, on that particular night I was so turned on I would have done anything for him. Why did that night happen to be the only night he didn't have a condom with him? I really wanted him inside me. It didn't happen.

My relationship with Henri became a game of cat and mouse. He sent me flowers after that first weekend we spent at church camp. We flirted, we played. Our conversations were filled with double entendres. I teased him until he came to orgasm while we were talking on the phone during one of our endless conversations. I listened to him play the piano. I hung around in the candle room waiting for him to show up. I was building toward consummation.

I discussed my situation with Julia. Our favorite place to talk was the communal bathroom on our floor in the dorm. We'd wrap ourselves in big towels and head towards a hot bath. One of us would sit on the floor while the other luxuriated in the tub. Then we would pour a new bath and switch. After an hour or more of relaxing conversation, we'd go back to my room and continue our talk. We talked about sex, drugs, and other advanced topics. We mocked the silly farm girls in our dorm.

It shouldn't have been a big surprise when we were summoned before the housemother one night. She told us we were on the verge of being expelled from the dorm for homosexuality. Our parents had been notified. After I got over my initial shock, I looked over at Julia. She was doing her best not to laugh, but she wasn't being totally successful. When my mouth twitched a little, she burst into laughter. The housemother frowned at us with disapproval. This was no joking matter to her. We asked what specific charges had been brought against us.

The charges were: running naked through the halls, taking baths together, and sleeping together in the same bunk. In fact, all three charges were perfectly true. However, I didn't know any more about what lesbians did than I knew about regular sex, so I didn't even know what I was being accused of, only that whatever it was, it was shameful and really bad. What did women do to each other anyway? Julia, the expert in all areas of sexuality, was able to defend us. She said that we talked a lot together and that neither of us was modest about our bodies. Almost every word of our conversations had to do with men. This closed old woman was finally convinced to give us another chance. We were forbidden to appear naked in the halls, to talk together in the bathroom, or to fall asleep in the same bed.

The First Time

Fall blew away in a wash of wind and rain, and I was finally getting used to the colder weather. Exams were coming up, and I liked to study in the candle room. Henri had given me a spare key that he had stolen from the church office. The only other key was kept by the minister, who used it rarely. Henri and I would meet accidentally in the candle room several times a week. While I studied or read, Henri would open his briefcase and bring out gin and tonic mixings. I never saw him study, but he did some drawing for fun. He didn't practice his music any more, either.

Julia had been working and working on me about "going all the way." We discussed whether or not we would bleed much when our hymens were torn, or even if they were still there to be torn. What did a hymen look like? Where was it located anatomically? I certainly didn't know. We also discussed the best types of birth control. Mostly we discussed how much more complete as human beings and real women we would be once we had participated in a complete sex act. Finally, I decided I was ready. I couldn't wait a minute longer.

It happened on a freezing February night. There was a crunchy layer of dirty snow on the ground. I ran into Henri at the church and suggested to him that we go for a walk. He never took me out on dates, so walking was one of our main activities together. I told him I had something I wanted to talk to him about. We walked several miles to Happy Hollow Park, an eerie dish-shaped valley scooped out of the hills outside of town. It was a popular place for sleigh riding because of the steep, sloping sides, but on that unusually cold night we were alone.

Somewhere along the way I said to Henri, "I'm ready."

"Ready for what?" was his response. I thought I was being so obvious. "You know," I replied. He looked at me and did a double take. "Are you sure?" he asked. I had been fighting him off for three months. I assured him that I had made up my mind and knew what I wanted. His response was less enthusiastic than I expected. We had both enjoyed our games with each other, and the reality of taking our relationship further might ruin that.

To get through the experience, I had hyped myself up, like a weight lifter pumping up before a contest. I felt like running a marathon just to calm myself down. I was burning with adrenalin or one of those other crazy hormones the body produces under stress. Mania kicked in for the first time since I had been in school. When a manic person wants to have sex there is very little that will stop her.

We skidded down the incline into the bowl of the park. The moon shone on the blasted crystals of the snow, which glittered and reflected the light back at millions of crazy angles. I was bedazzled by the rainbow colors; I felt that I had never seen the world so clearly, and that it had never been so beautiful. The wind zinged against my cheeks.

Henri dared me to roll in the snow. "I'll do you one better," I cried as I pulled off my coat, sweater, bra, boots, jeans, and panties and leaped into the icy drifts. I suppose I threw my own heat into the snow, because I felt not cold but a wonderful tingling on my skin, like being gently bitten by hordes of tiny mosquitoes everywhere at once. I was high, and before me stood an amazed and handsome lover. He said, "Why don't we go back to the candle room?" My intensity level was more than he had bargained for, and besides, he wasn't magically warmed up the way I was.

I put my clothes on and realized I was soaked from head to foot. We walked back to the church and went to the candle room.

Henri was uptight about getting caught having sex in the candle room. He said he knew a better place for my breaking in. The church was dark, and we didn't dare turn on the lights outside the candle room for fear someone would catch us. He grabbed my hand and led me past the organ to a small door behind the altar. We entered a crawl space crammed with an array of organ pipes of different sizes. There was barely clearance for us to get by, but he led me on in the dark until we reached a set of stairs. We climbed the stairs and then traveled back across the upper level of pipes, trying not to bump into them and set off a giveaway cacophony.

I felt like a mouse heading for a trap, seduced by the scent of exotic cheese.

Henri had a flashlight in his pocket, and he shone it on a small square door at floor level at the end of the passageway. "Here we are," he said cheerfully. We crawled into a rectangular-shaped room, little bigger than a closet. Henri pulled out a white candle and a stick of incense from his pocket and lit them both with some kitchen matches that had been conveniently left in the room. We dubbed this strange love nest "the organ chamber."

I stripped off my wet clothes, not slowly or sexily. I simply took them all off without glancing at Henri to see if he was watching me or not. I noticed my silhouette on the wall and thought, "Yep, my boobs certainly do stick out." I don't remember too much about our sexual communion, except that it hurt, and that I didn't bleed. I must have broken my hymen doing gymnastics or riding horses.

After it was all over, Henri licked his lips and said, "Now you've been properly broken in." He folded up the used rubber and stuffed in back into its wrapper, then shoved the whole mess into his pocket. God forbid we should leave any incriminating evidence behind. My wet underwear was hard to put on.

We headed carefully back to the candle room without setting off any of the organ pipes, and Henri announced that he had to leave. Goodbye, see you later. Now I knew what "slam bam, thank you ma'am" meant. I lay down on the dirty, cold cot, feeling empty. I didn't have a blanket, and all my clothes were wet from my romp in the snow, even my ski jacket. I started to shiver violently. I couldn't get warm, I was alone, and I had just given up my virginity to a cad who didn't care about me. I stayed there until I couldn't stand it anymore and then went to an all-night cafe, where I ordered bacon, eggs, and toast I couldn't eat.

An angry red sun poked its bloodshot eye over the horizon. At 6:00 a.m. the dorm was unlocked, and I went straight upstairs for a hot bath. I slept in my own bed for the rest of the day.

That night was the beginning of a series of roller coaster mood swings that would take me to heights and depths of emotion for the rest of my life. My experience with Henri confused and depressed me. As our relationship progressed, he taught me every imaginable sexual position and technique. But he could never teach me just to relax and enjoy it.

My feelings of self-worth plunged to new lows. What could I enjoy if not sex? Besides, I had been conned into the whole sexual experience by both Julia and Henri. I had never wanted to get involved with any of it. And what if I were to get pregnant?

Henri's band was booked for a gig at the student union. I wanted to go and see them, as I had never heard him play anything but classical music in the church. The night of the concert I showed up at the candle room, ready to walk over with Henri to the student union.

He stated matter-of-factly, "You can't go."

"What? I won't get in your way; I just want to hear you play."

"Forget it. I don't want you to show up."

I was insulted and hurt. I packed up my stuff and walked back to the dorm. I was too upset to stay home alone so I called Jordan, a friend from the church group Henri and I belonged to. He asked me to come over to his dorm room. "Why not go?" I thought.

Within five minutes of being in Jordon's room he was stripping off my shirt and then my pants. When he undressed in the late dusk light I could see his erection standing out like the arm on an umbrella stand. "What about your girlfriend?" I whispered. "She understands," he replied. Then we made love very impersonally while I was thinking, "Hmm, I didn't ask him to put on a rubber." He was so large he wasn't actually able to penetrate me fully, so I thought, "Perhaps it will be alright."

I skewed again and floated above my body during our brief sexual encounter.

Feeling guilty about my abrupt departure from Henri and my betrayal of him, I walked back to the candle room, where I lay down and thought, "This is getting kind of confusing."

Henri did indeed show up after his concert, and we made up and made love in the candle room. "Good," he said, "That's the best you've done so far," he whispered. It was by far the most relaxed I had ever been during sex with him, since I had just spent forty-five minutes getting stretched out by Jordon. And I "almost" came.

When my period was ten days late in April, I was frantic. I didn't even know what an abortion was, much less where to get one. I told Henri and his response was, "I thought one of those rubbers had a hole in it. Sorry, looks like you have a problem."

Of course I knew that if I was pregnant then Jordon, the African exchange student, would be the most likely father. I found myself tangled up like line in a fishing reel gone wild.

I saw a flier for a trip to the Deep South, a "race relations trip," and I signed up to go. Twenty other students and I boarded a bus for Arkansas, Florida, Georgia, and Tennessee during spring break of 1968. We slept on the floors of people who fed us grits, cornbread, and freshly fried chicken from their farms. For the first time I met angry, militant black people. It was my first experience with people who hated me for something I had not personally done to them. They frightened me, but more so they made me feel ashamed to be white person. Shame was a feeling I was getting used to.

We were preparing to leave Georgia for Memphis when Martin Luther King was shot. I had made a date to play tennis with some Auburn boys that day. After we got the news of the assassination, our racial relations trip was clearly over.

On the long ride home, my period came. By the time I got back to town, I was bleeding so heavily I might have been having a miscarriage. I don't really know. All I knew was that there was a lot of blood, and my insides felt like they were draining out of me painfully. Eventually the bleeding stopped and I vowed to give up men, especially ones who laughed at my inexperience and naiveté and teased me about holes in condoms. I would never again sleep with a man out of anger at another man. Most of all I would never make love without birth control. Better yet, I would just not ever have sex with a man again.

Maybe I could find someone less worldly and sophisticated. I suppose I thought all men would turn out to be like Henri. I knew one exception: somebody who was familiar, considerate, and loving. Yes, I would go back to Karl, my old high school sweetheart, who wouldn't force me to have sex with him in a dim and dingy hole in the wall.

When I got back to school I hid out in the candle room for three days and took a lot of Midol. I didn't tell my parents I had returned from the trip south, and they worried about where I was and what I was doing. I couldn't talk to them after my close encounter with pregnancy.

With relief I told Henri our relationship was over, and I spent a few months alone sulking in my room. Then I called Karl to help me out with the mess my life had become.

Repressed Memory

After I sent Henri away, I returned to the candle room one more time and jumped deliberately into the black hole.

In that moment between waking and sleeping I heard a sound from outside the room. I lay on the same dirty cot, covered with the same old scratchy blanket. I heard heavy footsteps approaching me from a distance. Thunk, thunk: someone or something with heavy boots was descending the stairway outside the door. The sound came from the direction of the organ chamber hidden above the room where I lay quietly, not daring to breathe.

Must be Kristen, I thought, coming to practice the organ.

But of course it wasn't Kristen.

My heartbeat increased until I could feel it booming in my fingers and toes, all the way up through my body to my eyeballs and to the roots of my hair follicles. I felt a stabbing pain at the base of my neck. I felt that I was surely dying here in this cold deserted room, before the end of my feeble attempts to finish what should have been the beginning of a hopeful and golden life, my first year away from home, my deciding of who I would eventually be.

The footsteps were upon me, just outside the flimsy door.

And I was transported to the backseat of the family car, lying in a fetal position on the floor, hoping to hide from the familiar monster.

The Ajax Man, at first so frightening, had become a regular part of my childhood, one that I lived in by myself, alone to face the monster that was more real to me than any family member: lovely mommy, happy daddy, annoying siblings, even my puppy Dinky dog.

I would just get up and leave. I would crawl up out of the hole and walk out. Somehow I would skirt past the maker of the footsteps.

I found I was paralyzed, from head to toe. I couldn't move my arms or legs, or blink my eyes, or even make a sound. I wanted to scream but when I tried to open my mouth the muscles wouldn't work. I heard myself shrieking at the top of my lungs but no vibrations entered my ears so I knew I had been unsuccessful at making the barest whimper.

The Ajax Man stuck his head in the backseat window of the car and said to me... "Let me fix your teeth."

Sex, Drugs, and Rock-'n'-Roll

A whole year of depression went by. I called Karl one night, and from then on I just couldn't leave him alone. Although I went back to him partly because he didn't demand sex from me, I couldn't resist showing him I had learned a thing or two.

When I tried out my newly learned sexual skills on him, he was bewildered, and we were ultimately even more frustrated than we had been before. Since we never used any kind of birth control, he would always pull out at the final moment. Our sex life was as messy as the sheets we left behind. It had been so much simpler and more pleasurable when we were only playing at the real thing, and we achieved mutual orgasms by rubbing against each other fully clothed.

Perhaps understandably, we turned to drugs. The first time I smoked pot was at the apartment of one of Julia's new friends. I was sitting in a rocking chair trying to appear knowledgeable about sucking in the harsh smoke and holding it in as long as possible. At first I coughed it all out immediately, but soon I could hold in the smoke for at least a few seconds.

I wondered what all the fuss was about. I didn't feel any different than I had a minute ago, even an hour ago, and now I had been rocking, rocking for three hours, and I wasn't high, when would I get high and giggle like everyone else? What I really wanted right now was to be left alone without the high anxiety I was feeling around all these strangers.

Then we were in the car going home, and the car was sliding around the corners. Surely it would fly off the road, and we'd all be killed and caught and arrested.

I taught Karl the pleasures of drugs and the severe paranoia that seemed to be an innate part of the drug experience during those early days of the "revolution."

My relationship with Karl bloomed and then died the summer after my sophomore year in college. We had been seeing each other all that year off and on in motels and parks, at the island, in his car. We smoked pot, drank seven and sevens, and tried to screw. We loved each other, and we confused each other. Karl said that we would either be married or say goodbye forever by the end of the year.

When summer came, Karl had made some drug connections of his own, and his friend Johnny Weir joined us in our drug experiments. We drove to Columbus, Ohio to Ohio State University and bought a summer's supply of pot, hash, opium, and mescaline. To temper our highs, we stole booze from my parents' ever-full stock in the cabinet under the kitchen counter.

My parents' influence on me at that time was as absent as the grownups in a Charlie Brown comic strip. On the surface I must have appeared somewhat normal. I was attending summer school classes at the University of Cincinnati, and I had to get up at 6:30 every morning. I slept only three hours a night and took afternoon naps.

Karl, Johnny and I would go on our adventures after our parents had gone to sleep.

The first night we took hallucinogens was on a weekend night. I had gone to a toy store and bought day glow paint, a black light, and a disco light. We called our basement The Catacombs because of the number of funny rooms that branched out under the house. It was a perfect place for a trio of amateur dope heads.

We began the evening by smoking hashish. Hash was a fine drug which left me in a mellow and quiet mood.

Then Johnny pulled out three small purple tablets from his pocket. We were about to embark on our first "trip." The tabs were supposedly top-grade mescaline. Later I learned that they were more probably speed mixed with strychnine. Ritualistically, and for me apprehensively, we each swallowed a tab and waited for something to happen.

Garden of Eden

According to Johnny, it would take an hour for the drug to take effect. We drank some beer and got out our paints and brushes. We mounted the silver disco ball on the ceiling and turned it on. We set up the black light on the floor in the middle of the room. We had walls and walls of gray cinder blocks to paint on. My idea was to create an extended mural of the Garden of Eden in the unused space.

I turned on the black light, and we started our masterpiece. I drew Adam and Eve and the apple tree. My snake turned into a fiery dragon with scales and wings. Karl painted the universe, and Johnny worked on the birds, beasts, and a stairway to heaven.

In less than an hour, I felt an excruciating pain stab into the base of my skull. The pain was such that I had to lie down in the black light. I closed my eyes and saw glowing colored balls. When I opened my eyes the dark vision was superimposed on the reality around me. Our painted universe had become one with my mind, a dream of an outer space world come to frightening life.

My baby sister Belle came in to see our mural, and she was impressed with our work.

Mother came downstairs and asked if we'd like a cool drink. "Sure," I managed to push out. I gathered Karl and Johnny into the TV room for mom's whiskey sours. The little men in the TV were speaking to me, and

I watched the amber drink flowing out of the pitcher, flooding out. "Enough," I cried to my mother, before a drop of the sticky stuff ever reached the glass. She looked directly into my eyes and asked, "Have you been smoking something?"

"No, no," I assured her, "We're just painting a mural in The Catacombs. Let's get back, guys."

We reentered our primeval universe. Eve was dancing in the grass, and the apples were red, so very red, the dragon was blowing steam, and the stars were twinkling in the sky. I watched one of the planets, and suddenly I was a planet, spinning in remote space, alone, cold, and trapped in a dark, sucking vacuum. "Karl," I cried, "I'm gone, where am I, where did I go?" Although Karl and Johnny had not been affected by the so-called mescaline as strongly as I had, they were not exactly in great shape, either. They were awed and jealous of my hallucinatory capability.

We left the house on some flimsy pretense. I lay down outside in the wet grass while a soft rain fell. I was so freaked out I thought I was dead, and I tried to explain this to Karl, who listened patiently. I had fallen into a dark hole, Alice Not-In-Wonderland, and there I would be stuck forever. He whispered to me that he loved me, that my parents loved me, and that my sisters and brother loved me, that I was loved now and forever. No matter what I did, I would always be myself, and being me was of value in this world. I became aware of the cool wetness on my skin and hair. If I could feel wet, I must still be alive; and my head still ached, that was pain and pain was sending messages to a brain. I crawled out of the hole I had fallen into. "Let's get out of here!" I suggested shakily.

Group Hallucination?

The rest of the night must have been a group hallucination in light of later evidence. Johnny drove, being the least stoned. We drove out toward the country with no specific destination in mind. After an hour or so, we saw a little country cafe and decided to stop for hamburgers. By this time I was feeling much better, and we giggled our way into a brightly lit restaurant. We were led to a booth by an old woman.

The woman was wearing enough makeup to sink a ship, but none of it hid the wrinkles on her face or the pouches under her eyes. She wasn't just old, she was ancient. She was clothed like a young girl on her way to the prom, a very poor girl who had bought her dress from a thrift shop for a nickel. It was almost like a cheap doll's dress with stiff, gaudy, gold-sprinkled lace and fraying satin. Her hair was wound into a beehive on top of her head.

We laughed and tried not to act obviously stoned while we talked about the woman and how weird she was. Johnny droned on with his thoughts on life and the universe. Then another woman came to take our order. This one was as young as the other one was old. She couldn't have been more than 13, and she was also dressed for prom night in a tight blue dress, not stylish, but not unattractive. She looked as though her great-grandmother had chosen her clothes, makeup, and hair style. Her dress with its revealing lines was totally inappropriate for her age. She looked like a cheap and inexperienced hooker.

We ordered hamburgers, fries, and cokes though I knew I would not be able to eat much. We decided we had happened upon a country-style whorehouse in the middle of the Ohio plains. The small cafe was a front to cover up the activities going on in the back rooms. There was a whole parking lot full of cars and trucks outside, but no other people were eating in the café. The young girl-woman came back with our check. She wrote only one figure on the slip and handed it to Johnny. Our meal came to $.92 for three hamburgers, three cokes, and three orders of fries. That was too cheap even for 1969, and Johnny surmised that she didn't know basic math. Why would she need to, in her line of work, ha ha?

We left with a vow to return and do some exploring later. Johnny went back a few weeks later. Instead of a small, charming, and lonely cafe he found a busy, bustling truck stop with a new name blazoned over the front door. Noisy truckers trundled in and out. There were no dressed-up, too old or too young waitresses. Had we actually seen what we thought we had seen? I wish I could explain that evening as a drug-induced trip, but it seems unlikely that all three of us experienced the same hallucination. I also wish I could say we quit taking drugs after that, but we didn't. From then on I was allowed to take only half-doses of heavy drugs, being trippy enough by nature.

Movin' On

Although I didn't freak out again for a long time, my life was bottoming out, and I was only 19. My family had lived in Cincinnati for six years, the longest time we had stayed anywhere. It was 1969 and nearing the peak of the hippie era. I would get high to relax, only to find myself tense with paranoia and a deep unremitting anxiety. I couldn't talk freely to anyone. Karl and I alternated between sexual frustration and wild bursts of passion, after which I would fear pregnancy. I flunked the philosophy class I was taking in summer school when I didn't make the deadline for a long paper I had written. I slept only during the daytime. I looked for jobs but couldn't find anyone who would hire me.

My father was traveling five days out of every week, and mother was irritable. She caught me making out with my sister's diving coach in the dark of my bedroom one night, and she was beyond disgusted with me. My acquaintances helped me drink up the supply of Scotch and whiskey in kitchen cabinet. I abandoned Karl completely; being around him twisted me in knots. I had reached one of those crossroads in life where I would be required to choose a path.

Julia provided me with a way out of my dilemma. She invited me to visit her in Chicago. I could look for a job in the Loop, and we would rent an apartment together. Neither of us wanted to go back to school. Julia had already landed a secretarial job with Prudential for the summer at $550 per month. That sounded like a fortune in those days. I made a reconnaissance trip to visit her.

Chicago and Independence

That summer Julia was sleeping with a drug-addled Jewish man named Dave. He irritated me to tears. He lived in a small apartment on Lincoln Avenue near Old Town just north of the Loop, a very trendy place in those days. He took a lot of different drugs; speed, LSD, opium, hashish, Quaaludes, and whatever he could buy on the street. He smoked weed every day. He worked for his father at an insurance company owned by the family. Fortunately he was not a heroin or cocaine user that I knew of.

I arrived in Chicago on a Wednesday, the week before my twentieth birthday. Julia conducted me to some of the high points of the city. We ate huge salads topped with creamy Russian dressing for lunch at the Empire Room. We walked over to Rush Street where I bought two dresses, one a see-through scrap of pink material which barely covered my ass and the other a diaphanous tent made from five royal blue paisley scarves. I called it my scarf dress, and I wore it until it was in rags. I spent $15. We sunned for an hour or so at the Oak Street Beach and then walked back to the subway along the shoulder of the Lake Street Expressway.

We stayed at home that evening with Julia's family and got plenty of sleep in preparation for the next day's activities. We started out the morning in Old Town, where I applied for a job at an art supply store. For $1.40 an hour I could learn how to frame pictures professionally. Then we went to Dave's apartment, where we all took tabs of a potent kind of speed. Speed was not the best drug for me in those days; I was already hyper enough. I was climbing the walls by the time we went to the grocery store to shop for dinner.

Later, while Dave was cooking the cheap steaks he had bought, Julia broke the news to me that she had already gone ahead and rented an apartment for us. We could look at it that evening. It would be ready for occupancy by the first of the month, only a few days away. I was stunned. Now I would have to find a job right away and face my family problems. I couldn't calm down. Commitments scared me then as they do now.

The next morning after a sleepless night I had to confront another problem. Julia's father left the house on his way to work and saw a pair of feet sticking out from behind the tree in the front yard. The feet were connected to a body, and the body was attached to Karl, who had come back to haunt me. He was asleep under the tree, waiting for the household to arise. Here I was trying to make a new life for myself, and my past was hanging on like superglue. After breakfast, Julia's mother declared her approval of the nice young man who had followed me to Chicago from Cincinnati, and who had slept under a tree to prove his faithfulness. I ignored Karl as much as possible, but I did allow him to accompany us on our adventures.

That day we met Freddie, a published writer who was Dave's cousin. Freddie was a mesmerizing, nonstop talker. He never quit pouring out verbiage the whole time we spent at his place. He was tall and gangly, with a caved-in chest and little pot belly. His hair was dark, curly, and receding from his high forehead. His eyes were a watery blue. He wore a navy blue Swedish fisherman's hat and a three-quarter length black cape when we went out. He was a chain smoker.

Julia was tense, Karl was jumpy, and I pretended to be cool during our visit. Dave decided to scout out Grant Park in his never-ending search for "good" drugs. He and Karl went off to the park while Julia and I ate herring and cream cheese on crackers with Freddie.

At that time Freddie had a 50-pound stash of homegrown marijuana pressed into wheels and stored in his refrigerator. There were seeds and stems all over the floor. He sold an occasional lid to partiers in the neighborhood, but he was not a great businessman. He was more interested in the story he was trying to sell to Playboy magazine and interviews he had gotten with famous people. He didn't even smoke pot himself--he just kept it around to be cool.

I had never met a real live writer. Karl didn't stand a chance in comparison. I was wearing my new blue scarf dress with no underwear on under it. Freddie asked me to stay for dinner. Regretfully I had to decline the invitation. Dave and Karl returned from the park with four hits of acid they had bought from street people.

We swallowed the tabs of LSD in Dave's tiny apartment. Dave talked endlessly about how some bad acid was going around, and how you never knew you had taken it until an hour later, when you dropped dead. The worst part was waiting out the hour after you swallowed the drug, wondering whether you had gotten the good stuff or the bad.

After that speech we were all pretty spooked. I was staring at the wall when suddenly the room started to shift and sway. The circles of my dress began spinning and whirling. The floor swept by me like strips of film through a projector. The world changed before my eyes. I was trying to learn how to deal with reality, and now I saw that reality could be changed at the drop of a pill. Why bother to learn to cope when obviously nothing was as it seemed? The world was nothing but a bad joke. I was right to have been a dreamer for all those years. The whole world was as skewed as I was.

I was too terrified to move. Finally the guys dragged me off the bed and out the door for a walk into what used to be my real world.

. . .

I would get through this experience and never again take another drug. I would stay away from Julia in her present phase and tell Karl to go home. I would arrange to see Freddie the next day. After I settled all that in my mind, I still had to endure 12 hours of tripping on some seriously potent LSD.

We went to Old Town and were kicked out of an ice cream parlor for being barefoot. We walked into the wax museum and all the head shops. We strolled into the park and saw imaginary cops behind every tree.

To my relief, we finally went back to Dave's apartment to listen to music. Karl kept playing the same record over and over, as if there were an important message he wanted to relate to me but couldn't express in his own words. I wasn't able to talk at all. In fact, I didn't say a word until midway into the next afternoon. I was too caught up in the rushing movement and beautiful visions appearing before me. If Karl wanted a declaration of love, this definitely was not the right time.

Eight hours later we were due to be home at Julia's house for bed. Karl assured us that he was fit to drive. How he managed to maneuver the car across the busy Chicago expressways while hallucinating wildly I don't know. He said later that he watched the white line and the speedometer. He dropped us off then went back to the park to sleep. No bed for him that night either. It was ten years before I could feel strongly about him again and understand the loneliness and sadness he felt after his ill-fated attempt to retrieve me from Chicago. He left the next day.

I arranged to see Freddie again immediately. We sealed a bond between us that night by sleeping together on the roof of his building. I had my period but that didn't deter him in the least. I promised to come back to Chicago after a brief trip home to see my parents.

I returned to Cincinnati to think about the way life was unfolding before me and to confront my parents. For weeks I dawdled and thought about what I wanted from life and what my goals were. Julia expected me to join her in Chicago. I had a job if I wanted at the art supply store. I could say goodbye to Karl again for the second or third time, but he still had visions of marriage and an apartment for us in Eden Park near downtown Cincinnati. I wondered who I was, really.

Then my father bombed the family again, as he had done every few years for as far back as I could remember. He had been transferred. Denver would be the destination this time. The family began making plans to move, and no one was happy about it, but by now moving was an accepted part of our lives. I promised my father I would help out in the moving process before I left for a permanent life in Chicago. He made me promise to give Denver a chance first.

When I told Karl I would be leaving Cincinnati for good, he burst into tears in the middle of the university cafeteria. I felt awful. We weren't ready for marriage, but my leaving would mean uncertainty and insecurity for both of us. I wanted out of the drinking, drugs, and unfulfilled sex routine, but living with my family in Denver would be Chinese torture. No, I would go to Chicago as Julia suggested after a token visit to Denver. I would find a job.

My father reacted to my decision with a bribe and a scare. He would give me $2000 to go to Europe if I would come back and live with the family in Denver. He assured me that living in Chicago meant certain and violent death for young, undirected women like me. I laughed at him and rejected his bribe. I told him I didn't care about how I turned out, as long as I didn't end up like him. I would go to Chicago where I would try to find my true self.

The night before we left for Denver I said goodbye to a small group of friends, all guys. We drank all evening in the tent in our back yard, and Charlie of my old English class pinched my left breast hard while no one else was looking. I was shocked and insulted. Was this the way men treated women when they thought they could get away with it? Henri had been bad enough, but this was worse. I didn't know where Karl was.

I was ready for a new life to begin. The next morning my brother and I drove west to Denver. I felt like a strange bird that had woven a ball of feathery wings around itself, a bird in a straitjacket. I had turned my wings into binders. I would figure out what to do next and how to fly again with the aid of nature and my own strength.

Revolution

Back before sophisticated calculators that cost two dollars at the grocery store, personal computers for everyone in the home, and women CEO's, the energy had begun to build for the coming of the New Age, or as sung by the Fifth Dimension, the "dawning of the Age of Aquarius." The leaders of this era were brilliant, odd, turned on. Some would be wildly successful, and others would choose to achieve their own small miracles with little or no recognition except from a narrow group of peers. Many of the followers of this renaissance turned on and tuned out for good and made their way through life in a permanent fog. Those unfortunate enough to be drafted went to war and came back damaged to be spit on and then ignored. Or they didn't come back at all.

On My Own and Looking For a Job

I stayed in Denver for a month, looking at apartments and not looking for jobs until I thought I would go mad. I watched TV on my parent's bed all day and nursed a very itchy, burning, vaginal infection. Freddie called me from Chicago and begged me to join him. There was no question that I would go. My parents bought me a plane ticket when it was clear that I had made up my mind. Besides, Julia had already rented us an apartment, and she expected me to join her.

The only night I ever spent in our apartment in Chicago was the night my mother came to visit. The day I arrived, Freddie picked me up at the airport and took me straight to his place. I kept the apartment with Julia in name only. My share of the rent was $75 a month, an amount I thought I could handle. I would find a job as a hardware store clerk. I had done that job summers and holidays in Cincinnati.

Freddie was wonderful in bed, and he surrounded himself with warriors and witches, models, and members of motorcycle gangs. He was friendly with everyone. Why should I go back to my empty apartment when I could be entertained all day and all night long at Freddie's place? I felt happier than I had felt in years, maybe even since I was a gawky 12-year-old playing hide-and-seek with the neighbor kids. I felt free of all the constraints and problems of my previous life. It was like being high all the time without the necessity of drugs or alcohol. I was at least hypomanic, which means I was bumping right up to the edge of full-blown mania, but not quite there.

My financial resources were nearly depleted after I paid my first month's rent and deposits for utilities; I gave my parents Freddie's phone number as the place where I could be reached. My parents were unhappy with me. I had flunked all my summer classes except the German play-writing class. I had never failed a class before. I began to look for work; picture framing at $1.40 an hour didn't sound like enough money to live on or enough of a challenge for me. Freddie was making even less than that, and we were always feeding hordes of people who happened to stop by. I realized I would have to find a job, fast.

I went to a job shop with high hopes. The first thing they asked me to do was take a typing test. That should have given me a clue about what employers expected from women in the job force in 1969. After chasing all over Chicago interviewing for jobs like "receptionist" and "accounting clerk," I got fed up with the agency Julia had recommended to me, which apparently was for female workers only. The job selection was terrible for a young girl without a college degree. It also didn't help that my whole wardrobe comprised four or five mini-skirts with tight-fitting tops and several suits that my mother had made for me that didn't fit quite right.

I answered an ad that promised "$750/month. We will train you." The ad was posted by the male counterpart of the agency for women that I had already tried without success. I walked into the place and didn't notice that I was the only woman in the room until my interviewer asked me what the hell I was doing there. I looked around and realized my mistake. Not a woman's face was in sight. To my credit, I demanded that he tell me about the $750 a month job. His response was to give me an IQ test. He was completely floored after he graded me; my score was higher than his own. In spite of my test results, he sent me back to the female placement agency. They gave me another typing test. I decided to look for job on my own.

After several more weeks of fruitless searching at insurance companies, big corporations, and a whole lot of other companies, I concluded that job hunting was a devastating and exhausting effort filled with futility and disappointment. I was refused at Kraft foods straight out because I was a woman. The human resources interviewer told me, "The guys at our company would never take orders from a woman." I was getting desperate as I had only $40 left, so I decided I would take the next offer made to me. In response to a newspaper ad for a bookkeeper, I interviewed at a printing company near Greektown. They offered me $440 a month to start, which sounded okay to me. I would assist the accountant in keeping the books, which was all done by hand back then. It wasn't a great job or a great salary, but it was something. The best part of it was getting there. I had to walk several miles to the central bus stop. Then I took two different buses to get to the corner of the street where the building was. Another three blocks of walking, and I was there. I've never been in better shape than I was then from all that walking every day. Of course, I had a lot more energy before my child-rearing years.

I was too young and immature to do a good job in the professional world. After I got a job as an Assistant Accountant I remember spending time entering numbers from invoices into a big book and adding up the long columns. That was about it for my efforts on the job. The employees took long breaks every morning and afternoon. We took an hour for lunch. I hid out in the bathrooms on days when my period was unbearable and I had taken six Midols at a time for the cramps. During the breaks and at lunch we played poker for money. I hated the job and was late for work almost every day. My hypomania began to wane.

Life at Freddie's

None of the people who hung out at Freddie's place had a dependable income. We celebrated with what we could get our hands on, usually cheap wine or low-quality marijuana. Every day at Freddie's was a party since almost no one worked. Before I started my job as Accounting Assistant, anyone who happened to drop by would be invited for home-cooked dinners, all the Coke you could drink, and whatever alcohol happened to be around. People wandered in and out. At dinner we ate vegetable soup, homemade biscuits, fried pork chops, hash browns, and fish with black beans. No one could talk and cook as well as Freddie.

Freddie and I managed some impressive gymnastics in the bedroom. I was still nervous about sex, so I put extra focused energy into wild, uninhibited caricatures of the way I thought sex was supposed to be. I was very flexible then and could do front and side splits. We should have gotten scores for the originality of our performances. "And there's a perfect 10 from the American judge," I could hear the announcer blare from the loudspeaker as sound echoed through the gym.

I was finally starting to enjoy myself in bed. Before then it hurt too much to be pleasurable. Freddie gave me my first vaginal orgasm. It came as a total surprise. Now I knew what everyone was talking about. I really wished then that I had run into Henri after I was more experienced. We could have had a lot of fun.

One of the regular visitors to Freddie's house was a computer programmer named Kevin. Kevin almost always wore the same turtleneck sweater that matched his slanting, luminous green eyes. His hair was the color of a copper penny and fell to his shoulders. He wore it loose and messy, never tied back in a ponytail. He was lean and wiry, and he walked with a graceful, slinky movement that rolled his skinny flanks in a catlike prance. I couldn't take my eyes off him. I fell for him before I even knew his name.

Kevin and I made an unlikely pair. We didn't look right together. We were the same height, but he was leaner and wirier and weighed a little less than I did. His face was large and rough-cut like Abraham Lincoln's. I was large and full-breasted, with scanty, usually greasy, dirty-blond hair that I wore down to my waist. I had a sturdy, broad, athletic body, which I used in a kind of knock-'em-over style. I looked like the kind of woman who could smother a man if she sat on his face.

Before I centered my attention on Kevin I might eventually have fallen in love with Freddie and married him, except he was going through his homosexual phase at that time, and all he wanted to talk about was Fabe, who was Freddie's best friend from the University of Illinois. He was a member of the infamous motorcycle gang known as the Outlaws. He had a girlfriend Donna, but he spent most of his time with the Outlaws, who had nothing better to do all day than work on their motorcycles and ride around getting in trouble.

Kevin worked at Argonne National Laboratories, a scientific facility west of Chicago, and he delighted in bringing us mathematical puzzles to solve that were generally beyond the brains of me and Freddie. The real game was the communication between me and Kevin, our eyes flashing subliminal messages. We began to know each other from unspoken clues, body language, and a desire to touch each other; he often grazed my elbows, knees, hair or the back of my neck seemingly by accident.

"Why are manhole covers round instead of square?" said Kevin.

It took Freddie and me eight hours to solve that one.

Then there were the Einstein, the three prisoners, and the ducks-on-the-bank puzzles. We were slightly better at those, and the nights flew by.

While Freddie was a confirmed bachelor who had sampled the delights of many women, Kevin had only slept with one woman, to whom he was married and separated. His wife was an artist, and according to him, schizophrenic. She had left him a year before, and he was glad to be free of her but lonely in the big old house his grandfather had bequeathed to him. The single life was not to his liking. His wife was convinced that he was gay, as their marriage was never consummated; this was something I didn't find out about for years afterward.

I was young, passionate, vivacious, and seething with untapped energy. I didn't tell Kevin of my attraction to him but I sparkled at him with my bright blue eyes and listened too avidly to the few things he talked about. It was hard to get a word in edgewise with Freddie around. After a while Kevin and I stopped listening to him and instead began focusing on each other.

One particular humid Sunday night before I got my job, the three of us waltzed down the street to Freddie's Volkswagen truck, with me snuggling between the two men in the front seat. We were going to visit Kevin's office at Argonne. He had generated our interest by rambling on about the computers he programmed and what they could do. Freddie was a linguist, so he cared most about the communication possibilities presented by the new cyber technology. I was happy to be part of the action, though computers baffled me in those days. If the men were interested, then I would be too. Besides, I was a talented mathematician in my own right; I knew I could figure out a way to keep up with them.

The drive to the lab took an hour; we were as comfortable as herrings in a tin. I was thinking I would have to tell Freddie soon that I didn't wish to share his bed or apartment any longer. He talked too much and listened too little. Sex was fine, but to me it was not as important as other kinds of attention. With my waning mania deserting me, I didn't feel very sexy.

We got to the lab around 1 a.m. and followed Kevin to his work area. The desk, where people dropped off their stacks of cards to be run on the big computer, was brightly lit with florescent lights and enclosed by floor-to-ceiling shelves. The Outbox was stacked with green-lined pages that were ultimately filed neatly on the shelves nearby and labeled with the names of the scientists who had written the programs. In those days, a program could easily bomb for a myriad of reasons, even something as trivial as a typo. Programs were being submitted round-the-clock to be run on the large computer that was run by computer operators. Kevin started out in that position since he did not have a college degree.

He took us behind the imposing operator center desk to the behind-the-scenes guts of the lab where the computers did their plodding work. Contrary to expectations, the area wasn't quiet. Visually it was almost too stimulating. The decor comprised electric blue walls accented with wide orange stripes. The computers were color-coordinated in the same blue and orange. It would not have been a good place for a quiet nap. I hadn't expected such a dazzling and noisy place for scientific work.

Kevin sat down at one of the consoles and began to type. The keys clicked and clacked in the cool room that echoed every sound. He invited me and Freddie to sit down at the adjoining keyboards.

"I'm going to give you both code numbers and then we can communicate with each other."

"Why don't we just talk?" I thought. I could send a message to either guy that would be hidden from the other so that no one knew who was talking to whom. This was before the Internet. The three of us proceeded to type messages to each other at a frantic pace. My messages were only for Kevin, my intended lover. Freddie couldn't wedge himself back in our conversation so he sat between us and watched us engage in what could only be considered computer conquest.

After a while Kevin and I realized that perhaps a better form of communication could be accomplished by actually turning to each other and speaking, or at least gazing deeply into each other's eyes. The three who left the lab were quieter than the ones who arrived. Still, I went home with Freddie, and Kevin went home to his cats. I practiced what I would say to Freddie when I told him I didn't want to sleep with him anymore.

I continued to live at Freddie's house and kept the apartment with Julia until the day she and her boyfriend took acid together and freaked out. Freddie and I were getting ready to go see a concert of Irish music. I realized when I was getting ready that I had left all my dress-up clothes at the apartment. A see-through scarf dress wasn't appropriate for a formal concert. Freddie and I walked to my nearby, usually-unoccupied apartment. As we approached the building from the sidewalk across the street, we noticed that traffic seemed unusually sluggish. Cars were stopped and horns blaring. It was a hot evening, and everyone was out of sorts. Then we saw

I'm Not Bipolar, I'm an Astral Traveler

the reason. Julia and Dave were stuck in the middle of the road, watching traffic go by on both sides of them. Dave was screaming. We watched as Julia tried to jerk him across the street. He would only go halfway, then turn around and attempt to go back to the centerline, where he felt safe. No cars could get past going in either direction.

Freddie and I threaded our way through the traffic and pulled Dave back to the sidewalk in front of the apartment. He continued to yell at the passing cars as though they were enemy tanks.

Before long, the landlady came out to investigate the source of all the commotion. She took one look at Dave and demanded to know what was going on. Dave grabbed her by the front of her lacy, old-lady blouse, and she started to squall. He panicked and started shouting, "Oh, the blood, the blood. I've killed her." That was the last straw for the old lady. She pulled away from him and ran inside to call the police.

While we were waiting for the police to come, Freddie was having his own panic attack. He had 50 pounds of fine homegrown marijuana stored in his refrigerator. What if the police decided to search both apartments?

The paddy wagon came and the cops made like tough guys. Even though Freddie and I were obviously straight, they threw us inside the paddy wagon for questioning. They decided we weren't stoned, and we were allowed to leave. Julia and Dave were transported to the nearest hospital for doses of Thorazine to bring them down.

Julia's parents were notified, and they came to pick her up. Freddie went into a flurry of activity to remove all traces of grass from his apartment. He took the pressed wheels outside and dropped them into neighborhood garbage cans. I swept the floors and closets clean.

The police busily raided the apartment in Julia's and my name and found a small quantity of grass. In those days possession of even a joint could get you a jail term. I was furious with Julia. I decided I would move my stuff into Freddie's place immediately. As it turned out, the police left both me and Freddie alone. He had thrown out his grass for nothing. Julia's parents made her move back home. Dave was busted for possession. When my parents found that I had moved in with a man, they tried to send me money for a motel room until I could get another place. I laughed at them. Life went on in Chicago very peacefully for a few more months.

Kevin began dropping by every night after he finished work. He worked as a help desk programmer and computer operator during the day and free-lanced for the physicists in the evening. He was the first person I met who seemed to feel that he was mentally superior to all the other people in the world. Freddie called him a Peter Pan because of his youthful face and slender, wiry body. He slept and bathed infrequently but after a while he cleaned up a little, I think for me. I flirted with him and tried to solve his puzzles.

No one in the group drank much but one night before Kevin came over, a friend and I finished off a half gallon of Bali Ha'i, a Kool-Aid-flavored wine product. By nine o'clock, I felt the floor begin to rock and sway as though in the throes of a violent earthquake. My head spun like I had been caught on a wildly out-of-control merry-go-round. There was a hole burning in my stomach, and hot green fluid was flooding my bowels. I went to the bedroom thinking that if I could just lie down on the bed, I would pass out quickly and be out of my immediate misery.

Lying down was a terrible mistake, as any good drunk knows. As soon as I hit the supine position, all the spinning and swaying of the world centered in the small area of my brain. The urge to both vomit and shit out the vile fluid I had so joyfully ingested was overwhelming. I knew I couldn't make it to the bathroom, so I lurched to the nearest window and spewed both my stomach and my guts down onto a poor unsuspecting Volkswagen parked under the window two stories below. I felt substantially better and settled back into the bed, where I soon passed out. When Freddie came in later I heard him say, "Phew, it stinks in here. I think I'll sleep on the couch tonight." You know perfectly well how I felt in the morning.

Eventually I began to have trouble with both Julia and Freddie. Julia and I had forfeited our apartment when she and Dave freaked out on the front walk, and she had moved back in with her parents. She wasn't allowed to see me anymore. I wasn't getting along very well with Freddie, since he wouldn't shut up about Fabe.

I couldn't exactly tell him I wanted to leave him because I suspected him of being homosexual. After all, up to this point we had shared a very satisfying sex life. I had never heard of bisexual people. Still, I was dissatisfied with my position in his apartment. I needed to find a place of my own. Rents in that area were about $145/month. I was bringing home less than a hundred dollars a week. Since I couldn't seem to get to work on time, I was being docked regularly. Some weeks I probably didn't clear more than $80 a week.

Kevin and I grew closer and closer, building toward the inevitable release through a physical relationship. He was hesitant to initiate a move on me, since he didn't know where Freddie and I stood with each other. It took some aggression on my part to push Freddie. By coincidence, Kevin ran into an old the situation over the edge. I wasn't inspired to attack until the night we attended a party in Old Town with Freddie. By coincidence, Kevin ran into an old friend from school named Cookie. What kind of name was that for an adult, anyway? She was short, dark and well-proportioned. Kevin ended up talking to her for hours. I wasn't at all manic, so I was shy with people I didn't know. I went to tell Kevin I was leaving. He looked at me perceptively, and said he would get our coats.

We walked back to the apartment, where we were alone together for the first time. We lay down on my mat in the living room and made out like a couple of desperate teenagers. I was wearing a velveteen orange mini dress that quickly hiked up around my hips. We were a picture of writhing, squirming, although fully clothed, humanity when Freddie walked in an hour later. He gave us a quick, embarrassed look but otherwise didn't react to the sight of us entwined on his living room floor.

I had some decisions to make, and Kevin made it awfully easy for me to go in his direction.

South Side

My clothes needed cleaning one day, and Kevin offered the use of his washer and dryer. He drove me south in his '57 T-Bird to the house where his grandfather had grown up. Kevin's wife Lara had done a beautiful job decorating the hundred-year-old white elephant. The mood of the house was warm and vibrant. Lara had papered the high ceilings with loud yellow and white daisies, which leered down at the room below. Gaugin and Modigliani prints were hung prominently in the living room and den. The couch was textured in fake black fur and was shaped like a welcoming, concave banana. A rattan table and chairs covered in hot red and orange flowers crowded the small dining area. My favorite room was the den, used as an office and furnished only with a walnut desk, a curvy blue foam chair, and a liquor cabinet filled with J & B, Kevin's favorite Scotch.

The house smelled of cats. Kevin had kept a beautiful calico cat left over from the failed marriage. Kevin wasn't home often enough to be bothered by the ammonia-and-shit smell of a too-full litter box, so the house stank of ripe decay. The cat was friendly and jumped right into my lap when I sat down on the couch, which seemed to suck me into its uterine depths. I lay back and felt deeply relaxed and contented with the warm, purring animal curled across my breast. Kevin looked at me with his slanting green cat's eyes and led me upstairs.

The mood of the upstairs was cooler and more austere. The ceilings and upper walls were painted a moody midnight blue. Below the ring of satiny trim was a vast light blueness. Lovely oak cabinets and drawers had been built-in when the house was originally constructed. The bathroom was relatively un-modernized, with a big, claw-footed bathtub. There were four bedrooms, mostly filled with the remainder of Lara's things.

The master bedroom was freezing. I didn't want to undress. Kevin said that for some reason he couldn't figure out, this room never got warm. Probably a friendly ghost lived here. While my clean clothes tumbled in the dryer, I slowly seduced Kevin, both of us covered with goose bumps, while the ghost watched.

Kevin was the first of many men I came to know who claimed to have been mentally abused by the women they loved. His wife must have put a hex on his prick, because that first time in the cold room, with the ghostly specter hovering quietly over us, Kevin couldn't get it up for me. I didn't mind; I can be turned on by a soft prick. I came as he fumbled and fidgeted and finally lay still over me, exhausted. "I'll take care of it," he whispered. I whispered back, "It really doesn't matter," and I meant it sincerely.

Partly because of the disparity in our looks and temperaments, no one in Freddie's crowd guessed that Kevin and I were having an affair, or at least trying to.

My last night at Freddie's apartment was on New Year's Eve, 1969. Freddie threw a big New Year's Eve party, to which he invited all the people who had wandered in and out of the apartment during the year. There were so many people the party expanded out onto the roof. At midnight one of the guests played Auld Lang Syne on his bagpipes. The sound was lost to the cold and bitter wind. Kevin and I kissed furtively among the shadowy guests on the dark roof. I felt no connection with any of the people there, and soon we left to join the happy ghosts in the south side house.

Kevin got it up that night, and he never faltered for me again.

The next day I decided to move in with Kevin into the comfortable old house. Freddie deserved at least a goodbye, but I didn't have the nerve to face him. He had been good to me in a misguided way. I sneaked in and out of his place taking my few belongings: clothes, paints, a few books, and the goat hair boots that Kevin had bought me for Christmas. I didn't see Freddie again for several months.

Kevin took some time off work to spend long, lazy hours with me. Now that his prick was getting hard again, we lived in the cold bedroom. I learned to have multiple orgasms. I phoned my boss at work and told him I would be out indefinitely with mononucleosis.

Kevin and I had another kind of disease: mutual nymphomania. I got out of bed for long enough to fix us bacon, eggs, and toast with jam, then we made love alongside the breakfast dishes. The china piled up on the floor beside the bed while we napped and fucked our brains out, like newlyweds. I found that I could screw and come to orgasm almost continuously, with small naps in between. Kevin was making up for a long-term celibacy and who knows how long of impotence. We lingered in the blue bedroom for six weeks.

One day Kevin said he needed to drop in at work to see how things were going, just for a few minutes. Argonne National Laboratory was 30 miles west of Chicago. Because the drive was so long, he tended to stay put once he got there. The other scientists there worked day and night, and Kevin's job was to keep their computer programs running. He was never at a loss for something to do there.

I had been able to save some money somehow, and in the spring of 1970 I enrolled in classes at the University of Illinois, Chicago Circle campus. The days went by, and I was so busy with school I didn't notice just how much time Kevin was spending at work until the night I took the wrong train and didn't arrive home until 8 p.m. I was worried that I had kept Kevin waiting for dinner. We usually ate out in the evening at the local IHOP. To my shock, Kevin wasn't even home yet. I worried about his car breaking down on the dark roads. All of his cars were pieces of crap, even though he was very proud how well he maintained them. Also, he had a tendency to run out of gas.

He waltzed through the door at 9 o'clock p.m. and breezily greeted me. I was angry, but I acted as though nothing was wrong. We went out to eat, and I mentioned that he looked tired. We didn't make love that night. He fell asleep as soon as his head hit the pillow.

That night became the norm. The nine o'clock arrivals stretched to two, three, then four or five in the morning. Finally, he started sleeping at work, so that some days he didn't come home at all. He reveled in being tired and overworked. His career was the most important thing in the world to him, more important than me or sex or his health. He got involved in a new project, and soon I saw him awake only if I went to work with him.

The evenings belonged to me alone in a house filled with moody ghosts. I masturbated, drank J & B, and ran around the house dressed only in one of Kevin's old shirts. I couldn't believe that work would win out over sex, but with Kevin that became the case.

I became interested in cultural and physical anthropology. I had a vision of our predecessors living in a warm dark cave, spending long hours joking, eating, and storytelling before a flickering fire. They were happy, and they accepted life as it came to them. Hunting and gathering were done casually. The earth, though capricious, provided all their needs, and its resources were constantly replenished. I wanted to go live in the great outdoors. I needed to get away from Kevin and get a life of my own.

Back to School

Anthropology was a poetic discipline, no matter how rigid the professionals tried to make it. My professors and their colleagues wanted to be accepted in the scientific world, and I don't blame them. Still, how much can you tell for sure about a few pieces of grain, stone, bone, or pottery? Visualizing the lives of ancient man requires a leap of the imagination. That's exactly what I loved about the study of this puzzling subject; I had an excuse to let my imagination run wild.

In the spring I heard about an archeological dig being conducted in Central Illinois by the Anthropology Department at my school. I just had to go. Kevin was gone most of the time. His nasty wife had shown up at the house one night, and because of my presence there now felt she had more ammunition for taking Kevin's house and money in the divorce settlement. I had a long talk with her, and she sneeringly called me Kevin's "little honey" and Kevin my "prince of peace." Those were the days before no-fault divorces. She would use my presence any way she could to get money out of him. I hated being in the house when I knew she could barge in at any time. She had a perfect right to enter: it was half her house, and she had left many personal items, including some of her original paintings.

I wanted to get out of there, away from Kevin and his crazy wife. A little physical activity and being outdoors for the summer sounded like healthy, though temporary solutions to my problems.

Too much sex with Henri had done me in and now too little of it with Kevin was doing the same thing. I figured that a road trip and a worthy goal would pull me through. I would earn 12 hours of credit towards my degree in anthropology. Amazingly, when I started the trip I was more depressed than manic. I zoomed upward as soon the shenanigans of the summer began at the camp.

Meds--Yes or No?

Most psychiatrists have no idea what psychotropic medications do to their unsuspecting patients. If they had a clue I don't think they'd be so quick to prescribe medications that seem to have as many side effects as people taking them. There's no question that the medications have improved since the days of heavy Thorazine and Haldol usage. Still, the meds I have taken for the last thirty years have caused some miserable side effects such as uncontrollable nausea and diarrhea, hallucinations, stupor, tics, mania, depression, excessive weight gain, tooth decay, high blood sugar, hypothyroidism, and diabetes. Through it all I have tried to achieve a normal level of stability, but at this point I realize that normal is relative.

Before I drank or took mind-altering drugs, my unique brain chemistry allowed me to get high pretty much any time I wanted to, given the addition of a few catalysts. When I was very young I found I could vastly improve my mood by seeking out friends who had a little more energy than most, a little more sparkle, and a little more daring. I avoided boring, compliant kids and instead chose as my playmates the ones who were unique, unpopular, troublemakers, or just really fun.

As I got older, I found that I could also make myself high by exercising to an extreme, breaking the rules and getting away with it, staying awake all night, reading exciting books, challenging my physical limitations, running away, driving fast, studying intensely, spending money, indulging in forbidden sex, and in general doing whatever I wanted as the mood struck me. Later on there was alcohol, pot, mescaline, LSD, speed, and even a lot of Midol to push me higher. The main thing was, whatever I did, I did to an extreme.

For years I have wondered if I actually made myself bipolar through my choices and not through an accident of nature. Once you start doing exciting things and taking risks matter-of-factly in your normal life, it's hard to go back to plain old everyday reality, even as a three-year-old. You're always on the lookout for a way to feel that euphoria again. You might say that you become a thrill junky, which is what they called Bill Clinton after his affair with Monica Lewinsky. You learn to pick out manic people in a crowd and gravitate towards them as second nature. You choose activities with a high potential for risk just to feel the danger and excitement. I've been doing risky things since I met Jeff before I went to school, and it's been hard for me to break that pattern. I rarely listened to warnings from adults once I learned to love the adventurous side of life.

Looking back, I see an obvious motivational pattern for most of the important events of my life: I sought the path that brought me the highest highs, the most stimulation, and the most orgasmic joy. When I was depressed I took antidepressants or simply slept. Those times were nothing more than preparation for the next manic high. Most times I came out of a depression only to go directly into mania. Anti-depressants aren't supposed to make you high. But if that's true, I have to ask why do you suffer withdrawal when you quit taking them? And why do you seem to need more in time to get the same effect? Anyone who's ever tried to go off antidepressants knows that you can indeed suffer weeks of nausea, sweating, extreme anxiety attacks, and headaches before you are totally free from their effects.

When I look at my young grandchildren, I see that babies are born happy. For them, life is mostly grand. Unhappiness passes quickly. What's wrong with wanting to be happy for the rest of your life? I can really do without depression. I can't see that feeling suicidal has ever had a purpose to further mankind along the evolutionary ladder. The problem lies in knowing the difference between happiness and being high. When you're happy, you're content with the way things are; when you're high, you just want to be higher and stay that way for a long time.

After countless destructive manic moods, I have a nagging fear that I'm not supposed to feel too good. "Feeling good will lead to mania," I think.

In my experience that is usually what happened. As I've gradually figured out which medications are the best for my overall mental health, I've come to realize that it's perfectly normal to be happy most of the time. But there's that fine line. I'm always asking myself, "Am I too happy? Do I like this medication because it makes me high? Am I just an addict at heart, looking for the best fix? Even though psychiatrists say that psychotropic medications are not addictive, why is it that I can't do without them?"

Brave New World is my favorite book, even though I don't agree with Huxley's vision of technology being ultimately evil. Why should our version of soma turn us into boring, bland idiots with no creativity or originality? The happier I am the more creative I get. I've used a cornucopia of prescription medications to keep me happy and productive, and yes, occasionally high. It's no wonder I have been so tolerant of putting up with side effects. The rewards can be so great and the failures so devastating. But I've also realized that there might be no end to the medication game.

Note: I wrote this book many, many years ago, and now I have discovered a drug regime that works for me that as far as I can tell has had no bad side effects with the exception of a gain of ten pounds. I can easily lose the ten pounds if I put my mind to it. I am thrilled that I have been able to regain my depth of feeling and creativity. I have now been able to mourn the loss of my father. I thought I was a monster when he died and I didn't even cry. My meds were dampening my feelings to the point that I felt very little. Though I realize there is no end to the medication game, I feel no resentment or anger about that, only relief that for me there is a solution to the riddle of my own particular chemical puzzle.

The Dig

I left Chicago with a small group of anthropology students on a bus for Decatur, Illinois early in June 1971. I felt listless and bored, unusual states for me. I was hot, and as a Northern girl, I've never done well in the heat. With what seemed a tremendous effort, I started a conversation with the woman sitting next to me. Her name was Mayellen. By the end of the long, hot ride, we were acquaintances. Mayellen was married, and her husband Bret would be coming down later to take photographs of the artifacts we uncovered. Mayellen had long, greasy, dark brown hair, and her mouth was shaped into a permanent pout. She was passive and talked with a lisp. She and Bret were broke; they hoped to be paid for the pictures Bret would take at the site. Mayellen was a typical child of the sixties. She had brought lots of drugs with her: speed, acid, grass, and hash. She needed some speed that day; she drooped like a nodding, wilted flower. She looked as depressed as I felt.

We arrived at the site late in the afternoon. The tents lay lifeless on the ground, a tangled mass of limp canvas and segmented posts. Unless we wanted to sleep under the stars, we were going to have to set up the tents before dark. No one knew what to do with these gigantic army tents, and we scurried around aimlessly like busy little worker ants without a queen. Our instructor was a professor named Ralph Laurent (no kidding), and he had brought his wife and four girls with him to camp. He had his hands full organizing his family for the night in their camper, so we were left to our own devices to set up the gear.

Ralph Laurent had the worst stutter I've ever heard, and it was literally impossible for him to give any kind of detailed instructions about how to get the tents up. It was so painful to hear him speak that we were relieved to be left alone to get the job done ourselves, even though we were making a mess of things.

There were two huge tents to erect, one for boys and one for girls. By the time we figured out how to make the clumsy structures stand up, we were stumbling around in the dark, screaming and cursing at each other. We ripped dozens of holes in the rotting material, which would have to be repaired if we wanted to stay dry. This group would be stuck together for the next two months, living, eating, sleeping, shitting, and of course fucking in the closest proximity to each other. We started out very poorly.

By eight p.m. we had done a barely adequate job of constructing our shelter. The posts wobbled, and only the major holes were mended, but we'd be dry and protected as long as there were no high winds or extremely heavy rains. We gathered around an impromptu campfire and assessed each other.

Already the people in the group fell into stereotypes in my mind. There was Richard, the macho man, who had brought his guns and Cora, the feminist. Cora was infuriated by Richard's constant lewd comments and attempts to bait her with obscenity. Sparks would fly between these two night and day for the rest of the summer.

Also in the group was a shell-shocked soldier who had just returned from Vietnam. The first sentence I heard him speak was, "Let me eat your pussy, please." I don't know why I was so horrified by that request; I guess I imagined some kind of exotic jungle rot flying from his mouth to my body. I declined the offer.

A husband and wife team, Lisa and Jim, had brought their two small children. They planned to trade off on the babysitting. Jim had a long scraggly beard that fanned out over his chest. Lisa was chunky and wore a braid down past her waist.

Of the remaining men, Greg was the best looking. He was 6'6" tall and weighed over 250 pounds. He made us all look like dwarves. Unfortunately, he hurt his back the first week and didn't dig again for a month. That first night he took great pains to tell us all what a great lover he was and that he had the largest penis in the world. I know now that people who talk big about sex usually don't follow through with action.

The rest of the group comprised a trio of women who giggled constantly and wore makeup to bed and a few quiet men who faded into the background. Altogether there were twenty-five of us. There was no doubt about it: anthropology seemed to attract some of the stranger people on campus.

Ralph Laurent divided us into work groups. My group got to make sawhorse tables. I discovered I was the only woman who was strong enough to use the big handsaw to cut lumber by hand. I felt like superwoman. I challenged the men to arm wrestling matches and beat all of them but one: the Vietnam vet, who tied me, then asked again if he could eat my pussy.

We spent the first week setting up and establishing a routine. Ralph Laurent told us that we would be required to keep a diary of everything we did. I took him literally; I was great at personal journals. As it turned out, I got a little carried away with personal information. After all, how much can you write about a few arrowheads and pieces of plain pottery?

That first week the group split into different flavored factions. The feminists led the pot-smoking crew. Greg and a quiet, soft-spoken, man named Colin formed the core of the drinkers. I had a problem choosing sides. I had given up drugs, but I felt more in tune with the potheads. On the other hand, the feminists were a little too strident for me; I was unfamiliar with their rhetoric, so I felt insecure with them. I cast my fate with the alcoholics. The groups were to remain unmixed all summer, except for a few uneasy sexual excursions between tents.

We began our real work the second week. Our job was to excavate a strip of ground overlooking a winding riverbed. Each person was responsible for a ten-foot-square area. Ralph Laurent had been given a grant by the city of Decatur to excavate the site and set up a small museum with the finds. We started out with enthusiasm and energy.

The painful monotony of archeology became all too apparent after our first week of digging. None of us were used to being in the sun eight hours a day, so we were all in various stages of sunburn. Cora, with her fair, freckled complexion, suffered the worst; even her scalp was a red, raw mass of peeling flesh.

The work consisted of carefully removing a tiny scoop of dirt from the surface of each square with a tool that looked like a garden trowel, then sifting the dirt through a fine screen. Whatever remained was carefully examined for archeological significance. We could work for hours, days, and weeks without discovering anything important.

A few seeds of unrest were planted in the group early on. After Greg hurt his back he spent the mornings resting on his cot. The days stretched into weeks of inactivity. His injury didn't affect his sex life, however. He was the first in the group to initiate a sexual encounter; he and Mayellen sneaked off to the woods every evening that first week. I was vaguely jealous that he chose Mayellen over me for a partner, even though I disliked him intensely. I would have liked first shot at turning him down.

Lisa and Jim began violent arguments about whose turn it was to babysit. Both of them wanted to work full time on the dig, and neither of them wanted to watch the children. The family camped out in the woods by themselves several hundred feet from the dig. They seemed happy and cheerful at the beginning of the summer, but as time went on it became obvious that they were headed for big trouble.

Ralph Laurent's children ran around wild and got in everyone's way. Our fearless leader's lack of direction and his indecisiveness drove us all crazy. His wife was a plain Jane, and she attempted to control the students but not her own children. An added irritant was that Ralph Laurent had definite favorites among the students. The favored few got the choicest assignments and the best grades. The rest of us were treated as drones, were forced to perform the nastiest jobs, and earned B's and C's for our efforts.

We found no artifacts for weeks. Our routine never varied. We got up at six and then ate a quick, hearty breakfast if we were able to roll out of bed at that ungodly hour. We were working at our pits by seven and then digging and sifting all morning until noon. Lunch comprised sandwiches and chips, then there was time for a brief snooze. Afterwards, we went back into the hot sun for another three hours. At four we were supposed to take time for writing in diaries and working on independent projects until dinner. Dinner was the big meal of the day, and we took turns preparing it at five. After dinner we were on our own.

In spite of the monotony and long hours of backbreaking labor during the day, I was full of zest and mischief in the evenings. I became a ringleader for the drinking faction. One night I suggested that we find a deserted spot for a private campfire party. Colin knew just the place. He had been wandering around looking for fossils on his own time.

Colin was our camp mascot. At 18, he was the youngest student enrolled in the summer program. He was also something of a celebrity in the department for his discovery of a unique new fossil that had been named for him. He was intense, single-minded, and unbelievably naive. All the women from both groups loved him.

As a specialist of paleontology, Colin scoured the area for interesting rock formations. He had discovered an abandoned quarry behind camp in the middle of the woods. It was a weird and eerie place: a jagged hole scooped out of a block of rock in the Illinois outback. There couldn't have been a better party spot.

One moonless night, Colin led us through grassy thickets and past dark shapeless forms to the brink of what appeared to be a cliff over the edge of the world. I didn't dare look down for fear of being sucked into the yawning hole. We quickly gathered some brush and sticks and started a sickly fire. Our uneasiness with each other was not quelled by the warm glow of the flames. Where was the camaraderie I had endowed upon my cavemen as they drowsed by the fire at the end of the day? Colin took out his flask and took a healthy swig of vodka. Greg asked for a sip. Lisa suggested a sing-a-long and led off with, "Michael Rowed the Boat Ashore." Our voices quavered weakly into the mysterious beyond. I realized how alone I felt, even when surrounded by other people. We walked back to camp accompanied only by the sounds of the night birds and bugs.

Before long, we all knew our way to the quarry in the dark. By unspoken agreement, the drinkers brought as much booze as we could afford to our hideaway. Our meetings stretched longer and longer into the night. We all started skipping breakfast for an hour extra of sleep in the morning.

One night the pot smokers stayed in the tent while the drinkers wandered off to the cliffs over the quarry. Greg was now free to come on to Lisa, who was fed up with her husband's lack of support in taking his turn at childcare.

Jim half-heartedly talked to a red-haired graduate student, but he kept glancing over to see what Greg and his wife were doing. A couple of unattached guys who would have welcomed any female attention were sitting around trying not to look horny. One minute we were sitting around the campfire talking and drinking. The next thing I knew, Lisa and Greg were both naked and maneuvering into the missionary position in front of us. They didn't even bother to creep behind a bush as the rest of us would have done. I tried not to watch them.

Not to be outdone by a cheating wife, Jim took off his pants and snuggled up to me. I wasn't drunk enough to fuck someone I didn't even like in front of an audience. No one else made any moves. Hedonists we were not. I wondered how I would face my classmates sober and in the light of day. I drank a pint or more of straight, warm J & B most nights while reading or writing by myself.

Halfway through the summer, my boyfriend Kevin tore himself away from his job in Chicago long enough to come visit me. We stayed in a borrowed tent and made beautiful, passionate love. I forgave him his workaholic lifestyle, and we talked about marriage for the first time. His divorce had gone through, and now he was technically free. He had lost his grandfather's house to his now ex-wife, and he was understandably bitter. He was making good money, though, and his ex had not been awarded any ongoing support payments. So, things were looking up for us, if I could only seduce him away from work some of the time.

Because his ex-wife had gotten the house, we would have to find somewhere else to live. We had a few ideas about where to go after I was done with the dig. In the meantime life was wonderful, wasn't it? And we were in love, weren't we? We stopped using birth control. I hoped the LSD I had taken the summer before hadn't ruined my chromosomes. I didn't know about infant fetal alcohol syndrome, so it's a good thing I didn't get pregnant that first month. If I was so happy, why did I feel so on edge?

After Kevin left I felt more alone than ever. I finally convinced Colin to meet me at the top of the hill outside camp one night after dinner. I talked a lot, and he said hardly a word. He drank vodka nonstop. I guessed that he was one of those man-boys who are afraid of almost everything: women, school, friendships, and intimacy. He felt most comfortable with rocks and dirt. Deep down, I could relate to his fears. The only difference between us was that I had developed a phony outer shell to carry me through the events of daily life. I liked Colin, so I seduced him, thinking it would be good for him to get over being a virgin. He didn't seem to have ever entertained a girlfriend, so it didn't occur to him to abstain from booze if only for the sake of having sex. I really didn't care: it took very little attention on his part to satisfy me. Being with Colin was like cuddling with a baby blanket.

After our attempted tryst we walked back down the hill into camp. Most of the crew was lounging about, snacking, and drinking. Colin put his arm around my shoulder. Without thinking, I shrugged it off. I could tell by the way he looked at me that he was hurt by my rejection. His familiarity felt too possessive to me, especially since I already had a serious boyfriend. And one attempted fuck does not make a relationship. After that night he withdrew from us and spent most of his time drinking alone. Halfway through the summer another woman, Anna Rapp, joined our group. She fell for Colin in a big way and took him under her wing.

They drank together, but I never asked her if she tried to have sex with him.

One night I took Greg on. He was indeed as big as he had bragged. He was so large that sex wasn't even possible between us, and we parted unsatisfied.

It never occurred to me to blame my cheerless promiscuity on the effects of alcohol. I never got visibly drunk; in fact, I seemed to be able to drink without much effect at all as long as I didn't drink too quickly. Maybe the physical activity of the day was washing all the alcohol out of me. My nighttime activities were almost dreamlike, as though they were being acted out by a person separate from me. I guess that's what I liked most about alcohol. It allowed me to dissociate from myself and do things I didn't normally dare. I could skew off in many directions and still feel somewhat integrated when I was drinking.

As the summer wore on, I had less and less fun and felt more and more dissonant with my real self. My thoughts of being skewed from the world reminded me of my experiences in early high school.

Being on the dig was the closest I would ever come to "dating." I never did really get the hang of it.

We moved to a new site. The old dig had yielded little in the way of archeological interest. Each of us had done a special project and turned in our diaries. I found an exquisite obsidian arrowhead, the only one of the dig, and it killed me to have to turn it in to Ralph Laurent.

I knew he would bury it in some storage area where no one would ever look at it again.

One night as I approached the dining tent, I heard the group laughing raucously at something one of the drugged-out women, Janice, was reading aloud. Curious, I listened outside the tent. I realized with humiliation that she was reading excerpts from my diary in front of the dinner crowd. As part of our coursework, I assumed that the journals were supposed to be confidential. I couldn't believe Ralph Laurent had exposed me to this mockery by giving Janice my personal notes for scrutiny by the group. After a particularly uproarious surge from the crowd, Janice giggled, "Is she existing in the same time and place as we are? Let's tell her she has to share whatever drug she's on with us."

I was furious, and I hated every last one of them. I hated Ralph Laurent for being a wimp, Janice for her joyous mockery of me, Cora for her shrill feminist certainty, Greg for his giant, useless prick, Lisa for her sex appeal, Colin for his timidity, the silly girls for their giggling immaturity, all the children for being pains in the ass, the Vietnam vet for wanting to eat my pussy, and everyone else on general principles. I borrowed money from Anna and bought more booze.

One night I walked alone to the quarry. The woods were full of mysterious shapes and sounds. A glowing, light-colored boulder materialized into a man-form before my eyes. I thought I saw a white man with dark hair and a full beard. He was handsome, still not someone I wanted to meet alone in the black woods. He appeared to be watching me. My imagination kicked in full force, and I ran. I ran through the thorny underbrush as fast as I could manage, hearing certain footfalls behind me. I tripped desperately into camp, claiming I was being chased by a phantom from the forest. Someone who looked like, well, Mayellen's husband Bret, who had joined us earlier in the week. My colleagues looked at me in disbelief. Most of them had been sitting around camp getting stoned all evening, including Bret. He thought my accusation was hilarious, and he impersonated the "Phantom of the Dark" every time he saw me after that. By then the constant drinking was really getting to me.

The climax of the summer occurred one moonless night shortly after we had moved from Decatur to a new site located ten miles outside Cairo, (pronounced Cay-ro) Illinois. We were uncovering an Indian village that had been abandoned for an unknown reason. We hoped to find a clue as to the motive of the obviously hasty retreat: it appeared that everything inanimate had been left intact. Although Ralph Laurent had dug here before with different sets of students, so far he had found no human bones.

I had fallen into bed exhausted after sweating my ass off on a day that could have rivaled the Sahara desert for temperature and an equatorial jungle during the rainy season for humidity. I had not exactly improved my physical condition after dinner with the consumption of nearly half a bottle of Scotch. At 10 p.m. I heard a scuffle and a muffled cry somewhere out in the night. The sounds seemed to float directly to my ears even though I could tell they originated from some distance away.

I heard more scuffling, then a howl. "Don't, please don't. I didn't do anything."

"You bitch; you've been fucking him again, haven't you?" There was a loud and sickening thwap, a sound like a boxer with padded gloves connecting with a ripe cantaloupe, and then the softer sound of something hitting the ground.

"No, I just went to the shithouse," whined Candy.

There were more thunking noises.

"I'll kill you both, but I'm going to kill him first," Jim said.

Then we heard the heavy footsteps of a booted man running on the dirt road in front of camp.

Greg of the giant prick foolishly tried to pretend he was asleep. By this time everyone in camp was wide awake. We were all paralyzed. No one knew what to do.

Jim entered Greg's tent and overturned the 250-pound man and his cot in the dark night. Greg, who had just arrived back in his bed only moments before Jim's furious entrance, made no attempt to defend his relationship with Lisa. He denied everything in the face of Jim's maniacal anger. Everyone who heard the scene feared for Greg's life. Jim had a gun.

Greg spoke slowly and calmly to the madman. "Jim, you're wrong about me and Lisa. She loves you and you alone. She'd never do anything to harm you. She's a faithful and loving wife."

Greg's strategy worked, if only because Jim wanted to believe in his wife. As a matter of fact, Lisa and Greg had been balling each other's brains out every night for over a month. And Jim, the hypocrite, had approached me in my small tent and tried to put the make on me that very night. He had given up after a few futile attempts with the mournful line, "I want to fuck my wife."

There may have been a strange sort of logic underlying all these peculiar events, but if so, it was not a logic I understood. Lisa and Jim were asked to leave camp the next morning. Before they left, Jim asked me plaintively if I thought he was a bad person because of what he had done to Lisa in the night, which had been to beat her to a pulp. I said no, but secretly I had lost all respect for both of them: Jim was no more than a bully wielding his power and Lisa was the willing victim who groveled before him but slept with another man behind his back. I didn't feel much sympathy for either of them.

Jim and Lisa returned two weeks later with their children to finish their coursework. Lisa's arm was in a sling and her face still showed the bright blues and yellows of healing bruises. No one commented or attempted to interfere. After that summer, I realized that human nature could be very bizarre when the normal restraints of society were released. We should have done an anthropological study of ourselves and turned it in to Ralph Laurent for credit.

The heavy drinking I had been indulging in all summer finally took its toll on me. I got behind in my required class work and skipped a few days of digging to catch up. Then it began to rain heavily, and we were stuck inside with busywork. I despised the process of cataloging artifacts. It was too detailed and painstaking for me. I invented excuses not to appear when it was my turn to write numbers on pieces of pottery and paint over them with nail polish. I began to suffer miserably from hay fever. I stole antihistamines from Ralph Laurent's medicine stash and swallowed them by the handful.

One night after swallowing about ten of the antihistamines and drinking a pint of Scotch I blacked out and didn't wake up for four days. I hadn't lost time since my sophomore year at Purdue, the night I had seen the movie *Ulysses*. I remember Anna coming to get me out of bed for dinner. I asked her what day it was. She said "Thursday," and looked at me quizzically. I felt as though I was coming to consciousness after a long sleep. I couldn't remember what I had done that day, or yesterday, or the day before that. The last I remembered was Monday night. It scared the shit out of me. I wasn't hungry or thirsty, but I went to dinner with Ann. It seemed strange that no one commented on my absence from the field. Had I somehow kept on functioning without being conscious? That didn't seem likely. Had I stayed in bed for the whole time pretending to be sick?

I tried to carry on a normal conversation with Anna. I hoped she didn't notice that my hands were shaking so badly I couldn't hold my fork. I ate a few pieces of fish and a cupcake and went along to my bunk to read and ponder what happened to the missing days. I had never been skewed for days in a row. The psychiatrists call what had happened to me a fugue state, but I think skewed is a better description.

Maybe the aliens had come to take me to their spacecraft that week and they poked and prodded me for their education. That seemed as likely as anything else to have happened. Next time they come to get me, I'm going to ask them to keep me conscious while they study me.

Wedding

The sweltering summer of 1970 was finally over. Kevin spared me the bus ride home by coming to pick me up in his black '57 T-Bird. We spent the last night at camp in a musty old barn, sleeping on a damp, skittering pile of hay. I didn't sleep well, thinking about all the wildlife we were disturbing; but no living thing bothered us, and we made confident love. The next morning I finished up my scanty classwork diary that came directly from my imagination, since I had stopped taking notes on my findings about halfway through the summer. "Nothing here for anyone to mock," I thought bitterly. With a huge sigh of relief, I turned in my assignments, and Kevin and I were off to a new life together.

I was noticeably less than enthusiastic about the anthropology program after that. I graduated the next year, barely, only because there were reduced requirements for graduating at that time. Most of the students were still demonstrating against the war, and all you had to do was show up for class to get passing grades.

Kevin and I had nowhere of our own to go to. Kevin's cousin, a psychiatrist at the Loyola Medical Center, offered us his home as a last resort for the time his family would be on vacation. We decided to take him up on his offer and headed towards Oak Park, a charming suburb west of Chicago. We disappeared into the rambling, disordered house for two weeks of absolute inactivity other than lovemaking and fast food jaunts. Sooner or later we would have to surface and make plans for our future. For the time being, we lost ourselves in each other.

I realized I would have to call my parents to tell them where I was. After all, I wasn't lying dead somewhere, but they didn't know that. The phone conversation between my mother and me was surreal to the point of being hallucinatory. Somehow she got me to agree to come to Denver with Kevin. Kevin wanted to get married so we would have legitimate children. With all the screwing around we were doing, I could get pregnant at any minute. I was quite sure I didn't want children right away. I was 20 years old and had never changed a diaper or held an infant. I was understandably terrified of motherhood.

For a while I had been a popular babysitter for older children in our suburban neighborhood. I was smart and good-natured, and I only charged $.75 an hour. That was a good deal even for the sixties. Throughout my high school years I made enough money babysitting to pay for my whole first year of tuition at Purdue.

As I thought about the kids Kevin and I would have, I felt a shiver of unease. I remembered some incidents I had conveniently blocked out.

Like the summer of 1966, when it was time for the World Series playoffs. My maternal grandma had instilled in me a love of baseball. (She was the one who got me started on Scotch, too). I wouldn't have missed the first game of the series for the world. Sandy Koufax of the Los Angeles Dodgers was going up against Whitey Ford of the New York Yankees. I had butterflies of excitement in my belly just thinking about it.

I don't know exactly how it happened, but my mother did not understand how important this game was to me, and she promised a neighbor that I would babysit for her three-year-old boy the afternoon the game was going to be televised. I figured I could watch the game while I was taking care of the kid.

The kid's name was Jeff, and he was the child from hell. His mother left for a shopping trip just as the game was starting. She seemed really relieved to be getting out of the house. I turned on the TV and started to watch the game. Sandy Koufax was more of a hero to me than The Beatles or any singing group. Jeff was running around like a little wild man, throwing his toys and ignoring all my pleas for him to play quietly. Every time I spoke to him he shouted at me and ran away. He was my first genuine ADHD charge; I had no idea how to deal with him.

So I did what most teenagers would have done: I ignored him and went back to watching the game.

Then, my heart dropping, I heard music in the background: it was the ding-a-ling of an ice cream truck. When Jeff heard the tinkling music he disappeared out the door before I could grab him. The last inning was coming up. I simply couldn't miss the game at this point. So I let Jeff run to the ice cream truck, and I didn't chase after him.

What happened next was inevitable. Jeff's mother walked in the door while my eyes were glued to the TV, and her child was nowhere to be seen. Now I was going to be in trouble, and worse, I was going to miss the end of the game. She was startled into speechlessness when I told her Jeff was gone and I had no idea where he was, and no I was not out looking for him but watching a baseball game. She paid me and I ran out the door as fast as Jeff had run when he heard the ice cream truck. Strike one for letting me be a parent.

Strike two was as bad or worse. I was babysitting my youngest sister's best friend and her brother and two sisters. Belle's friend seemed quiet and shy, so I figured I was in for an easy evening. I fed the kids at five, and they were much more unruly than I expected. We played games for hours and then I read them many bedtime stories. They didn't seem to be getting tired. Finally it was nine o'clock, and I decided it was Really Time for Bed. They began running up and down the stairs. I figured at least I could get the littlest one in bed, but she kept popping out every time I turned my back.

I chased them all over the house and they shouted at me that they would never go to bed. I was getting really frustrated. I grabbed the oldest one, whose name was Sarah, and I dragged her upstairs to the bedroom. She began spitting in my face, and that pushed me over the edge. I sat down on her bed and put her over my knee.

Then I spanked her, just like I occasionally got spanked at home. She started to scream and I spanked harder, four or five times.

The spanking didn't do a bit of good, and when the parents got home just before midnight, the kids were still up. That was my first experience with permissive parents. I wondered how a family could live like that. I found out twenty years later that the kids never forgot the spanking, as their parents had never done it to them. Apparently they were quite traumatized by the experience.

And Kevin wanted me to be a mother? As my inevitable pregnancy grew nearer, I became more and more alarmed. I didn't dare tell Kevin how I felt, as having kids seemed so desperately important to him.

With feelings that I was compromising myself to the standards of the straight world, I headed west in the T-Bird with Kevin to get married. I don't remember much about the trip except that we had a fight over chocolate milk and that Kevin scared the shit out of me by hot-rodding with other drivers at speeds over 120 mph. With my predilection for mania, you would think that traveling at extremely high speeds would have given me a real thrill. The truth is that mania resulting from speed only happens when it is under your own control.

The air around Denver was thick with smog due to temperature inversions up against the mountains. My contacts were not wearable, my face broke out in a frenzy of pus-filled boils, and I had a terrible headache. I had gained weight from those weeks of bed-ridden sloth. I was cranky and irritable. My mother wanted to know where the glowing bride was. She had not seen me in such a terrible state for years, maybe ever. Actually, this state wasn't an uncommon one for me. When things get that bad, I have the sense to stay away from the rest of humanity until the mood passes.

As soon as we arrived in Denver, my parents began trying to control our lives. My mother arranged for a minister to marry us in the back yard, and she made doctor and dental appointments for me. Dad planned a camping trip for our honeymoon. He packed enough food for us to live on for a month. Is it any wonder it's taken me so long to grow into a capable adult in my own right?

Mom and I had a screaming match over what her wedding gift to me would be. She ended up getting me a very fancy food mixer, and she made me two of the most beautiful dresses I had ever seen for my wedding: one a peacock blue and purple scarf dress that I wish I still owned, and a sophisticated beige pants suit with an overlay of a filmy, crocheted material. How she could be so right one moment and so nasty and controlling the next was beyond me.

The dentist fixed my teeth while I quietly passed out, as usual. When I was unconscious I found myself floating above the ground over a snow-covered, pine-scented mountain retreat. When I came to, I felt like throwing up. Actually, I had felt that way a lot lately. Maybe what was wrong with me was that I was pregnant. I visited the family doctor who gave me a pregnancy test and said there were several signs that the test was positive. He would have to let me know; those were before the days of instant do-it-yourself pregnancy tests. The necessary amount of time passed, and I turned out not to be pregnant after all, but I did have some kind of vaginal infection. In those days we had never heard of herpes, AIDs, chlamydia, genital warts, or PID, but we had heard of syphilis and gonorrhea, and that's what I figured I must have.

Actually, I had noticed no unusual vaginal symptoms, but if you're a creative thinker you often suffer the worst afflictions you can imagine even if nothing is wrong. I figured Greg had given me gonorrhea, forgetting for the moment that hadn't actually penetrated me or even really touched me very much. My doctor treated me with antibiotics without even examining me: that's how uptight even doctors were back in those days.

I was just glad that the miserable summer was over, with its frustration, embarrassment, and alcoholic haze. I felt that I was done with drugs, illicit sex, and alcohol for a long time. I would get married to Kevin, and we would live a straight, happy, and constructive life. Ready or not, it looked like we would have kids sooner rather than later.

I didn't get pregnant for another two weeks.

We were married on my twenty-first birthday on a dry, sunny afternoon in the back yard of my parent's

Denver home. No one took a single picture. The minister who performed the ceremony was nervous and ill-at-ease. Ours was his first wedding. After the ceremony, the family went to a place called the Writer's Inn. My parents reserved the bridal suite for us. Later on in the opulent room, as we finished making love, Kevin murmured in my ear, "Don't you think sex is better when you're married?" I wondered what the hell he was talking about. Hadn't sex been wonderful before that? This was one of two or three statements Kevin made to me that caused me to wonder whether I was making a mistake in joining my soul with his.

Kevin and I headed for the mountains with our stash of food and a large tent. It should have been an idyllic honeymoon. We lasted all of three days in the mountains. We left the tent for a walk only once. The rest of the time we spent eating, playing silly card games, and making love repeatedly. My period came with a blast of maroon goo. We didn't mind too much. I came up with the bizarre notion of shoving a tampon in my vagina just before sex, thinking it would minimize the mess. It didn't seem to interfere with our enjoyment of each other. On the third day we rose again and heard that a snow storm was expected that night. We packed up and left, just like that.

My parents were surprised to see us back so soon. Truthfully, my husband was already bored with our new life. He wasn't much interested in becoming well-rounded. His strength was in his ability to understand

and manipulate computers. The rest of his life was so much background noise. For some reason, I never could resist an extremely technical man, one who was really smart and told you so. I vowed to learn how to survive in a relationship in which I was second fiddle to one kind of machine or other.

We left for Chicago with no specific destination in mind. We didn't have a house or apartment to call home, and Kevin's cousin had returned to his messy house with his wife and six children, who no doubt would mess it up even further as time went on. We decided to visit my old friend and lover Freddie when we got into town; we could stay with him for a little while until we could find an apartment.

The Outlaws

We got to Freddie's place and surprised everyone with our shiny new gold rings. We hadn't told anyone about our plans to get married. I was surprised at the reactions of our few friends. Were we so badly matched that no one could conceive of us together? We whipped up a plan for all of us to move in together into an old, deserted house for rent in Newtown. The house was due to be torn down to make way for a high rise, but for the time being it would be empty until the necessary paperwork was completed.

We all trooped over to the house. I had never seen any place like it. It had been built around 1880 for the Fire Chief of Chicago. No expense had been spared. There were huge fireplaces in every room, embellished with intricate and colorful mosaic designs on the hearths and around the edges of the mantlepieces. The house represented to me something romantic spared from a long-lost past. I wanted to move in as soon as I saw the parquet floors. The others agreed.

The house might have been beautiful, but it was also definitely not modernized. The bathrooms and kitchen were surely below the standards of any relevant city housing codes. We cheerfully cleaned and mopped, shined and scrubbed until the floors, walls, and porcelain fixtures were at least bearable. For cooking, we used a monstrous gas stove that had been abandoned in the huge kitchen long ago.

From the beginning there were problems. Kevin was the only member of the household who earned any money legally. Gary, one of our roommates, had just been fired from his father's rubber hose company again. Fabe's only source of income was the money he stole from the Outlaw's treasury, and he didn't exactly want anyone to suspect he had a secret source of funds. So Kevin paid the rent. Not that the rent was very high. In fact, it was less than $150/month. Still, there was also food to buy and utilities to pay. Winter was coming, and the house would eat up heat with its twelve-foot ceilings, four stories, and large, drafty rooms.

To further complicate matters, I found myself pregnant for real this time. Every morning I woke up with the feeling that I was on high seas in a small boat. I thought I would die all through the morning. Immediately, I started swelling up like a big pink balloon, and I gained twenty pounds the first two months. I foolishly had enrolled in school that quarter and was struggling with an hour-long el ride each way to and from classes. I had signed up for Russian that quarter and thoroughly enjoyed the study of that language, which sounded almost musical to me. Morning sickness was like nothing else I had ever experienced.

All at once I was no longer able to be a nice person all the time. Maybe for the first time, my true self stepped forth. I didn't know what was going on or what to expect from pregnancy. All I knew was that once again life seemed to have played a cruel joke on me. I had quit drinking and doing drugs, so I was feeling uptight, repressed, and cranky as hell.

When I was feeling well, I studied Russian vocabulary in the sunny, cheerful bedroom. Our days there were numbered, however. The last straw for me came the night Fabe invited the Outlaws to the house for a blowout party. The party lasted for three days, and only ended because everyone was passed out on the floor by then.

When Kevin started back into his twenty-hour-a-day work mode, leaving me in that house alone, I freaked out. One day when he came home late I gave him an ultimatum. I told him I wanted out of there immediately; I couldn't wait another day.

We were lucky enough to have some friends on the South Side of Chicago, near where Kevin and Lara's house had been. These friends were Richard and Deedee, and they welcomed us into their home. We would share expenses and sleep in one of the extra bedrooms upstairs. So that is where we stayed while I grew bigger and bigger...

Beautiful Baby

We enjoyed our stay at Richard and Deedee's house. They were game players, just as we were. We played Yahtzee, Bridge, and Pounce for stints of twelve hours or more. Sometimes we played through the night and went to sleep at nine the next morning. We were evenly matched at all the games, so competition was always fierce. After a few months, I started feeling a little better and got into the swing of being pregnant. In the early spring, Kevin and I looked for an apartment on the west side of town, which would be an hour nearer to Kevin's work. We found an apartment in Forest Park, and we moved in February of 1971.

I was five months pregnant and still hadn't visited a doctor. I've never been crazy about doctors. And of course, when I finally got the courage to go, the doctor stuck me with needles for all sorts of blood tests. I wasn't doing so well. I had gained thirty pounds and I was only halfway done carrying the baby. I had toxemia, which caused water retention, high blood pressure, and ultimately convulsions in both mother and baby if not controlled. The doctor gave me specific diet restrictions. The main thing was to eat no salt in any form.

The new apartment was fine, but I was not happy about the long, lonely hours I spent there with no company but the two cats that were getting crazy with claustrophobia in an area smaller than they were used to. I took walks to the grocery and walks in the fields near Kevin's office at the Fermi National Accelerator Laboratory (Fermilab), where he now worked. He had gotten a fancy new job and was so pleased with himself. He was writing computer programs for the circular atomic accelerator that was under construction in Batavia, Illinois. His friends were world-famous scientists. He could barely stand to leave work at all for fear of missing something important. I guess I was proud of him, but I didn't feel very important. I continued to gain weight, and I cheated on the salt-free diet, which worsened my high blood pressure.

I read and slept, ate, and walked. Kevin was hard to reach at work. I was afraid I would go into labor and not be able to reach him. My dreams were horrifying. In the worst one, I gave birth to a tiny Thumbelina baby who fell into a milk shake I was drinking and drowned in the frothy bubbles. I had almost given up talking to my family: my mother was too hysterical to deal with. My father, however, came to see us just before Kassie was born. He took us out for a perch dinner, where I overate, as usual.

When my weight reached 190 pounds, the size of a medium-large football player, my doctor put me in the hospital. My blood pressure was going through the roof, and I was so nervous and jumpy I could barely function. The day before I went into the hospital, I had gone to Marshall Field's and bought a crib and a few baby clothes. I felt that I was as ready for this baby as I would ever be. I had no idea what was going to happen to me during labor. My fear of this unknown experience was almost unbearable. Lamaze was unknown then, and Kevin and I had no idea what we were getting into. I thought I was losing my mind. I had no close friend to talk to, so I just worried about everything alone. For once I was not either manic or depressed, but in some state of anxiety that was so stressful I could barely stand to stay conscious. I slept and read most of the time.

Kevin took me to the Loyola Medical Center. I was shown to a cheerful room, where I promptly overturned a heavy blood pressure monitor. Gobbets of mercury bounced all over the floor, and I thought, "My baby will be poisoned, she'll be born dead, that's the meaning of all those bad dreams, they were a premonition, and get that stuff out of here, NOW." Another nurse came in to clean up the mess. She ordered me into bed immediately and said, "Don't Get Out."

Once again Kevin left me alone for days. I didn't see him again until the day my delivery was scheduled. The birth of my baby girl was to happen on June 12, 1971. I rested and ate bland food and waited with dread for the coming event.

On the appointed morning, Kevin joined me at 6 a.m. in the labor room, bringing with him a copy of *Cat's Cradle* by Kurt Vonnegut. I had read it before, but I felt it was well worth another look, especially under the present conditions. I needed something to distract me from the smell of medical equipment and the job ahead of me.

The last thing the night nurse did for me was to shave my pubic hair and give me an enema. It wasn't so bad. Someone had warned me to expect those procedures. The new shift came on, and I tried to prepare myself for what was to come.

I still had a psychotic hatred of needles. I had never been hooked up to an IV before, and when I realized the nurse was going to stick a big, long needle into my arm, I resisted for all I was worth. Of course, the end result was that she couldn't get the needle properly into the vein and so had to stick me repeatedly. The needle went everywhere except into the vein. My arm flailed as she screamed at me to lie still. By the time she gave up on me, there was a lot of blood and no needle threaded into my arm.

The doctor on duty was a florid, chunky man with greasy, blond hair like my own. I had never seen him before. I had no idea where my kind and sweet Doctor Takagi was. This man looked at me with no sympathy whatsoever. He grabbed the IV needle with one hand and leaned on my arm with the rest of his substantial body. Without a moment's hesitation, he rammed the needle into my vein, where it stayed. He taped the needle into place and told the nurse to set the Pitocin drip. And that was that. I hated to admit it, but he hadn't hurt me at all. Next, he shoved what felt like his whole arm into my vagina and broke my water. I looked down and saw what appeared to be a whole bucket of yellowish water rushing out of my body. The liquid dripped down from the table onto the shiny floor, a veritable river of nutrient fluid. No wonder I had gained so much weight. He confirmed that I was dilated three fingers. I had to get to ten.

I began to feel a little better as I realized that phase one of the bizarre baby-bearing process was now over.

Kassie

I read my book while Kevin worked on a computer program. The morning passed calmly and quietly while I waited for something to happen. By noon Kevin and I decided it might be time to start thinking about girl baby names. I knew this baby was a girl, even though I hadn't had an ultrasound. She just felt like a girl. So we thought of just the right name for the brilliant and beautiful girl who was about to be born.

Kassiopoeia, her name was to be, spelled that funny way to set her apart from the crowd. And still nothing happened. The afternoon wore on, with hourly visits from various doctors and half-hourly visits from the nurses. Every once in a while I would feel something that was like moving fingers tickling me all up and down my midriff. I wanted to laugh; this couldn't be what all the fuss was about, could it?

By seven o'clock that evening, when I supposedly had been in labor for twelve hours, the doctor decided to pull the plug for the night. We would try again tomorrow. This isn't so bad, I thought. The worst part of it so far had been the constant pressure on my bladder.

Kevin left, to get some well-needed sleep (not surprisingly, he had been at work steadily for the last three days). I tried to relax on that stiff, hard table. I tossed and turned most of the night, not exactly dreaming but not conscious either. I began to be impatient for the whole ordeal to be over.

The next morning I tried again. The nurse who mutilated my arm was back, and so was the doctor with the tree trunk for an arm. After a while, the nurse gave me a sedative by injection, and this time it was Kevin who folded: he fainted gently and laid his head on my swollen belly. The nurse laughed and said that happened all the time. That's why they didn't let the daddies into the delivery room.

The morning passed, and I finished my book. Suddenly, Kevin couldn't work on his programs anymore. The doctor started coming in more often, and his explorations of my insides grew rougher and more painful. Goddammit, couldn't he be a little kinder? Nothing was happening; the contractions didn't even hurt yet. The doctor ordered a speedup of the Pitocin drip.

One o'clock came, and still nothing was happening. The tingling fingers were back, but there was still no significant movement off ground zero. At two thirty, a woman doctor came in and sat down next to us. She said that they didn't want to wait any longer. For the sake of the baby, they would have to perform a C-section.

I really didn't know anything about Caesarians, but one thing I did know: to do a C-section, the doctor would most certainly have to cut me open. I envisioned him standing over me with a huge butcher knife and slicing me open like a loaf of bread. Naturally, I panicked.

This would be a lot worse than facing a needle, which I couldn't stand.

The doctor left to make preparations for the operation. In seven minutes, I felt an earthquake erupt in my womb. I was stunned into silence by an overwhelming pain that hit me like a tidal wave. I hadn't gone to Lamaze classes, so I did all the wrong breathing; I could only hyperventilate in stuttering gasps. The pain ebbed and flowed in my being for what seemed like hours but in reality was only minutes. Then all at once I felt an undeniable, intuitive urge to Bear Down. When the bear-down feeling hit me, I obeyed it. I bore down for all I was worth. It was a wonderful counter to the waves of torture battering me from the inside out. Then the waves receded. Kevin was screaming for the nurse, who came in time to see the baby's head crowned. She yelled at me to stop bearing down, it wasn't time yet. The anesthesiologist rushed in with another big needle. I was beyond fear at this time and well into a deep, unreachable madness of elemental pain. I was given an epidural, which is in essence a shot in the back using a foot-long needle. It seemed to take effect very quickly. I didn't have a chance to get into any good screaming fits.

Then I was in the delivery room. The world looked underwater to me: the nurse had taken my glasses. I quit hyperventilating. In no time at all, my legs were straddled into the upside down saddle. The doctor split me open to make way for the baby, and I didn't mind at all; I couldn't feel a damn thing down there.

The doctor with boxing gloves for hands smiled at me and held up a pink squirming mass from the foot of the table. She was my daughter, and she was perfect. She didn't scream, she wasn't misshapen, and she wasn't a horrible color. She was pink and round and the most beautiful sight I had ever seen. The nurses cleaned her up and laid her in my arms. A tiny trickle of tears strayed from my eyes, and then the trickle was a pool, and suddenly I was bawling my eyes out. Having this baby was the best thing I had ever accomplished, and I was filled with an almost tangible joy. My world was illuminated by a sunny-colored light. I was so high I thought I was floating above the table, looking down at the scene below. The doctor looked at me sharply and asked if I was hallucinating. "No, of course not, I feel just fine, better than fine, on top of the world," I told him. I found out later that hallucinations are a symptom of eclampsia, which is when the mother goes into convulsions after having a baby. I wasn't hallucinating; I was just high on life.

As the nurses took the baby from me and put her on the cart to be wheeled into the nursery, I swear I saw my little Kassie smile at me. Her eyes were wide awake and alert. She looked around her as if to assess this new situation. I was aware of her as a sentient, feeling being. It was almost spooky. We connected or bonded at that moment. I knew that Kassiopoeia would be a joy to me from then on until forever, and I felt like the luckiest being alive.

Everyone wanted to see the new baby: family members, friends, neighbors, and even the hard-boiled scientists at the lab. Kassie loved to travel; she was always on her best behavior when we were visiting. When she was four weeks old, we went with Richard and Deedee in their van to see the car races at Elkhart Lake, Wisconsin. The screaming engines didn't bother her a bit. She slept through the whole weekend.

We planned to take a vacation together to my grandparent's cottage in Minnesota. Kevin, of course, was supposed to come with us. He hadn't had a vacation in a while and was still working nonstop to get the programs ready for the startup of the accelerator. It was mid-July in Chicago and hotter than blazes. Kevin had an hour-and-a half drive to and from work in a non-air conditioned car, so he had just stopped coming home. I hadn't seen him for several days when mother arrived to pick us up for the drive to the lake. I called him at work and told him we were ready to go. I was packed, and the baby was freshly diapered. Kevin said he would be right home, so I fixed some sandwiches and fruit to eat in the car. We sat down to enjoy the air-conditioning and my new Rattan furniture. An hour-and-a half passed. Kevin would be here at any minute. Maybe he had run into a little extra Friday-afternoon traffic.

Kassie lay down for her afternoon nap. I was breast-feeding her, and it seemed that all she did was eat and sleep. She slept like an angel for almost two hours, and Kevin still wasn't home. My mother suggested nastily that maybe I ought to call him and remind him we were waiting. I felt awkward: I was not a nag, and I didn't like to tell him what to do. Nonetheless, I called. He said he had just a few details to finish up and would be home by dinnertime.

He wasn't home the next morning, and I couldn't reach him at work. Yes, he was there, but he was busy with something out on the floor. Yes, the message would be conveyed that he was supposed to get his butt home.

He called that afternoon and said that he wouldn't be able to get away. Something big was going on that he needed to be present for. Could we wait another day?

The next day my mother took matters into her own hands. We packed up the car, and she drove us to the lab. The guard on duty recognized me and let us past the gate. We trailed into the ring part of the accelerator and found Kevin working on the East Computer. He looked at me quickly and said, "Look, I just can't go. Why don't you go without me?" I looked at him tearfully and in my saddest voice said, "Please, please can't you come with us?" I felt like I was in a boxing ring standing between two heavyweights going at each other. What was supposed to have been a relaxing getaway was turning into a tug-of-war between Kevin and my mother. He must have seen some of the struggle of my face, because he finally said, "Oh, all right," finished printing up his program, and dragged himself away from his computer with a reluctance he didn't bother to hide.

Mom drove to Minnesota while Kevin slept and I entertained my beautiful baby. July is a good season for Minnesota: it's not nearly as hot as everywhere else, but it's warm enough for swimming and water sports. Grandpa had died of cancer several years before, but grandma and Uncle Daniel spent every weekend at the lake in the summer.

We arrived in the evening and were greeted by relatives I knew and relatives I didn't know. Grandma served her normal bounteous spread at the dinner table, and I felt happy to be there. Kevin was totally out of it. I don't remember him speaking a single word to anyone. He didn't have any puzzles to offer or the desire to play games. He hadn't showered in a week, because he hadn't been home in that long.

The rest of the vacation passed uneventfully. We played bridge, I fed Kassie every three hours, and Kevin rebelliously refused to take a shower.

By now my moodswing downward was getting worse. After experiencing that horrible pregnancy I fantasized every day of going to see a psychiatrist and talking to someone, anyone, about what was going on with me. I felt I was so out of control that I would never be able to take care of a baby. I never got the courage up to call anyone, even though Kevin's cousin was a psychiatrist and could probably have helped me. I spent every waking moment caring for the baby, and I maintained a constant vigilance of her. I was so afraid I would do something wrong I cried with frustration every time any little thing happened to her, like when the little piece of umbilical cord fell out of her belly button. I had no idea how I was going to be a good mother to this perfect child.

Blue Baby

When we got home from the hospital, I started getting some funny back pains. I had never had a back pain in my life. It was time for my six-week checkup at the gynecologist, and I had Kevin drive me there for what I've figured would be a routine checkup. I was still breast-feeding Kassie like mad, so I hadn't bothered to start back on any kind of birth control. Kevin and I made love all the time when he was home, but since that wasn't very often I didn't even think about the possibility that I might get pregnant again so soon after Kassie's birth. When the doctor told me I was pregnant again, I burst into very sincere tears. I was crying when I came out of the office to tell Kevin. He was absolutely thrilled. He said, "Good, we'll have a boy this time." I didn't quit crying; in fact, I cried and cried for the next three days. Obviously, I would have to get an abortion. Who could go through that ordeal again when the memories of Kassie's birth were still so fresh? Besides, it was unnatural to have kids this close together. According to the doctor, this one was due exactly eleven months and one week after Kassie was born.

Kassie was getting prettier and more alert every day. She smiled, kicked, and waved her arms, and before long she was flipping over from front to back. One day she scared me by stuffing a whole fistful of blanket fuzz into her mouth and almost choking herself. I knew I would never be able to have an abortion. The next baby would be as wonderful as Kassie was, and I would die if anything happened to her.

Once I decided to have this baby, I became directed and determined not to make the same mistakes I had so foolishly committed the first time. I followed the salt-free diet down to the last milligram. I baked my own salt-free bread. I didn't eat anything but fresh fruit and vegetables, with a little chicken and fish thrown in for good measure. I felt marvelous. The puffy, flabby look I had carried over from the first pregnancy was gone. I took long walks with Kassie in her stroller. The time seemed to fly by.

Kevin worked as much as ever, in fact, maybe a little more, because the accelerator was quickly approaching startup time. Kassie and I spent some time with Kevin at work; the men looked at me strangely as they noticed the radiation badge pinned over my swelling belly. As far as I could tell, there was no danger of radiation leaks; nothing was actually operating yet. I enjoyed visiting the site with its bizarre, science fiction-like equipment. There was a big machine called a Cockroft-Walton, a voltage generator that accelerated hydrogen molecules around in a large ring and then smashed them into a target to see what particles might fly off.

The scientists were all practically wetting their pants in anticipation for this system to become operational. Kevin wasn't about to be left behind. He always felt he had to work harder than everyone else to prove himself worthy of being included in the company of the great physicists who had been invited to do experiments at Fermilab. Kevin had flunked out of engineering school after a few quarters, so he had no credentials other than his reputation. He worked himself into a position of respectability by doing good work for the sharpest of the scientists. So, of course he had made a good many enemies along the way by stepping on other people's toes. When he came home, he was often full of frustration and bitterness, when one or the other of these enemies had thwarted him in some way. I was a good wife: I listened and sympathized.

However, I had no shoulder to cry on myself. I was trying to complete my own education. I was having a hard time staying motivated to finish up the last few courses I needed for a degree in anthropology. Kevin helped out while I attended classes in the mornings several days a week. I took two finals the week of May 18, 1972 while Kevin stayed in the car with Kassie. My sister Janie came to help me type up the papers that were due at the end of the quarter.

I had only gained 17 pounds during this pregnancy, but my stomach was still sticking way out to there. People don't realize how big a pregnant lady really is during that last month. Fortunately, my professors were sympathetic. I realized that after all these efforts, I would be one credit short of the required number of credits for graduation. "Well," I thought, "somehow I'll get that last class taken this summer, after the birth of my baby boy."

Once again, the doctor scheduled me for an induced labor even though I had controlled the toxemia this time by following a salt-free diet. My mother and baby sister came to take Kassie to Alton, Illinois, where my parents were living. Kevin and I again trekked into the hospital at 6 a.m. The same nurse who had covered my arms with bruises the year before trying to get the IV in did the same thing this year. Unbelievably, the same intern, who was now a real doctor, came in to save the day by decisively and quickly sticking the needle in a vein on top of my hand. The similarities between the births ended at that point.

Almost immediately, I began to feel pains. By noon I was scared to death that I would freak out on the table, make a huge fool out of myself, and somehow lose the baby as well. At 1:00 my regular doctor, a man I trusted and had a warm fondness for, entered with a short, thin, bespectacled medical student. My doctor told me they would be giving me a new kind of anesthesia. He promised me it would be wonderful: I wouldn't feel another pain until the baby was born, which he predicted would not be for another three hours or so.

I felt no other pain except being stuck in the back with what was the largest needle I had ever seen. How many times did I have to tell these idiots that I really didn't like needles?

The medical student was shy and insecure. When I started wriggling like a worm on the hook, he really should have taken the needle away from my body and waited until I calmed down. Instead, he tried to stick it in my back, anyway. That was a big mistake. The needle went right through the epidural space and into my spinal column. A pain like a knife slicing my brain into two pieces hit me, and at the same time I felt a warm fluid streaming down my back. The doctor screamed at the poor med student, who probably decided not to go through with medical school after all, that he had blown it and to get that needle out of me immediately. He had inadvertently given me a spinal tap, and my brain had crashed against my skull when the cushioning brain fluid flowed out of my back and onto the floor, where it did me no good at all. The headache was so severe that I almost wished for the next labor pain instead. The doctor told me that I had to lie flat and stay absolutely still. How was I supposed to be in labor without moaning and screaming and moving all over the place? Worst of all, my doctor made this quivering young man do the whole thing again.

I was astounded, but I kept my mouth shut. The doctor was going to give the guy another chance to mutilate me. I was sobbing steadily by this time and my head ached like the devil. This experience was getting worse and worse. I became convinced that nothing was going to go right. I had been lucky enough to have one beautiful baby, but there my luck ended.

My tormentor began again. He pounded in a little template farther down on my back from the previous scene of carnage. He pushed the needle in with a firm tap, as if he had used a little hammer to pound it in. So far everything was going well. But this was just an IV to restore the lost fluid. Then he went through the whole process again to administer the anesthesia. I didn't wiggle this time. Soon I was numb from the waist down. I should have been glad; instead I felt flat and lifeless. The experience had barely begun, and already I was done in. I wasn't even sure there would be a baby at the end of all this; I felt unreal, like a paper doll with a lump at her middle.

Donne

Three incredibly boring hours passed. Kevin must have been there, but I don't remember what he was doing. We didn't even try to think about baby boy names; I was too tired. Then the doctor told me I was dilated far enough and it was time for the baby to be born. What did I know? I couldn't feel a goddamn thing except for the pain in my head. I didn't want to be there on the table, in that antiseptic room.

They wheeled me into the delivery room and set my legs up in the saddle. Then they told me to push. Push with what muscles? It's hard to will your muscles to push when you can't feel them; it's like trying to move a pencil telepathically. I tried and tried, but nothing was happening. Then the doctor was yelling at me, "You have to try to push."

"You try, you moron," I yelled. My attitude was very poor, and I was not getting the job done. I guess he used forceps to pull that hesitant baby out, because finally out he came, a beautiful, but very funny-colored baby. As beautiful as Kassie had been, this one was as hideous. They had assured me that I wasn't going to have a blue baby, but this one was so blue a mama robin would have loved him. Actually, he was more of an indigo than a robin's egg blue, like a stormy sky, sort of a bluish, purplish gray.

They took the baby away somewhere immediately. I didn't get to hold him. In fact, I didn't even see him again for three days.

Kevin told me the baby was in an incubator. He told me there was a tube down his throat. I'd get to see him later, when he came out of the incubator. I should just rest and not worry about anything; the nurses were taking good care of him. Dad sent yellow roses, just like he had the year before. The hospital food was outstanding.

My roommate saw her baby every four hours. She wasn't breast-feeding, but she gave the baby his bottle at those times. I wondered who was giving my baby his bottle, and how often he was eating. My milk came in with an almost orgasmic rush on the third day after he was born, and surely they would bring my baby in this time around.

They didn't bring my baby in on the third day, either, and suddenly I knew why. He had died in the night, and they didn't want to tell me. Kevin hadn't been in to see me since the first day, and he wouldn't tell me, either. He was too chicken. I started crying in that helpless, droning way so characteristic of a person who has given up all hope; an endless monotone of sobbing. I went on that way, trying to cry as quietly as possible, until one of the nurses heard me and figured out what was wrong. She happened to be a very kind and perceptive young woman with two children. She told me that my baby would be fine now. He had indeed gone through a crisis in the night, teetering on that delicate line between life and death. He had been born with a disease called Hyaline Membrane Disease, now called Respiratory Distress Syndrome, a condition resulting when a baby is born with underdeveloped lungs. This disease is common mostly to premature babies. It is the same disease that killed Jacqueline Kennedy's first baby.

My baby was born blue, because basically he was not able to breathe; his lungs were not able to process the oxygen in the air. Each breath sounded like someone trying to breathe underwater; a mucousy, phlegmy sound. The nurses had to suction out the fluids threatening to choke him and hope that his lungs would develop soon. The baby had remained a deep purple color into the second day. On the third day, he got worse, and his color turned sickly gray. The nurses realized he would live or die in a matter of minutes; either the lungs would suddenly start functioning, or he would die. As they watched over him, the gray turned to a deep purple, and the purple to an indigo. This baby was like a rainbow. Then the blue became pink, and the pink a yellowish cream, and he was going to make it. The Taurus baby was a bull after all.

I took him home on the next day, with instructions to put him in the sun to cure his slight jaundice. I should have been the happiest mama in the world. My baby and I had survived a miserable ordeal. I soon as I entered our modest apartment I began to cry. Kevin hadn't changed the cat litter for two weeks, and the cats had pissed on the couch and in the baby crib as their revenge at this new intrusion into their lives. I made Kevin change the cat litter and put a new sheet on the baby's crib, crying all the while. He left for work immediately, and I sat down with my new baby to ponder my life. It did not seem good.

Kassie came home. When she walked through the door at eleven-and-one-half months old, she greeted me with the words, "Hi, mom." She also knew her colors; that was something new. She didn't seem to mind at all that now there were two kids in the family. I think she was too young to realize that by all rights she should have been the only kid for at least a while longer.

We had finally named our boy after a character in a science-fiction book Kevin and I had finished reading that spring, *Patterns of Chaos* by Colin Kapp. Actually, I had named the baby myself while Kevin was at work. The character's name was Donne. We chose Donne for a first name and added Kelly as a middle name to keep in line with the other K's in the family: Kevin, Kris, and Kassie. After he got over being sick, Donne was healthy as a horse. He sucked on my boobs constantly. I couldn't keep him filled up. He would eat for an hour, then fall into a deep sleep for an hour or two, and then wake up starved again. He never cried; he was an angel baby, just like Kassie had been. While he slept I played with Kassie. She got smart very fast, and she could solve all her shape puzzles and toys. Fortunately, soon both kids were sleeping through the night, so I wasn't totally exhausted juggling my attention between the two of them.

Postpartum Blues

The kids and I rarely left the apartment. We rarely saw Kevin. One afternoon in August, I received a registered letter from the University of Illinois. They had waived the one missing credit and granted me a degree. I was ecstatic. That was the best news I had heard in a long time. Maybe there was justice and kindness in the universe after all. But I had not been able to shake the postpartum depression that had clung to me like one of the babies since Donne's birth. The future had no meaning to me; I withdrew into the tiny world of the apartment, the two babies, and the occasional visits home by my husband. When Kevin did come home I would be crabby and demanding. I made him go out for pizza, gourmet pies, or whatever I craved at the time. I gained weight again. Once I even made him take me for a driving lesson during rush hour. I hadn't driven for almost five years and had lost my confidence. The experience wasn't fun for either of us.

Kevin's mood wasn't so great either. Once the accelerator started up and all his operating programs were in place, I think he felt that his job at Fermilab was done. He began talking about finding a job in California. I encouraged him; we both definitely needed a change.

The glow of my second pregnancy had definitely worn off, and my mood plummeted and darkened further. I gained 40 pounds, cut all my hair off, and bought some ugly wire-rimmed glasses, which didn't suit me at all. The kids and I watched Sesame Street three times a day and didn't do much else except survive. I did some drawing with colored chalk, and made a huge mess all over Deedee's living room carpet. I absentmindedly left shitty diapers all over the house, which Richard inevitably stepped on in his new shoes. I arranged to meet my mother at Marshall Field's one day. I wandered around wondering why she was so late. As it turned out, she had been there on time, but kept walking away from me because she didn't recognize me. My sex life seemed to be all over. When Kevin and I did get together, I had absolutely no feeling at all, either physically or mentally.

Let's Move Again

I knew something had to give. Kevin said over and over he would go to California to look for a new job, any time now. Once he actually packed a suitcase and left for the airport, only to end up back at work for three days. I knew I needed to see a psychiatrist. I began to think the word "divorce." I knew I wouldn't have the courage to go through with it, but just thinking about getting away from my insane lifestyle made me feel happier.

As far as I was concerned, my marriage to Kevin ended sometime during that period one morning with he came home after a long siege at the lab. Kassie was now two and could be a stubborn little monster when she wanted to be. I don't know what she did, but I looked up from the table where I was sitting to see Kevin grab her by her right arm and swing her with a good amount of force across the room. She slammed into a wall, then slouched to the floor and started to whimper. My normal wimpy self was suddenly gone, and I screamed at him, "What are you doing?" I still didn't cuss then. I scooped her up and took her upstairs to the bedroom, where I wept for our lost freedom and my unhappiness. I blamed everything on Kevin: it was his fault we were in this mess. If he wanted to go to California, why didn't he just go and leave us alone?

Not too many days later, Kevin left for California. He was going to visit some people he knew and see if he couldn't line up a new job. He called from California and sounded happy. "Thank God," I thought, "he's found a job." He said, "Get ready to go; we're moving to Boston."

We jam-packed the car with toddlers and other necessities and nervously headed east. The movers had come earlier and packaged all our valuables around the looking-its-age '57 T-Bird. The car and all our furniture and boxes took up only a quarter of the moving van. Better to travel light, we figured.

The trip went much better than I expected, at least at first. Donne slept most of the way, and Kassie, strapped into a car seat in the back of the Chevelle, drew on the ceiling with her colored chalk while she babbled to her creations. I admired the Indiana, Ohio, and Pennsylvania scenery and thought that maybe we would make it all the way to Massachusetts without incident.

Kevin's luck with cars followed its normal course, though, and somewhere along a straight, hot stretch of highway in New York, the car suddenly took matters into its own hands and decided to quit.

Kevin spent two hours fixing whatever was wrong. I don't remember if he had to walk somewhere to find a part or not, but the wait in that burning car with a baby and an active toddler was no fun for me, either. We got back on our way and soon were skirting the city of New York, an eyeful of busy, colorful sights rising and stretching off in every direction. We got through the city and Kevin chose a seedy, scary motel for us to stay in that night. There were noisy comings and goings outside the door throughout the night, and once I'm sure I heard someone rattle our doorknob with a frighteningly flimsy, tinny sound.

The next day one of the children started throwing up in the car, an orange and milky foam of slimy spew. I was enthusiastic about Tang for the kids but that spell of trying to clean up a huge quantity of the stuff mixed with just enough milk to make it seem like a kind of vile, stinking, orange milkshake in a limited space with limited cleaning materials was enough to sour me on the astronaut's drink forever.

Next it was my turn, and I threw up spaghetti from the night before, a huge plateful of it. With all the red and the orange flumes of vomit flying through the air in that burning car, we must have looked like carnival flame throwers. Not to be left out, Kevin and the other child joined in the fun with sympathy vomiting. Only once or twice in my life have I ever felt so horrible: I honestly wished I was dead for a moment or two.

We arrived in Maynard, Massachusetts and checked into a Holiday Inn. Kevin's new company, Digital Equipment Corp. would be paying our living expenses for the first month after our move. We all took long, hot baths, even Kevin, as our first act in our new home state. We would be cooped up in a single room for a month: the company paid for two rooms, but we decided to save the money and make do with one. In the meantime, we would look for a house to buy, and the kids and I could enjoy the pool during the days while Kevin was at work. I still wasn't a legal driver, so we'd have to eat our daytime meals at the Holiday Inn restaurant.

I never realized how small a Holiday Inn room was until I tried to control the behavior of two toddlers in one of them. The days were endless as the kids literally climbed the walls, fell off the beds, unpacked all the clothes from our suitcases, banged their heads on the undersides of tables, played in the toilets, and found daddy's shaving materials fascinating, among many other creative amusements. There was no way I could take both of the kids to the pool at the same time, nor could I leave a sleeping child alone in the room. So pool activities were out, at least until Kevin got home from work. By the third day in that tiny room, I was ready to attack my husband the minute he walked through the door at dinnertime.

I talked Kevin into taking a few days off work to seek out a realtor and begin the job of house hunting. Surely the people at his new company would understand that we needed a place to live. We had saved up about $8000 and felt very rich. We thought we could afford about a forty-thousand-dollar house, which at that time would buy a nice middle-class home.

House Hunting

The realtor we found was a jolly, roly-poly man dressed in a manner reminiscent of a Leprechaun. I didn't like him very much, but at least he was easy to talk to, and he listened carefully when we told him our requirements for a house. We visited several old, run-down houses, some brand new houses, and one house that had just been sold. Then the man took us over the river and through the woods to a neighborhood surrounded by forest except on the west side, where there was a beautiful, clean little lake with a beach. I was entranced by the neighborhood. I had a hunch this was the place for us.

I was right. We entered the house and climbed a small set of stairs to an airy, cheerful living room. I imagined curling up on the couch next to the picture window, reading a good science fiction book, listening to classical music, and every once in a while looking out the picture window at the woods behind the house to see if any wild animals were stirring back there.

The living room led to a well-lit kitchen, which was small but efficient, with all new appliances and cupboards. The kitchen was complete with a built-in dishwasher, one of my top requirements for an acceptable house. A bright, spacious den filled the lower level, where the kids could have their playroom. There were three adequate bedrooms on the upper level. We visited the lake nearby and learned that swimming lessons were offered every summer for children in the neighborhood. I thought I could live happily ever after in this house and never be troubled with mood swings again.

We put down a thousand dollars earnest money on the house then and there. The realtor was so pleased he could not stop smiling. I went back to the motel to wait for the house deal to go through. In those days it took a month of shuffling paperwork before the final closing day. For us, thirty days turned out to be way too long.

Swap

I wasn't sure if I would be able to endure a month of watching game shows, screaming at kids, and eating motel food. Kevin came home with a solution one night: at work he had made a new friend with a family that included five small children. They would welcome visitors, since they were also new to the area and hadn't met many people. They were Pat and Nancy Gallen, and they lived in Concord near Walden Pond.

Pat turned out to be a gangling giant at six feet, six inches tall with a deep, booming voice. In spite of his size, he had a kind and gentle demeanor. Even so, the kids were scared to death of him and hid behind my legs when he approached.

Nancy was built like a fertility goddess, with breasts that stuck straight out in front of her (she didn't like bras) and spreading hips. She would be monstrous when she got older, I could tell. As it was, she probably outweighed me by thirty pounds and was about two inches shorter than I was. I can't remember what color her eyes were, but they were shiny and intense, as though she were about ready to cry or send sparks out at any minute.

Kevin and I hadn't met any people this laid back since we left the house we shared with the motorcycle gang. We had left behind our pot-smoking, LSD-tripping, flower-children friends after our own children were born.

The only people we hung out with were stuffy physicists or way-out-of-it computer programmers.

Since I had nothing else to do, I began visiting Nancy in their three-story rented house every morning. I must have had Kevin drop me off on his way to work, because I still wasn't a legal driver. Soon the mornings stretched to afternoons, and then Kevin started coming after work to the Gallen's house, where Nancy and I would fix something cheap for dinner.

I had not had a true woman friend since Julia, and I missed the deep talks and shared confidences. Nancy was warm and open, and she loved to analyze people, just as I did. She and Pat had a multitude of problems, so she was seeing a psychologist, which I had wanted to do for a long time but hadn't had the guts to actually follow through with. I was curious about what went on in a shrink's office. Did you really lie down and talk about your dreams? Did they hypnotize you and make you remember buried sections of your past? Did they accuse you of all sorts of faults you weren't aware of? Nancy could fill me in on all these details. Also, Nancy was a practicing Scientologist who had met L. Ron Hubbard. I had no idea what Scientology was or who the hell L. Ron Hubbard was, but I knew it had something to do with alpha waves and machines that could measure your brain activity. Nancy seemed to be a skilled psychologist herself or, if not that, at least a very good manipulator.

I shared with my new friend some of the feelings I had wallowed in during the previous winter, particularly those about wanting to leave Kevin. I spilled my guts to Nancy, just for the sheer relief of purging my mind of stale, unwanted, negative thoughts. I didn't really want to leave Kevin; I just wanted to tell someone I had thought about it. I wanted to do some professional work with him. I was sure we could come up with a project to do together. One of my ideas was to write a computer program to translate German into English. I knew we could be a successful team if we just devoted some time to it. I didn't tell Nancy about the positive side of our relationship; I told her only the negative things. She believed me and secretly took my husband's side. She was another betrayer of women's confidences, just like my high school friend Judy had been.

The Gallens were desperately needy financially due to the high child support payments Pat paid his ex-wife. Kevin and I were desperately needy spiritually due to the lifestyle we had adopted over the last two years. It was inevitable that we would get entangled with the Gallens in a sick, codependent relationship. Melodie Beatty, where were you when I needed you? *Codependent No More* didn't come out for many years after this time.

The Gallens asked us to move in with them while we were waiting for our house deal to come through. It seemed like a perfect temporary solution to the problems of our living situation. We would pay them a small amount of money for living expenses, which would help ease their financial burdens. They would give us a large room on the third floor of their spacious home.

We would share expenses for food and utilities. Both families would come out ahead, and I wouldn't have to go crazy in a small motel room for another three or four weeks.

During the long days of that Massachusetts Indian summer, Nancy and I shopped for groceries, went to the mall, and played with the children in a nearby park. We fixed simple but adequate meals. A few times in the evening we hired a babysitter and went out for a fancy dinner. I loaned Nancy my favorite red dress to wear one night out: she didn't have any dress clothes, and I was kind of tired of the red dress, anyway. Too bad it was too tight on her. She wore it anyway and looked like she was going to pop out of it any minute or split a seam. There was not a hint of trouble between any of us until about the second week we had been staying in the house near Walden Pond.

I'm not sure exactly how the trouble started. The beginning may have been when Pat and I took over the cooking, with the arrogant attitude that Nancy cooked well enough when it came to macaroni and cheese, but she should leave the real cooking to the experts, namely me and Pat. Or it may have started when Pat and I made it a habit to take the children to Walden Pond every evening for a swim, since neither Kevin nor Nancy liked the water. Then again, it probably started in Nancy's cunning little mind when she got me to admit that sex hadn't been too good between me and Kevin lately due to my depression, his overworking, and the demands of two toddlers on a set of tired parents.

Before I knew it, I found myself fascinated with Pat. He was so much more normal than Kevin was. He was a programmer too, but he didn't obsess over his work the way Kevin did. His childhood hadn't been so hot. His father was a doctor, and he had screwed up Pat's metabolism by giving him a growth hormone in an effort to make a second testicle drop. In Pat's case, that wasn't possible, because he only had one testicle to start with. The effect of the hormone was noticeable in the stretch marks around his middle and his height. He was the only person I ever met with stretch marks as bad as mine. He looked as though someone had grabbed him by the head and feet when he was a baby and yanked in opposite directions until his body was almost pulled in two. In any case, my heartbeat sped up and I got a little breathless around him. I make up excuses to touch his arm, his shoulder. When my mood started to turn upward after a two-year depression, the desire for sex became almost overwhelming, and my husband didn't seem very turned on by me. I wanted to throw Pat on the ground and ravish him, if that was possible.

Meanwhile, I didn't exactly notice that Nancy was making a play for Kevin, but they started having long talks together. One afternoon they went upstairs for naps in separate rooms, supposedly, which lasted five hours. Kassie and Donne started getting hyperactive and demanding, as though they felt they weren't getting enough attention.

The formal beginning of our dual affairs commenced the evening when Nancy and Kevin announced that they had a Plan for the Future of our families. No matter how strong my feelings for Pat were getting, I was still taken aback by the nerve of those two, plotting my future for me. Pat felt the same way. The outline of their scheme was that Pat would continue his work at the Digital Equipment C. I would find a job as soon as possible, since I obviously was not suited for motherhood (according to Nancy, a real mother). Kevin and I would give up the house we had bought together and look for a farmhouse big enough for both families. We would all live together as a small commune. Nancy and Kevin would stay home and take care of the kids and animals. Kevin would do contract programming if we needed extra money. Most important, we would switch our marriage partners, since obviously the original partners were so mismatched.

Actually, Kevin and I were far better suited to each other than Kevin and Nancy were. She was domineering and a nag: two traits I didn't think he'd be able to tolerate for long. Later on I pieced together what was going on between them. At the time, I did not have a clue as to what their attraction for each other was all about, except that I knew Nancy had her eye on his relatively large salary. She was sick of seeing most of Pat's salary go to support an ex-wife and kids.

Walden Pond

Pat and I slipped out of the sweltering house one evening after dark. The neighborhood, full of historical sites, was undergoing a prettying up for the next year's centennial celebration. We didn't talk about it, but we both knew we were looking for a quiet, private place to make love. Everyone seemed to have lit up their yards with spotlights for the express purpose of exposing our lust. I felt paranoid and furtive, as though I were about to break some ultimate taboo in front of a jury of my peers. No spot was just right, and we kept on walking for a long time. We discussed how off-the-wall Nancy and Kevin were to try to control our lives. We discussed how it was obvious that they had already slept together. We discussed everything except how nervous we felt with each other. I truly wanted to sleep with the man, but the situation made me very uneasy. The relationship needed time to mellow: we had known each other less than a month.

The night was aging quickly, and we had to hurry up and get it over with; if we didn't act now we would look like chickens, which is exactly what we were. A dark yard surrounded by low bushes loomed up just in time. This would be our trysting place. There couldn't have been a less romantic setting. The grass was dewy, and the bushes barely hid us from passing cars. Neither of us was relaxed, so the mechanics of our coupling was awkward and uncomfortable. We tried and tried, but couldn't get a rhythm going. After a while Pat just kind of wilted, and we lay in the grass, frustrated. We were much happier talking to each other than fucking. In time, we would have been good friends.

We walked home and entered the house with pretend smirks on our faces. Nancy and Kevin beamed with approval. Now they were free to continue their burgeoning relationship without guilt: we had been manipulated like little children into exactly the position that suited their needs. They retired to the master bedroom to enjoy the king-sized waterbed.

Pat and I were left with the air-conditioned third story bedroom. The furnishings consisted of a double mattress on the floor and one of the children's dressers painted brightly in blue and green. The coolness was heavenly. The children themselves were scattered in rooms on the second floor. Each one of them sensed problems looming ahead before any of us were consciously aware of impending chaos, and they started to act out their feelings of unease.

Donne screamed into the wee hours of the morning, scared of nightmares or monsters of his imagination. Kassie found some magic markers, the kind that don't wash out, and decorated the library walls. Kyrie, Nancy's four-year-old, talked back to the adults like a teenager with a foul mouth. Zoe, the baby, clung to Nancy with all her might and refused to leave her mother's lap. Nancy's younger brother and sister, who were staying with us in the house for a week, came down with horrible staph infections, which resulted in open sores up and down their legs. Kassie caught this lovely disease on her bottom just under the line of her panties, which made life torture for her. Five-year-old Josh wandered around in a daze, regressed to a pre-speaking age, and grunted his wants to us in guttural howls. You can't say we didn't have plenty of psychic warning to get out of that house.

We lived the high life for a while.

Tension rose as Nancy and Kevin slept in the waterbed and plotted, while Pat and I continued our platonic friendship. After another attempt at sex under water one eerie night at Walden Pond, we never tried again. Pat said it would be best if he just went back to Nancy. But now Nancy had her hooks buried deeply into Kevin, and he walked around like a lovesick Zombie. Most days he didn't even bother to go to his new job. My birthday came and went: my parents sent a healthy rubber tree, and I thanked them by phone, assuring them that everything was wonderful in Concord, Mass. Kevin and Nancy gave me a butterfly mirror, which is the only artifact I have left over from my marriage to Kevin.

I began to feel cold and alone, in spite of the 90-plus-degree temperatures. Nancy raved on about every subject imaginable, the highlights being that the intelligent should inherit the earth by having the most children, and everyone else should be sterilized. I don't know where this woman got her politics; she was obviously spouting off something she had heard at a Scientology meeting. She wanted to be the mother of dozens of children herself, including mine and Kevin's. She encouraged me to go out and find a good job. In fact, why not go to San Francisco, a city I had dreamed of visiting for years? She, Pat, and Kevin would take good care of the children. She thought I was too distracted to be a good mother. Besides, I had told her I didn't particularly dig motherhood all the time, anyway, hadn't I?

One morning I woke up to all of the classical systems of a migraine. My brain felt like it was crashing into my skull. There were rainbows all around the lights. When I tried to get out of bed, I fell flat on my face onto the floor. Down was up and up was down. A new symptom appeared halfway through the day, which I spent stock still in bed trying not to move a muscle and jar my head into reverberating pain. I began to hear voices coming from the walls. All afternoon I listened to arguments between Kevin and Nancy about where to take the children after they kidnapped them. Nancy was in favor of an old cabin near the beach, and Kevin favored a place nearer to work. Of course, neither Kevin nor Nancy was home at the time: Pat was babysitting while the two of them went to see a movie. My motherly skills didn't totally desert me even then, however. Kassie came in with poopy panties towards evening and I managed to clean her up in spite of my dizzy disorientation.

The strange thing was that she'd been potty trained for over a year.

Nancy and Kevin bopped into the bedroom after their movie and asked how I was feeling. They entertained me with lighter tricks. I still thought they had been plotting behind my back to steal the children, but for a few moments I was won over by their efforts to include me in their fun. They bounced up and down on the waterbed where I had been lying motionless all day. They were being so palsy-walsy I should have been suspicious. Instead, I welcomed the attention; in fact, I ate it up like a starving refugee. Nancy started talking about how terrible a father Pat was to the children, and how secretly he wished he was still married to his ex-wife. She continued that we three were true friends and would be forever. To prove it, she would share Kevin with me for this night, just to make me feel better. Kevin and Nancy took off their clothes and crawled into bed with me. I felt comfy cozy, like a small child in bed with her loving parents, allowed to stay up late as a treat one night. I cuddled Nancy's soft bulk and Kevin's angular boniness.

Then adult needs intruded and Nancy was pressing her crotch into my hand and squirming in slow circles. I got the idea and continued rubbing her clitoris uncertainly. I had never stroked a woman other than myself before, and I didn't exactly know how to go about stimulating her. So I just pretended I was doing it to myself, and soon Kevin joined in our circle of pleasure.

I don't remember what role Kevin played in our game, but I know that before long I wanted to have Kevin all to myself, without the intrusion of the silly blond woman who seemed to have pulled the wool over his eyes. When he got on top of me, I grabbed his erection rudely and tucked him inside me. Now he was mine to do with as I pleased. We bucked and rolled while Nancy watched, with passive, jealous eyes on us. I was triumphant; I had won him over with my brilliant body. And the experience was not all physical, either. Kevin and I had always had a deep, psychic bond, which we both sensed during the moment of orgasm. Nancy witnessed that and was furious. Her control over Kevin wasn't all-powerful after all. As Kevin and I lay back contentedly on the bed, she abruptly rose and said she had a splitting headache. She left the room. I had no words of comfort for her. Serves you right, you bitch, I thought. That's what you get for being a fat slob and a traitor to your best friend. Thus, the trio dissolved before it even began.

The next day I was very friendly to Nancy. I felt I could afford to be nice to her now, renewed since I had reclaimed at least a little bit of my husband's attention. She rejected me and her efforts to urge me out of the house intensified. Kevin continued his support of her and her wacko ideas. She flat out told me that she hadn't been satisfied by our ménage a troi experience, and that she plainly wanted my husband back all to herself. Didn't I want to take a long trip to anywhere? My headache had been banished by the satisfying sex and attention I had received from Kevin. But I was totally freaked out by Nancy's efforts to sabotage my self-esteem and drive me away from Kevin and the children. I had proved I could have Kevin back if I fought for him and played a little dirty pool. But the trick was for him to voluntarily come back to me on his own. And he wasn't doing that. Nancy was doing some new kind of Scientology mind trip on him; I could tell by the way he started to look at me with hate in his eyes, as though he was looking at his mother. I couldn't stand the thought of being rejected by him, or by anybody.

I talked to Pat about what was going on, and he encouraged me to get out of the situation for my own mental health. He himself planned to see a psychiatrist as soon as possible. He'd like to have Nancy back, he realized, but he feared she considered Kevin the better catch.

I prepared to leave; what else could I do in light of the pressure being exerted on me by my husband and his lover? I was unwanted, unloved, and obviously a horrible mother. I called the train station and reserved a ticket to San Francisco. I bought a backpack and took $180 of the $7000 we had deposited from Kevin's and my joint bank account after putting money down on the house. I would be a waitress or something until I figured out what I really wanted to do. Kevin and Nancy and Pat would have to keep the kids for the time being.

Everyone came to see me off. Nancy pretended a few tears but the kids were as happy as ever. Kevin looked at me blankly and said, "Take care." I've always hated it when people say that to me: it's so impersonal. I felt as though he had really said, "Why don't you go off and die quietly somewhere?"

Escape and Help from Friends and Family

I got on the train with a sense of wrongness. I didn't realize what a mistake I had made until I saw a mother herding her two young children to the dining car on the train. The sight of the two little ones made me burst into tears. I rushed to my little room and couldn't stop crying. I cried my way across New York, Pennsylvania, and Ohio. When I got to Chicago I knew I could not go any farther. I would stop and talk to Freddie: he'd have lots of advice for me. After all, when did Freddie ever shut up? He was still my friend in spite of our rocky past, I was certain of that. With trembling hands, I looked up the number of my former lover and called him at work.

He was at his desk at the Sun-Times, and he answered briskly and cheerfully. Why couldn't I have such an efficient and positive life? I was a broken-down wreck of a woman who had just let her children be stolen out from under her by another woman. Why did I always seem to have these kinds of problems? I tried to tell Freddie what had happened, and the explanation came out a jumbled-up mess. But he grasped the situation almost immediately: Freddie has an extremely quick mind and talent for comforting others. He gave me his house key and told me to go to his place and rest. He would see me after work.

When I got outside the building, a dizzying wave of vertigo struck me, and I walked around and around the building trying to decide how to get to the elevated station. I was barely able to stand upright. Freddie watched me from a window upstairs, debating whether or not to come down and direct me. I knew that area of downtown Chicago very well after years of using the public transportation system, so eventually instinct took over and I found my way to Freddie's home. I let myself in with a feeling of peace and relief, and I retreated into a troubled sleep.

When Freddie got home he sat me down at his warm and friendly kitchen table. While he cooked, I told my story.

At the end of it, I found that I had done the impossible; that is, I had rendered my wordy friend into speechlessness. He listened to me for hours until I was all talked out.

I needed all the allies I could get. The next friend I sought out was Kevin's cousin's wife Cathl. Her psychiatrist husband had left her and their six children for one of his patients. She made me cry and cry until I was pretty much all dried up. Then I took a very big step: I decided parental aid was required, and I called home. I decided I would speak only to my father. My mother was too hysterical to handle an emotional emergency.

My mother answered the call, damn it all. I knew better than to give her any information. I told her that I needed to talk to dad about a serious problem. She played it very cool but I knew she would pounce all over me if I gave her any indication about what was going on. She asked where I was and where the children were. I refused to give in and tell her any more. She told me that dad and Derek were on a camping trip in Canada and would not be back for several days. She said she thought she might have a number where he could be reached. I urged her to try to locate him and to call me at Freddie's as soon as possible.

Miraculously, dad called me back within half an hour. His response to me as a daughter in terrible trouble was so unemotional and rational that I had no problem blurting out the whole story. He made me feel calm and sensible. I had run into a problem, and I had taken steps to solve it by leaving and getting help. He was so reasonable; I even told him all the messy sexual details. I couldn't see him, but I knew he didn't bat an eyelash. He said that he would meet me in Chicago. As soon as he got his flight numbers he would call me back.

The deep woods fishermen hadn't been in the wilds of Canada after all. For some unexplained reason, they were camping out in a plush motel somewhere in the states. Dad had left the number of the motel, which mom mercifully had saved. After beating a hasty farewell to his fishing buddies, dad planned to meet me at the Chicago airport. From there we would get a connection to Boston. What was to happen in Boston would depend on Kevin's reaction to me. At the very least, we intended to pull the kids out of a nasty situation. Who did Nancy think she was, anyway, to take my children away from me? It was a criminal act. In my mind I was already split from Kevin: I would from now on function as an independent entity. A wrong had been done, and I would right it with the help of my father. Kevin didn't stand a chance. Once I get stubborn about something, I hold on like a lamprey to a trout. And at that point, I wasn't anywhere near to admitting my own responsibility for the disaster.

Stormy Weather

I met dad at the airport, and we booked passage to Boston. He still looked as cool as ever. He had rushed to catch the plane without even packing a suitcase. When we got to Boston, we'd have to find a department store where we could buy him some clothes. He didn't feel like helping me steal the children back from Kevin in a camouflage suit. I have always been amazed that he was more worried about not having the proper attire than he was about what was going on.

The flight to Boston went smoothly enough. I couldn't stop talking about what had happened. I kept going through the story in my mind as though I had another chance at controlling the outcome. The only time I stopped talking was when I saw a mother or father accompanied by young children; then I started sobbing hysterically again, like a parent whose child has just died. Because I couldn't eat, I started to lose some of the blubber I put on during my depressing marriage.

We rented an economy car and took off for Concord. Dad and I are separately the two worst navigators on the face of the earth. Together we are so bad that we almost always get lost and have to drive hundreds of miles out of our way to get where are going. This trip was no exception. I picked some wild, roundabout route to Concord, which was all wrong. It took us three hours to get there from the airport: it should have taken 45 minutes. Along the way we stopped at a five-and-dime store where we bought dad some hideous shirts and cheesy underwear. It's a good thing my father has a strong positive self-image, because those crappy clothes might have made a lesser man feel pretty tacky. We hurried on, using the confusing New England merry-go-round roads. Just outside of Concord we rented a room in a comfortable hotel. By then it was late evening. I would wait until morning to pop in on the lovebirds.

I entered the Concord house the next morning to pack clothes for the kids and myself and to retrieve any belongings I could fit into one suitcase and a carry-on bag. I threw in a few toys and left behind my journal and poetry notebook. I left behind the cape and culottes outfit my mother had lovingly made me for Christmas the year before. I left behind all my jewelry and my choir pin from sixth grade. I left behind my collection of agates, gathered through the years from lake bottoms in Minnesota.

Pat was the only one up when I got there. I talked with him briefly, and he said that everything had gone to hell after I left. He supported me fully in my decision to take the kids out of a terrible situation.

Nancy and Kevin slept on in the master bedroom while I got the children ready to go. The kids were excited to see me. We left after a quick breakfast of cereal and milk. I regretted my decision to leave without saying goodbye, but I felt justified. After all, who the hell was upstairs in the bedroom, oblivious while the children were being spirited from the house?

I confronted Kevin later that morning in the parking lot of the motel where dad and I had spent the night. The air was hazy and muggy. I felt strung out and dragged down by the events of the last few days. I was no good at making demands. Besides, what did I really want from Kevin? My life would be a whole lot happier and simpler without him around. I was meeting him for the sake of giving him a last chance to make demands on me. I was there to find out what he wanted to save from the dregs of our marriage.

What he wanted was a total surprise to me. Nancy had been brainwashing him about perpetuating the world's geniuses; he said he wanted more children, and that Nancy was willing to provide them. I had made it clear after Donny's birth that I needed a rest from the childbearing game. I was knocked for a loop by his so-called desire for a big family: he spent a minimum amount of his free time with the two kids he already had.

"Well, okay, what next?" I asked. He wanted me to move in with him and Nancy: I could be the kind, loving auntie to all the brilliant and beautiful children he and Nancy would have. Who was he kidding, anyhow? I tried to be straight-faced, and told him I would think over what he said. My only message to him was that I might return to him if he got rid of Nancy. He asked me not to leave town immediately, that he had to go back to talk to Nancy before he made any agreements with me.

Dad called the airport and found out we would have to leave within the hour if we were going to get home that day. I called Kevin on the way to the airport to tell him we had to leave after all. The line was busy: I figured he was talking to Nancy. That thought burned up all my compassion for him. It seemed to me that he had made his choice between the two of us, and I and the children were not it.

Even dad cried with me as we prepared to leave the state. Kevin hadn't had a chance to say goodbye to the kids. No matter what had happened, I still believed that he loved his children. He had forced me into this situation by being such an ass over Nancy. I had to get the kids out of the state right away, before I got sucked back into the situation.

The tunnel under the bay to the airport was jammed with traffic. It seemed as though fate was conspiring to make us miss our flight. The kids were whiny and restless. I was still crying from both guilt and grief, and a small measure of relief as well. But at least I had taken some action, and I felt better for that.

We made it to the airport in time, only to find that our flight was going to be late, very late, as it turned out. I didn't try to call Kevin again. The kids were enough to keep me occupied as they raced back and forth in the crowded waiting room, glad to be expending some of their pent-up energy. We waited and waited for the plane, our vehicle of escape.

I can't remember what turned out to be wrong with the plane, but it finally landed three hours late. We would barely be able to make our connecting flight. We boarded the plane with the feeling that this trip was being jinxed by an evil genie. We had been forced to book first class accommodations. Too bad we couldn't completely enjoy the champagne and gourmet dinner. I half-heartedly attacked my Beef Stroganoff while the kids gladly chomped on Chicken Kiev. Halfway through the flight, the plane started gyrating like a drunken go-go girl. I felt like I was on board an elevator caught in a tornado. One particularly nasty lurch sent Kassie flying out of grandpa's lap. He grabbed her arm just in time to prevent her from flying across the aisle. She started to cry and cradled her arm as though it were broken. Although x-rays later showed no broken bones, she nursed her arm for weeks afterward. Her sore arm seemed to symbolize for her the whole horrible flight from Massachusetts, which seemed to me like another bad omen.

The storm outside increased in ferocity, and we were side-tracked way off course to Detroit. By now it was late at night. The safety and stability of home, any home, was so far away as to seem unattainable. Even natural forces were conspiring against us. Dad and I, in a very rational discussion, concluded that Nancy must be a witch, and she had cursed our trip. We prayed that we would make it off the plane alive with our precious cargo, the two children. In a sense we had stolen them from their father, who had been mesmerized by Nancy's strange power. Witch or not, basically what I wanted to do to her was rip off her tits and stuff them up her smelly snatch. I figure Kevin was being punished enough by having to take her and her miserable kids in place of his own dear family.

Getting Fit

In the fall of 1974 I went to work at the YWCA for $1.05 an hour. Money didn't have much meaning to me in those days. I had no hobbies, no car, and I hated shopping for clothes. Mostly I lived in my bathing suit. Grandma took care of all the kids' needs. I was a natural foods fan, which meant we ate a lot of fruits and vegetables and avoided expensive prepared and junk foods. I baked breads, cakes, cookies, or muffins several times a week. I made my own yogurt and sweetened it with honey or fruit. I took vacations on the train once every six months or so to visit Freddie in Chicago. I was thin and physically fit from all the exercise I was doing at the Y. It doesn't sound like a bad life, but there were cracks in it which would yawn wide open sooner or later.

I didn't know it then, but my marriage was finally over when I decided that even though I was not the world's best wife, the one thing I couldn't tolerate was another woman in my husband's life. Once I decided that, my decisions became very easy. All I had to do was ask Kevin, "Are you still seeing Nancy?" If the answer was yes, then I felt justified in refusing to see him or to negotiate visitation rights. He felt justified in closing out our joint bank account and blocking me from getting any of the money we had saved. I think I decided then that no matter what he did at this point, nothing would erase the fact that he had preferred another woman to me. I've never been so stubborn about anything before or since then. More than anything, I think I was suffering from hurt pride.

He got up the courage to come back to see us one last time. Kassie shrieked with joy when he walked into the house, "Dada, dada," she said, and ran into his open arms. He cried, and I cried, and we tried to forgive each other. We tried to negotiate a life together again. But my mother got him alone the second night he was there and ripped him to shreds. "You'll never be as good as Kris's dad." I heard the whole conversation, but I didn't try to stop it. I was still mad at him and wanted him to be punished. You had to give that to mother; she really knew how to lay into someone she hated. He left immediately, without even saying goodbye to the kids. Now it was his turn to have his confidence demolished.

So, within two days, he was gone, and part of me was dead. Circumstances had conspired to drive us apart, and now I felt more alone than ever before.

I built a life around the children and getting physically fit again. It felt so good to exercise. In the building of my muscular frame, my spirit reshaped itself into a workable and even cheerful form. I swam and attempted gymnastics in the morning. In the afternoons I helped out in the Y nursery. When the kids were safely in bed I took classes in Judo and afterwards indulged in long, leisurely walks in the dark.

Because I was not living in a vacuum, it was inevitable that eventually I would meet another man and ruin the calm rhythm of my days.

Charlie

I met Charlie in the most unlikely of places: the YWCA where I worked. He taught gymnastics to the hordes of little girls who were enrolled in the competitive gymnastics program. Charlie had a weight-lifter's build and was my first African-American friend in town. His moods varied almost as much as mine did. At first I was scared of him, more because of his caustic wit than his appearance or demeanor. When he was angry, he roared like a big, fluffy black lion. I sensed a deep vulnerability in him, and we started running into each other regularly during the day and in the evening while I worked or exercised at the Y.

One night I was invited to a birthday party at our minister's house. I wanted to go, but I had promised to meet Charlie after Judo class. I didn't think he would be interested in going with me to the party, so instead we took a drive out the river road along the bluffs that rose up over the Mississippi River just outside of town. We found a stony overlook hanging over the river.

Charlie wasn't much for small talk. Before I knew it, my head was in his lap. I unzipped his jeans. He never wore underwear, so it was an easy matter to caress the velvet smoothness of his penis with my mouth. I sucked him gently, like a baby sucking a bottle. This simple action soothed me as much as it excited him. The tensions of the day, week, and year faded from me into the dark river flowing below us. He came with a quiet shudder, and I was almost sorry. I hadn't given a man head for over four years. I wondered why not. It was just like eating an exotic tropical fruit. Kevin, for some strange reason, wouldn't let me give him blow jobs.

Charlie and I saw each other off and on for the whole next year. Then my sister was home, and she was working with Charlie teaching gymnastics. One night we got sisterly smashed on Tequila Sunrises, and Janie admitted she had a crush on Charlie. In a fit of generosity, I invited her to try him out, as though he were mine to give way at will. He didn't mind much, and then baby sister Teri was home and she was just so beautiful, who could blame him for sleeping with her as well? We shared Charlie among ourselves for several years more. In the end I think he was hurt by our cavalier treatment of him, but maybe not. As far as I could tell, he was completely amoral, and we three sisters were without many boundaries at that time. I wonder where he is today. I'd love to see him again.

Charlie wasn't the only man we three sisters shared. We all shared Steve, until Teri finally married him, and Janie and I shared Bob and Walt, and then later I shared Jim with Janie in secret. I admitted my affair with Jim in time, but Janie and I haven't talked about him in so long I question whether she remembers my confession to her. I'm not about to bring it up. Or maybe I just dreamed I told her I had an affair with her husband.

Blue Collar Work

I heard about the job at the refinery by accident. My father knew the plant manager, and he told dad that the company would be hiring a new group of process operators. The pay was the highest in the area for unskilled labor. Although the job would be physical, I was in pretty good shape from my two years working at the Y as a swimming and aerobics instructor. Like a lot of educated people, I romanticized the idea of working as a laborer. I fell for the old cliché that working by the sweat of your brow is somehow nobler than earning a living at a desk, with good clothes on. What I forgot to think about was how the other workers would react to me.

Amoco Oil Company of Wood River, IL called me for an interview in September 1975. I don't remember what was going on that year. I hadn't read a newspaper in years, I didn't have time to watch TV, and my concentration was so poor that I hadn't even read any good books in a long time.

The year 1975 was not a good year to live in a fantasy world or to be waylaid by extreme moods. My children were three and four and absolute terrors. No wonder moms go quietly mad. You know you have to get through the difficult years with your kids, but if you actually try to figure out how you're going to manage it you'll go bonkers even without the handicap of being mentally ill. I suppose being a single parent didn't help. Even so, I was living in a household with six other adults besides myself. You'd think we could have managed the kids better. I baked a lot of bread to stay sane.

The Refinery

So, in 1975 I applied for a job as Process Operator at the Amoco Oil Refinery in Wood River, IL. My salary of $1.05 an hour at the Y was not even beginning to support my little family. There was not a single female process operator working at any of the three large refineries in the area, and there were very few women working at any of the other factories. With the typical grandiosity of a hypomanic person I felt as though there was no job I couldn't do physically.

To pass the interview, first I had to take a math test. It was easy, though I only scored the second highest grade on the test (I never did figure out who beat me). Next I had to climb a ladder to the top of a water tank nearly a hundred feet high (on those slippery plain metal rungs that go straight up the side of the wall and are just skinny narrow tube-like bars), carry two 20-gallon buckets of oil about a block, carry a thick heavy fire hose up a ladder and onto a small platform on one of the towers, and last but not least, figure out how to load a barrel of oil onto a dolly, transport it a distance away, and then set up the barrel on a stand.

I accomplished all of these tasks, but I was still nervous as a cat. For my last trick, I was required to open a huge valve with a very large wrench. Thank God someone told me which way to open valves: right-tighty and lefty loosy. Strange how you can grow up in the world for 26 years and still not learn that crucial bit of information.

In October I learned that I had gotten the job at what was Standard Oil's third largest refinery in the world. I was one of only four women who applied. All four of us were hired. I assumed the other women did just as well as I did on the practical test. We were pretty strange specimens of womanhood. One of the women looked so much like a man that I didn't recognize her as a woman until months later, when someone jokingly whispered to me, "I wonder what hormones she's taking." Another of the women was at least a hundred pounds overweight. I have no idea how she managed to pass the physical. Although I considered myself normal at the time, when I look at pictures of myself then, I'm not sure I even recognize the tough, coarse woman I see dressed in Oshkosh b'Gosh bib overalls and carrying tools in the leg pockets. Nobody ever told me I suffered from multiple personality disorder, but when I look at myself in those pictures of me on the way to work, with my black lunch bucket and denim jacket, I have to wonder. I stepped into that alter ego as easily as jumping into a lake. I was skewed off into an entirely new part of myself I hadn't known existed, a female macho role.

I was practically unconscious with fear the day I started work. Not because I was afraid of what I might have to face physically. It came down to the simple fact that I was deathly afraid of looking stupid in front of a bunch of men. I had always felt equal or better among most groups of women, although not for the reasons you might think. The main reason was that I was much more adventuresome than all the women I knew except for my sister Janie, who was even more talented physically than I was. I walked down the streets of Chicago with a mini-dress on at night, and didn't have a moment of fear that someone would attack me. It never even occurred to me that I should be afraid. I had had my share of sexual misadventures, but in truth, when they had happened I was so dissociated by drugs or alcohol, that it didn't seem that it was I who had done them.

In a group of blue collar workers, I was afraid I would do the wrong thing. I feared humiliation and embarrassment.

As my first day of work went by, I began to fear total loss of rational thought; then I promptly lost it. Eventually, I even feared loss of control of my bodily functions. Finally, I went into a blackout state or fugue and can't remember what happened the rest of the day. Later I learned that we were taken on a tour of the whole refinery; however, the places we visited I remembered later only as surreal landscapes in a cold gray dream.

This overwhelming stage fright must be the same feeling football players get before a crucial game or performers before the curtain goes up. All I knew was that I could barely hear, see, or move. What I needed was a big dose of Valium. I can only imagine what I must have looked like under my hardhat and behind my ugly black safety glasses. The refinery was no place to worry about fashion. I wondered if my paralysis was visible to the other workers. My fear was so strong I felt it must have been painted on my face.

As the weeks went on, I relaxed, at least relatively. I would never feel totally comfortable in that setting, but at least my brain started to function and I proved myself a quick student of the antique equipment we were to operate, maintain, and sometimes even repair. Working in a power station suited me much better than I ever would have guessed. I even made friends with some of my co-workers, although most of them would spend the next year or so testing me for any signs of feminine weakness.

Right away it struck me that the most important traits needed for success at blue collar work were courage and a willingness to get dirty and perform the shittiest jobs so as to spare the more experienced workers from having to do them. Also, the newer operators were expected to show up early and to leave late. Newcomers were severely chastised for leaving tasks undone that fell at shift change time.

It followed that if you arrived early and did all your regularly scheduled jobs as well as the extra dirty, difficult, dangerous, and discouraging jobs you weren't really supposed to be doing, you got grudging respect from the old-timers. If you gladly performed a few of the next guy's jobs so he could drink coffee for an hour longer at the beginning of his shift, if you freely socialized with all the old geezers even when they made rude passes at you or grabbed your tits or ass, and if you did all these things with good nature and no complaints, then you would eventually earn a grudging acceptance from even the younger workers. I learned not to trust any of the other new guys because they considered me a threat to their chances of quick advancement. There were no minority supervisors or managers at this refinery, and everybody thought that you had to be African-American or a woman to be promoted. Too bad I didn't stick around for long enough to become a Chief Operator or Shift Supervisor. I probably would have been the first woman power station operator in the world to rise to those positions.

Understand that I was the first woman to set foot in the power station since the war years, when women took over all the refinery jobs. The Rosie Riveters performed these jobs quite capably: it was the men who made the biggest mistakes in the history of the refinery. For example, it was male engineer who caused the first Catalytic Cracker to topple over on its first day of operation by testing out a large turbine with water instead of steam on the fourth floor platform. When the structure fell over, it took the whole unit with it, from top to bottom. That must have been quite a sight. Lots of other crazy things happened at that place. Not to say I didn't do some dumb things.

Working at Amoco turned out to be much more educational than I ever dreamed it would be. I wish now that I had stayed there. At least I'd be richer; most of the refinery workers I knew retired with a million or more dollars after working thirty years.

My sister Janie would later join me at the refinery, where she worked for a while in the much despised chemical plant on the site. She didn't last a year. But I was there for a whole three years. We worked there because we both needed the money, and the refinery jobs paid a lot more than office work. I think I started at $6.60/hour plus extra for overtime, more than six times what I had been making at the Y. I felt like I had really taken my life in my hands and showed everyone I could do a tough job, right up there with the guys.

Kevin never sent a penny of child support; in fact, he disappeared from the planet for a while. I didn't find out where he was for years. His mother wouldn't tell me where he had gone, nor would his sister. He feared having to pay me so desperately that he would quit jobs and move often just so that I couldn't find him. I honestly didn't look for him very hard. I had proved I really didn't need his money. Also, I was afraid to ask him for money--it seemed to me that what I had done, taking the children away from him so sneakily, was such a shameful deed that I didn't deserve to receive child support. The kids didn't see him for another six years.

Blue-eyed Jim

The next part of my story makes me feel corrupted and stained. I hadn't gotten in any trouble sexually for a long time. I was overdue for a romantic disaster. I told you before that my sisters and I liked basically the same kind of men, and we shared them with no conflict. Until Jim.

I couldn't understand what had gone wrong with my relationship with Jim. He and I seemed to have everything in common. He was comfortable in my house--he had recently rebuilt a carburetor in my spare bedroom. I idolized him, as did my sisters. We thought he was the perfect man. He was six feet tall with piercing blue eyes. He looked great in light blue denim because it was the same color as those eyes. He was our mechanic, and he had taken care of all our cars for years.

One day he showed up with Janie. They were holding hands. I couldn't believe my eyes. He was my friend, not Janie's.

I couldn't believe I had let him get away. It was hard for me to accept the fact that Janie got the man because for the first time in her life, she got aggressive. I wanted to tell him how I felt about him, but I had a sudden lack of self-confidence. I might have thought that he genuinely preferred her sexually. But I still thought, No you can't have him; he's mine."

I thought of my relationship with Janie through the years. When we were teenagers, I always wanted to wear her clothes, which were probably a size too small for me. I remember a green and pink culotte dress that I wore to a party one night in Eden Park in Cincinnati. I was wrestling with one of my many boyfriends at the time, and I tore the dress under the armpit--I ripped it completely apart at the seam. Janie was furious. Mom mended the dress, but Janie refused to wear it again.

Jim and Janie moved in together and were married the next summer in Michigan at my parent's house on the beach. Janie didn't seem overly thrilled about getting married. I couldn't look Jim squarely in the eyes. I cried when they were saying their vows.

Jim worked at the refinery, too. He was a talented mechanic, and he did well at Amoco. But then the refinery was shutting down and all the workers had to find another place to work. Janie and Jim decided to move to Casper, Wyoming, the same town where my mother's parents had lived and died. When they left, Jim kissed me goodbye. That kiss told me all I needed to know. It sent electric sparks flying through my body. I remember crying afterwards and thinking, "How did I let this one get away?"

Then Janie was pregnant, and I began to think of enrolling in engineering school to escape from the refinery. I was thrilled at the thought of going back to school but also terrified again that I might not be smart enough to pass engineering classes. I knew I would love Jim forever but he had fallen out of my reach.

Off to School

In lots of ways I was happy enough living in my twelfth state, my twenty-sixth home, and working at my seventeenth job. I had long ago realized that I was destined to be a nomad, either by choice, upbringing, or genes. I was not searching for my soul. I told myself that I moved so often because moving is thrilling. I had grown with each new upheaval. Every new place brought to me new entertainments, pleasure, and educations. When I started to feel like a piece of old moldy bread, I knew it was time to move on.

One thing I could say for sure: there didn't seem to be a man alive, a job, or a town in the whole wide world satisfying enough to fill me up. The best experiences I could think of were the ones that snuck up behind me and yelled, "Boo," or pinched me in the ass. I had learned that these things could happen at any time, in any place, and with the most surprising people. So why should I try to set them up? Settling down for me would be like agreeing never to have another birthday party. I simply couldn't imagine staying put anywhere. After three years working at the refinery I realized it was time to move on.

Do You Drive Trains?

I never really got used to shift work. We worked midnights to afternoons to days, and often 16-hour shifts. In time, I was on a schedule with a shift of men I was compatible with who didn't approach me sexually. I was dating one of my co-workers, a hyperactive man younger than I. I knew by then that I wouldn't stay much longer at the refinery.

I had begun to study math at home in preparation for applying to engineering school. I started with algebra and worked my way through geometry and trigonometry. There is nothing like the goal-driven activity of a manic person. It took a certain amount of mania to work a swing shift with a bunch of men in a complex manufacturing facility. I always had to be at least hypomanic in order to do the job. I forced myself to be a superwoman and found it was not that hard to do with my overabundance of energy.

I applied to school at dad's alma mater, the University of Minnesota at Minneapolis. I didn't hear from the office of admissions for months so my mother, who happened to be in St. Paul visiting dad's relatives, dropped by the school office to see if she could find out the status of my application. The woman she talked to just happened to have my application sitting on her desk in a pile of documents labeled "What do we do with these?" My mother must have been very convincing because I was accepted into the University of Minnesota engineering school the spring of 1978.

I was so excited to be moving up in the world I could barely breathe. The children went to visit grandma and grandpa that summer while I packed up our possessions. With lots of help from friends and family I loaded up a truck and headed from Alton, IL to St. Paul, Minnesota. Dad helped me drive, and we moved on my twenty-ninth birthday. Jim showed me how to disengage my car's drive train so we could pull the car behind us. Driving the truck took some getting used to; it was a double-clutch model that I had never used before. After a few miles down the road, we got used to the strange transmission. We ate candy and slowly made our way north. As I told you before, Dad and I are the worst two navigators in the world. At one point, before dawn on our second day, we got stuck in a junk yard after I missed an important turnoff onto the highway in the dark. We spent an hour trying to turn the truck around at a dead end, all the while dragging the car behind us. Somehow, we got out of there and once more were underway. We arrived in St. Paul at the dinner hour, with the temperatures hovering above 90 degrees. My aunt Dorothy had prepared dinner for us, and I looked forward to moving right into our new house.

I got an unexpected shock when I saw the new house. It was painted a dingy puke green. My house in Alton was a cheerful lemon yellow that had always made me happy. I have always hated any shade of green, probably because it was my mother's favorite color. The porch was painted an equally depressing dirty gold. The house was a duplex we would share with another family. The hundred-year-old structure looked its age. The neglect showed in every detail of its form, from the broken window panes with no storms, the sagging door at the front, the crumbling concrete stairs up to the porch, the total absence of any grass in the front yard, to the trash heap piled high in the back yard.

If I thought the outside was bad, I was even less prepared for the inside. The woman who had lived there for the past five years was a single parent whose life was obviously out of control. She was still moving furniture when we arrived. She spent no time cleaning up, so when we finally entered the house, the smell of the place alone was enough to make me want to turn around and go back to my cheerful home in Alton. Imagine the smell of unchanged cat litter boxes, spoiled food, animals corralled behind peeling radiators, and fermenting garbage; all intensified because of the lack of air movement in the house. Flies and mosquitoes buzzed around our heads and all over our sweaty bodies. Even at seven in the evening, the heat was unbearable. We were all hot and cross and hungry.

The previous tenant was finally gone after we finished dinner across the street at Aunt Dorothy's house. I hoped I wasn't putting too much of a burden on dad as I watched him sweating and straining to lift the other end of the living room couch. The late afternoon sunlight was dwindling as we unloaded the truck and finished moving the furniture as best we could, in between the piles of garbage our predecessor had left behind her. The best and most hopeful part of the move was that on both sides of us were kids Kassie's and Donne's ages.

Three weeks later, I was still cleaning up the house and yard. Meanwhile, the men in the family decided to knock down one of the kitchen walls to make more space. The plaster dust settled everywhere, as thick as desert dust, and I had to clean the house up all over again. My classes were scheduled to start the last week of September, and I worked like a maniac to finish with the house before school started.

The hot weather continued, and we took a break to attend the Minnesota State Fair, which was set up only a few miles from us. Then it was time for school to start. I set off for classes on my bike in shorts and a T-shirt. Halfway through the six-mile trip, a cold rain started to fall, giving me my first glimpse of the tricks Minnesota weather would play on me for the next five years. Cold and wet, I attended my first engineering class.

A New Way of Thinking

I had signed up for classes in subjects I hadn't thought about for more than ten years. The first day, I knew I had jumped in over my head without the requisite skills to stay afloat. My transcripts placed me in the middle of second quarter calculus and first year engineering physics, for starters. As I looked over the textbooks for these two very basic engineering classes, I felt like I was in a foreign country. I stuck out the classes for a week, not comprehending any of the subject material presented to us by the patient engineering professors. I would have to either quit before I had gotten started, or drop down a notch or two in subject matter. I dropped all my classes and enrolled in the prerequisite classes, so I was in pre-calculus and general physics, an easy introductory class to the real engineering physics I would have to master at some point. Suddenly the world was alright again. I was afloat in my new world, able to tread water at least for a while.

I had to drop another class, engineering drafting, because I couldn't yet visualize and manipulate shapes in my mind the way all the other engineering students could do. Kassie and Donne laughed at me when I cut up potatoes into shapes so I could draw the shapes at new angles. This was before the days of CAD-CAM, and I would have to learn this new skill in my head. I'd spent most of my life thinking in words, and mentally playing with pictures was as strange to me as Swahili. Whatever had possessed me to give up my comfortable life to attend mechanical engineering classes and enter into realms not yet even envisioned by me in my wildest dreams? My parents were both gifted in visual thinking, but they had not genetically blessed me with any of their capabilities. I was left wondering where my mind came from, anyway. It was obviously a result of some powerful cultural influences.

My brother came to visit, and we put up a false ceiling with new lights in the kitchen. I wasn't able to figure out how to cut the tiles so they would fit in the odd-shaped corners of the ceiling. My brother crowed at me--finally he had found a talent he possessed that I was downright lacking in, for the first time. He has never let anyone forget how bad I was at spatial relations.

In spite of my handicaps, I got an A in pre-calculus and a respectable B in physics. I was on my way in engineering. I would retake the drafting class later. I was so excited to have found some measure of success that I even started dressing up for classes. My self-esteem soared, at last. I devoted myself single-mindedly to study. I found that if I really tried, I could understand all the technical material I would need to know as an engineer. It was like growing a new and useful limb on my body. My technical mind emerged from the depths of my unconscious. I had skewed into yet another consciousness I wasn't aware that I possessed.

It was a new and thrilling world. I felt really intelligent, maybe for the first time in my life. I had never had to try to achieve in school. Memorizing things was second nature to me. But this new thinking skill was almost erotic in its effect on me. I felt like I was glowing with some kind of inner light.

My best thinking always happened early in the day, though I spent each evening studying. I had so much homework to do all the time I felt that I was under pressure constantly. I didn't even have time to read for fun. The kids took up a lot of my evening attention, too, so I always felt like I was behind in my coursework. Some nights I would take the kids to the library with me, and we'd study together. I could bribe them with food from the machines to get through a few hours of study.

I Betray My Sister

By 1982 I had only one year left of engineering school. I decided to take a break in the summer after my classes were completed. I had been going straight through school, and I decided I needed a vacation.

At the beginning of the summer, Kassie had flown to Wyoming to visit Janie and help her take care of her new baby, Christopher, who by then was about six months old. My mother agreed to drive with me to Wyoming to pick up Kassie and to stay for a little visit. I didn't think about Jim anymore, at least I thought I didn't. I had moved on to a new and satisfying life, with a world full of hope ahead of me.

We got to Wyoming, and Janie was completely preoccupied with her new baby. She could barely put him down to take a bath, and when she did put him down, he cried. I was feeling high on life. Engineering school had done much to build up my confidence.

One day Jim rented a pontoon boat, and we went for a ride on one of the rivers near the Alcova Reservoir. I sensed that there was trouble between Janie and Jim. They argued over little things, and I never saw Jim holding the baby. Janie didn't want to take the baby on the boat, so she and grandma stayed home while the rest of us drove out to the reservoir.

We docked the boat in a cove along the river, and jumped into in the freezing water. I was happy and carefree. My life was working out, the kids were happy as could be, and I would soon be done with engineering school. Jim and I swam across the river and climbed up on a rock, where we sat together in the sun. From the way he was watching me, I knew for certain then that he and Janie were not getting along. I radiated towards him and thought, he's thinking the same thing I am. We looked in each other's eyes and saw, well, paradise. Then across the river, we saw Janie and mom standing on an outcrop of rock. They were watching us. Janie had the baby in her arms. They had driven to the reservoir to be with us after all. I had no idea how they had found us. I wondered if Janie would notice that I was sitting in the sun with her husband.

We boarded the boat and took it back to the dock. I was breathless with excitement. Now I had a secret. I've made a career out of hoarding forbidden thoughts. What I was thinking now was forbidden, indeed, in many of the cultures on earth.

On the way home, Jim stopped at the local liquor store and picked up several cases of beer. One of the brands was Red Dog. I had never drunk red beer, so I was in for a real treat. I loved the beer, and downed one bottle after another. I probably drank eight or ten beers, which was way over my limit. Jim drank even more. My drinking life at school had been sporadic; I'd go on binges on weekends, but I didn't drink at all during the week. By nine o'clock that evening, Jim and I were laughing and joking and having the time of our lives. No one else was drinking.

Janie, mother, and the baby went to bed. On some pretense Jim and I left the house together to take an innocent walk. I needed to clear my head, which was spinning. We walked down the street towards the little river that enclosed the subdivision. It was dark along the banks, and there was no moon to light our path.

I said, "What the hell," and threw off my clothes. I piled them in a heap beside the creek and jumped in. The bottom was mucky, and my feet sank up to the ankles in the sucking ooze. I ducked under the surface of the water and came up smiling. "Come on in," I urged Jim. He didn't need much encouragement and soon he was beside me in the cool water. I felt clear-headed and sparkle-eyed. I could feel the water on every inch of my sensitive body. I was not surprised when Jim threw his arms around me and I felt his comforting warm bulk enclosing me.

I was so high that after a while I began to feel numb, the way a mosquito bite feels when you've scratched it raw to make the itch go away. My mind had taken me up the mountain and over the side of the cliff. I felt like I was falling. The sound of crickets scraping together their long legs intensified in my ears. I was dizzy with feeling, high on the night, and I wanted sex from my sister's husband more than I had ever wanted anything. I felt an uncontrollable urge to jump on his body, impale myself on his penis, and ride him into the sunset. The urge was uncontrollable, so I acted on my impulse and mounted him on the banks of the river. We were on a small hill, so the angle was just right. I rode him frenziedly but after penetration I didn't feel a thing inside me. I had committed myself, so it didn't occur to me to say, "Let's stop this. This is wrong. Let's go home and forget it ever happened."

I was so over-stimulated that I couldn't have an orgasm. He was so stimulated that he had one right away. I had climbed up to the highest height of my senses and leveled off at the top. I had the feeling that I was just about ready to go over the edge, but I never actually fell over. I could screw the man all night and still never come to a climax. I think this is the true meaning of the word nymphomaniac--the inability to be satisfied by sex, no matter how much of it you get. It was enough to drive me batty. Our lovemaking didn't last more than a few minutes. We didn't draw out or savor our pleasure. We just plunged into our passion and briefly reveled in the feeling of being higher than high. I felt like I was above the physical laws of the universe. What we had together was worth all the shit we would have to take if we were found out. So what if I didn't have an orgasm. I could go on like that all night, until I was raw and bleeding. The hard part was going to be facing the family with the guilty knowledge of what we had done.

We put our clothes on and walked home. The kids were downstairs watching a movie. I put on my jammies and joined them on the floor, propped up with a big pillow. I had on a thigh-length robe and was just barely decent. When Jim joined us downstairs, I could barely keep my hands off him. I wouldn't be satisfied until I had had my fill of him, and I was a long way from that. We watched to the end of the movie until the kids were asleep on the floor.

Then he was over me and we were kissing, and he was stroking my breast, and I was back on the banks of the river, and maybe I could come this time. We kissed and cuddled for more than an hour.

At some point I looked over at the kids lying asleep on the floor, and suddenly I saw Donne's eyes opening, and he was looking at me, looking at us, and my robe was thrown wide open, and Jim was in my arms, and all he could say was "Oh, mom," with the most judgmental tone in his voice. Jim and I pulled apart, but we knew that it was too late to hide what we were doing. Donne rolled over and looked at the wall. I hadn't felt ashamed of what we had done until that moment. "We'd better go to bed," I told Jim. He went upstairs and I headed towards the bathroom. I realized that my period had come in a rush.

What timing, I thought. I was suddenly bleeding big clots onto the floor. I would have to go find a tampon. As I flitted past the stairway to the upstairs, Janie was there, looking down the steps with a confused look. She was holding the baby. She saw me rush past and I saw her from the corner of my eye as I passed the stairs. I thought, "Oh, no, don't tell me we've been caught again. Had it all been worthwhile?" I ran for the bathroom, shoved in a tampon that I found in the cupboard and took four Midols to drown the sudden cramps I felt. What would happen next? I could only imagine the scene between me and my sister. I stayed awake for a while, letting my imagination run wild, and somehow managed to fall into a restless sleep for a few hours.

The next morning I dozed on the sofa bed in the living room. Everyone else had gone out for breakfast, and I was alone in the house. Then from the wall I heard my mother's voice, like the witch's voice in *The Wizard of Oz*, accusing me of horrible crimes, saying I deserved to die for them, that a worse person had never been born. The voice went on for a long time, and I tried to shut it out, but it was concurrently outside and inside my brain. "You slept with your sister's husband!!!!!!!!! How could you do such a thing?"

I began to tremble and wondered how well I could fake normality, the way I had always done before when I had done horrible things.

The family came home, and Janie didn't say a word to me. Jim said, "Good morning, sleep well?" I waited for the dam to break and for them all to pour out a torrent of abuse on me. How could I survive what was about to happen to me: being exposed for all my evilness to the people I loved most?

What an anti-climax when nothing at all happened. I wasn't going to be punished for my sins. Soon it was time for us to pack up and leave. We took pictures in the front yard before we got in the car. I still have the pictures from that trip. I looked happy and vibrantly alive. There was a sort of spacey ecstasy painted on my face in all the shots. In one picture Jim and I are hugging. This would be a secret I'd have to keep to myself for the rest of time.

There was no future for me in a relationship with my brother-in-law. Mom and I drove the rest of the day. I got us terribly lost in a small town called Dixon. I think Ronald Reagan was born there. Mom was quite put out with me. I had wasted an hour being lost. We stayed in a Holiday Inn that night. The kids and I swam before dinner. The water was cold, but not as cold as the river water I had leaped into the night before. I took Midols all day to dull the pain of my menstrual cramps. Well, at least I knew I was not pregnant by my sister's husband.

Disconnected

Now I was in a real quandary. I had fallen in love with my sister's husband. My feelings of guilt and shame faded away as I studied thermodynamics, heat transfer, and industrial engineering. I couldn't call Jim on the phone because Janie would answer and think it was strange if I asked to talk to Jim. I thought about him day and night. I schemed and planned and imagined. How could I get him back to Minnesota? Sexual obsessiveness was a clear sign of mania for me. Being manic helped me get through my engineering classes but soon all I could think about was sex, like a teenaged boy.

Jim wrote me letters and said that he had taken a post office box number and that I could write him freely there. We wrote back and forth for months. He sent me a picture of a pile of stones that read "I love you." Then suddenly he was there with me in Minnesota. He told his wife he might want to go back to school and that he'd like to see the University of Minnesota. Then my mother was visiting too, and she slept like a bird---in fits and starts--on the living room couch. My bedroom was on the third floor at the front of the house. To get to my bedroom you had to pass by both of the kid's rooms. How was I going to meet my lover with all these people in the house?

We waited until everyone was asleep, and I met him at the top of the stairs. Donne had given up his room so

Jim had a place to sleep. My mind was not completely clear on why suddenly we were on a hard wooden floor, fucking, and I couldn't feel a thing again, and then he was done and we were whispering to each other in the dark. We took a long walk the next day, and fantasized about what, a future together? I was starting to have my doubts about this relationship. I went numb around the man, and I couldn't think straight. I only lived for the moments when I was with him, and that seemed like enough at the time. I couldn't see beyond the present. What we had already done was enough for me. He whispered messages in my ear, saying he loved me and he would return somehow. I knew it would never happen.

Crash and Burn

As time went on, I studied and hoped I could finish school. My classes weren't going very well. I got a few D's and had to retake some classes. I was discouraged. Jim and I wrote each other several times a week. My enthusiasm for him began to wane, and guilt attacked me with a vengeance. How could I have done such a thing to my own sister? Jim had had his chance with me years ago, and he had picked Janie. Now he had a baby and sure, it was sad that Janie had ignored him since the baby's birth, but what could I do about that?

I went to see a therapist at the university. There was a free therapy service for students. I saw a large motherly black woman and poured out my story of my love for my sister's husband and how things had gotten out of control, and how I felt stuck and guilty.

"Get away from that man as fast as you can. Don't write him, and don't call him, and for god's sake don't see him again." She didn't have a moment's doubt about the right thing to do. I knew she was right. I couldn't see Jim anymore, and I'd have to stop thinking about him. He would have to work out his problems with Janie on his own.

He sent me flowers on my birthday, and I didn't even thank him. I stopped writing and imagined him dejected at the post office when he didn't find a letter.

I wondered if I would ever find a free-and-clear man of my own, who would accept me as I was and love my children as I did. Through a friend I met in physics class I met the man who pushed me over the edge. His name was John St. James.

John was a fascinating man who caught my interest right away. He was over six feet tall and broadly built, like most of the men in my family. I was attracted to his wide, firm butt. His dark hair was starting to recede, and like me, he wore glasses. He was an archeologist whose unique talent was the ability to make arrowheads in the original Indian way, by chipping the edges of flint rock to a point with a special chipping stone. He was always chipping rocks. He showed me some beautifully crafted arrowheads he had made. I was impressed.

He had been a teacher at an Indian reservation, and had gotten fired for reasons he didn't elaborate. John was paranoid about everything. The idea of AIDs would have driven him bananas, which is no doubt what he is now. He talked at length about a girlfriend he had left who was cruel to him and with whom he never managed to have sex. John turned my world upside down, even worse than Kevin and Nancy had.

John was completely narcissistic, and he demanded that the people around him live according to his wants and needs. He didn't eat or sleep much. He ate only boiled potatoes and hot dogs, plain and cold. He was broke, and his car was falling apart. I was drawn to his intensity and his volubility. He never stopped talking all day and most of the night. We started staying up till four or five watching late night shows and revealing our innermost secrets. I told him about my job at the refinery and my manic tryst with three men. He told me about his lifelong impotence and his failures with women. I saw his problems as a challenge to me, and I encouraged him to get a sex life. I had had some dealings with impotent men, and I realized that often acceptance from a kind and understanding woman was the key to getting a man over that problem.

I bought a case of beer and a fifth of vodka one day. John and I began to drink, and we were easily able to down the whole case in one night. Four beers was normally my limit, but when I was with John, I was a bottomless pit of alcoholic need. Then we started on the vodka, because it was cheap. Before long, we were drinking and talking all night every night and sleeping only a few hours in the day.

I began skipping all my engineering classes, and the ones I did attend, I didn't understand. I passed electrical engineering lab, but failed all the classwork tests. I couldn't seem to remember the simplest calculus problems that I had been working on for the last five years, day and night, year in and year out. I had been doing very well in Materials Science, but I never finished my final project. John encouraged me to skip classes and whispered to me at night that I didn't really want to be an engineer, did I?

He was certainly right about that. I was learning that although I could do passably well in any technical class, my heart really wasn't there for the long term. Engineering was more of a game and a challenge to me than a calling. I'm not sure why it took my encounter with John for me to realize that. Engineering was interesting to me theoretically, but not practically. When it came to building things, tinkering with machinery, or even assembling simple household items, I was lost. How could I have ended up in school for mechanical engineering? John brought out a side of me I had buried. I was interested in books, literature, anthropology, and journal writing, none of which I had paid the slightest bit of attention to during the last five years. I realized that I must have tried to study engineering to please my father.

Donne started to scare his fifth grade teacher when he began writing poems about suicide. He said something about welcoming death while sitting on a blanket in the back yard. I was at the other extreme of the spectrum emotionally from where he was. I was flying high on booze, sex, and emotions of happiness and joy, the like of which I had never experienced. Mixed with my euphoria, though, was a sense that the future was hopeless for me, that now was all there was or ever would be. All I had planned for my life was going up in smoke because of this man John, who was slowly pushing me to the breaking point. In truth, though I was pushing my own self to the point of collapse.

I met with Donne's teacher and a social worker, and I agreed to see a therapist. What did I care, I was feeling on top of the world? The therapist gave me the Minnesota Multi-Phasic Personality Test to take at home when I had the time. I took it one afternoon in March. John had been staying with me for six weeks. I hadn't slept a whole night since the second week he was there. It took me several hours to complete the 400 or so questions.

John and I decided we would get married. I wanted him to meet my parents. We would drive to Michigan, where we could stay at my brother's house. John was on his best behavior, and he even changed out of his flannel shirt and jeans to meet my family. We stayed in my brother's guest room. I was still bruised all over my body from the night before, when John and I got into a tickling match. The tickling was so violent that we were both covered with ugly yellow and green bruises. At my brother's house, upstairs in the guest bedroom, we finally consummated the sexual relationship we had been building toward for the last six weeks we'd spent together. John was no longer impotent. I was sexually a demon by that time, and once we got started, I was eager to have sex morning, noon, night, and in-between.

We told my family we were getting married. What could they say? John and I were very convincing about our happiness together. John was an intellectual and interesting man, someone who was smart enough to keep me on my toes. None of us realized how manipulative he was and how unbalanced.

On the way back to St. Paul, John got the children alone in the back seat while I was in the bathroom, and he told them they'd better get used to him, because he was going to marry their mom whether they liked it or not. They were terrified of him. He told them they would have to stop being such spoiled, rotten brats. They would learn to behave, or else. I should have noticed how scared Kassie looked in the car ride home, as though the happy world she had known up till now was breaking into a thousand pieces. I was so emotionally out-of-control that I allowed a man to interfere with my relationship with my kids, who had always been the center of my universe, and also to destroy all my ambition and drive to find my place in the world.

I had made the mistake of telling John my life story and trusting him to keep his mouth shut. I should have known better. He took all my dirty secrets, which I had written down for him, and he would later broadcast them to the world. In short, he decided that it was his job to uncover the real truth about the ugly side I had hidden from my family and all the emotions I had kept repressed.

I was brilliant at the art of covering up my fears and my deepest feelings and of course, all my horrendous misdeeds. If there was a point in the predestined pattern of all things, then my attraction to John was an effort of the divine power to get me to open myself up to the world. At that time, I didn't realize how far my feelings would go.

When we got back to Minnesota, the weather was cold and bleak, not at all like spring, though it was March.

The kids were actively hostile towards John. Kassie rearranged his carefully ordered rocks, which he had laid out on the kitchen table in some pattern known only to him, and John flew into a fury. I've never seen anyone that angry before about something so trivial. Good thing Kassie wasn't in the room when he discovered she had ruined his project, or I don't know what he would have done to her.

There was still a lot of snow on the ground. John and Donne went sledding the night Kassie ruined his rock piles, and I thought, "Oh great; at least John and Donne are finally bonding." What actually happened was that they got into a snowball fight, and Donne threw an ice ball that hit John in the face. John retaliated by shoving Donne into a snow bank and grinding his face into the sharp ice crystals. When John finally let him up, Donne's face was scratched and bleeding, and he began to cry.

Donne and I had always been particularly close. He ran to me with his bloody face, and I looked at him with an incomprehension that can be achieved only by someone who is so greatly dissociated from her true feelings that she can't see reality at all but only how she wishes it to be.

In my manic world, there were no tears, and blood wasn't allowed. The kids never even skinned their knees. With John around I was spiraling higher and higher as if I had been snorting ever increasing amounts of cocaine. If I felt this good how could the world be so wrong? Wasn't everyone else as happy as I was?

If I were to trust the feelings of invincibility and joy I had when I was around John, then I would have to ignore the reality of Donne's bloodstained cheek. Staying on top of the world was the most important thing. As long as I was high, I could continue to make these right decisions; wasn't I smarter and more perceptive than everyone else? Didn't I need to be with someone as unusual and unique as myself, who made me feel this way? Hadn't I always admired the eccentric and different people who were capable of the same kinds of highs I was?

I thought the kids would get used to John in time. They had never liked any of my boyfriends, anyway. They always wanted all my attention for themselves. It wasn't fair that I never had time for men; I knew I would have to make compromises if I were to let a man in my life. Besides, how could John not love my children? How could any human with any perception or intelligence not love them?

Every rationalization in the book went through my mind as I looked at Donne's bloody face and brimming eyes. It took me shamefully long minutes to realize the truth I had been hiding from myself. As screwed up as I was that day, I suppose it's to my credit that I could finally see that truth at all. The horror that finally dawned on me set off overwhelming waves of nausea and dizziness in my body and a blazing feeling of deep shame in my mind. What in God's name had I been doing? Was I so far gone that I had allowed a stranger to turn me against my own children, whom I loved more than life itself?

Donne began to babble like a little child. I don't remember exactly what he said, but then Kassie was hugging me with all her might, "Mom, we love you, just get rid of him, get him out of here before he kills us. We want you back."

I looked around the house; it was no longer my own. I had let a strange man into my home, and I had let him change my life. I had let him hurt my children. I had let him ruin my concentration, my thoughts, my sobriety, and my sanity. All so I could stay high and have sex a few times. My high slipped into a new state: fury. It wasn't much of a transformation at all, just the opposite side of the same coin.

The kids were crying, and then John was shouting. He was telling me that Donne had deserved what he had gotten, that the spoiled brat had hit him in the face with an ice ball. Didn't I know how to control my own children? If we were going to be married, then I would have to start listening to him.

I pushed John downstairs. As he staggered backwards I felt a sense of doom, of the world flying apart with me on the outer edges. I had been sleeping with the boogie man. The normally non-confrontational me disappeared. For once in my life, I made a good decision based on my emotions. I envisioned him falling down the stairs and breaking his neck. He stumbled but managed to grab the railing before he went down.

I could barely breathe, but I managed to choke out the words, "Get out of my house. Get out and don't ever come back." He couldn't believe his ears. He said he couldn't leave because his car was broken, and he didn't have money to fix it or even any money for gas should he even be able to leave. I was at the limits of my emotional endurance, and I began to hallucinate. I saw him twisting Donne's neck, with Kassie watching helplessly. I'd been eating, drinking, and fucking with a psychotic murderer. I had to get the man out of the house. I was afraid it was too late, that the kids and I were already dead.

He said with a calm desperation, "You don't want me to leave, Kris; you know you need me. I'm the best thing that ever happened to you. We're going to get married, and you'll never be unhappy again. You want to fuck me, day and night. You can't get enough of me. You'll never find someone who fits you like I do ever again."

"Get the fuck out of here," I managed to scream out. He must have seen the murder in my eyes.

"If that's what you really, want, I'll go. But you know you'll ask me back."

He grabbed his rocks and his few items of clothing and left the house. His car started after all. When he left, I took the kids, and we went to my fourth story room, where we slept in my big bed. The kids fell into a quick and exhausted sleep, but I stayed awake all night, hypervigilant, with the fear that he would return. I didn't dare close my eyes. I felt like I would never sleep again, even though I was tired, so tired. How could I sleep when there was such evil in the world, and I seemed to be so susceptible to it?

The next morning I found a flannel shirt John had left behind in the kitchen. I sniffed the soft cotton, and the lingering smell of him made me feel more alone than ever before. I was afraid of what he might do to us in retaliation for rejecting him. I locked all the doors and listened continually for the sound of his car outside. Were we safe after all? Had he really gone back to Indiana, where he lived with his mother? I hoped so.

You're Sick!

By chance, I had an appointment with a psychiatrist at the University of Minnesota the next day. The results of my personality test had come back. I was shaking and on the outer edge of awareness. I was so tired suddenly that I could barely stand up. Once I started telling the doctor my story of the last six weeks, I couldn't stop talking. I told her the whole truth, probably the last time I did that with a psychiatrist for a long time. I was still not initiated to the intrusive spirit of psychiatry. After I was finished with the story of six weeks of no sleep, excessive drinking, uncontrolled sex, and even my hallucination that John was going to kill my children, without any hesitation she and the other two doctors who were with her proclaimed me to be in the throes of an intense manic episode. She explained that I needed to be brought down and that I needed to take a medication called lithium. "But that's for manic-depressives," I said with disbelief. "Exactly," she replied.

A whole lot of things clicked together in my brain. I remembered being in a hallway ten years ago, reading a medical book. I was reading about the causes and symptoms of manic-depression. The book said that children of parents who were chronically ill throughout the child's early years often became manic-depressive because of the up and down nature of the parent's care for the child. I remember thinking, "But my mom has been chronically ill for my whole lifetime. Hmmmm." And I remembered the man I had picked up at school after a physics test who said he was on lithium, and how he had tried to convince me that god was the devil and the devil was god.

I was shocked that a doctor could label me so effortlessly, so unthinkingly, and so immediately. I thought of all the movies I had ever seen that featured crazy people and all the books I had enjoyed so much, like *David and Lisa*, *I Never Promised You a Rose Garden*, and *One Flew over the Cuckoo's Nest*. I couldn't picture myself in any of those roles as a mentally ill person. The doctor recommended that I enter the hospital voluntarily, where I would receive immediate treatment. I vociferously objected--I had two kids to take care of at home.

The doctor said that if I would take some medication before I left the building, she'd let me come back for a psychological evaluation at the hospital the next week. She sent me to the lab downstairs for a complete blood workup, to check for drugs in my system. The technicians forced me to wait for the results of the lab tests. I was behind locked doors, so I couldn't have left if I had wanted to. I was clean and even sober, I knew that. What was wrong with me wouldn't show up in my blood.

After the lab results came back clean, I saw another doctor who gave me two cylindrical pink pills, and watched as I swallowed them down. She recommended some books for me to read. I was beyond being stunned. I just wanted to get home to bed.

Somehow I pedaled home the six miles on my bike, and I fell into the house with a deep sense of relief. I had my kids back, wonderfully spoiled and amazingly unharmed. In fact, I would spoil them every day for the rest of their lives. I wanted to erase every second of my experiences of the last six weeks. I needed to regain the mental capacity I had lost in the past weeks. The doctors had told me that I wouldn't see the effects of the drug for a month or more. In any case, I went upstairs to sleep and slept for a long time.

When I woke up, I could finally face the kids again. I was calm. I was not hallucinating. I would do what the doctors recommended: I would take the pink pills, see a therapist of my own, come back to visit a psychiatrist once a week, and find out everything I could get my hands on about manic-depression. Also, I would go to AA meetings and take my children to see therapists, if they needed it after my treatment of them. I would stay in control of myself for the rest of my life.

The next week, I presented myself at the University of Minnesota psychiatric ward. A whole team of doctors examined me for hours. They wanted to know every detail of my life. They tested me to see if I could count backwards from one hundred by sevens. They asked me who were the last five presidents, and what did the statement mean, "A bird in the hand is worth two in the bush?" One of the doctors asked me if the scars on my face were from acne or from a chemical accident. At the end of the day, they seemed satisfied that I was in control of my mind and not about to go out and kill myself or anyone else. They let me go home.

I stopped going to my engineering classes. I couldn't concentrate on any serious subject. I couldn't remember any of the calculus or physics I had been studying for the last five years. I started going to a group on the psych floor. The doctor had to let me in with a key. I went to an AA meeting, and poured out the story of my life. The people there kindly, but politely, told me I was at the wrong place and that I needed to find another group. How many people do you know of who have gotten kicked out of AA?

I saw a team of three psychiatrists once a week and a therapist another day of every week. I went to a DMDA meeting for depressed and manic-depressive people. I took Donne to a therapist once a week and Kassie to a psychiatrist who told us that she was as healthy mentally as anyone he had ever met and that she didn't need to come back. Donne was moodier, but I think he had suffered more from the terrors inflicted on him by my boyfriends and by the absence of his father. The psychiatrist told my daughter that she might as well get used to being the parent in the household, because I would never grow emotionally older than a child.

I was deeply distraught at that prognosis. Although there are many good things about remaining childlike for the rest of your life, including seeing life as a fun adventure and being wildly imaginative, being a parent does not lend itself well to being a child yourself. Kassie was downright belligerent with the doctor, and I was proud of her for standing up to him.

Recovery, Sort of

In a few weeks after I was diagnosed as bipolar I was feeling steadier. I began to look for work. If I wasn't going to finish school, I would have to find a job. It was 1983, and the economy was terrible. There didn't seem to be any technical jobs for which I was qualified. My friend Bob was too poor to hire me as an assistant. I was just a year short of finishing my credits for an engineering degree, and no one wanted to hire someone who was just going to leave a job and go back to school at the first opportunity. In spite of my bad luck at finding a job, I was starting to feel some joy again in life. I had a good time with the kids that summer, and we made plans for them to continue in their gifted program at school, where they were getting a tremendous education at no extra cost to me.

My problems with alcohol were over for the time being, but my behavior had badly damaged my credibility as a parent to my kids. In desperation, I took a job selling expensive solar panels for homes. It was a strange career for a person living in a state that was snowbound six months out of the year and gloomy most of the time. I sold one panel and made only $100. I was happier, but I wasn't yet able to function as an adult in American society. We ran out of money. I owed $10,000 to the University of Minnesota hospitals. At least I was feeling better. The pink pills kept me calm, although I had not come down totally from my manic mood. I was still higher than usual: everything looked brighter and sharper, and I began to see a future for myself again. Doing what, I had no idea.

I had stopped paying rent in order to keep up with my credit card payments and doctor bills. My father had been sending us $440/month for the last year, during which time I was supposed to graduate from engineering school. I sold some of my engineering books and didn't take the practical engineer's exam, because it cost $30 I didn't have.

The sun slowly warmed the frozen earth, and I spent long afternoons lying on a blanket reading Stephen King novels and playing with our kittens. I didn't work very much. Soon my father declared that if I wasn't going to work, then I would have to come and live with him and mother. I kept getting bills from the hospital and the psychiatrists. I decided that the bills must be in error. I had paid one set of bills; the new ones I was getting must be duplicates. I got so confused I gave up paying them entirely.

On my birthday of that year, I was 33 years old, Jesus' age when he died. I had been studying engineering for five years without getting a degree. I was out of money and didn't have a job. The night of my birthday, when I was celebrating with a few girlfriends, my father and brother arrived at the house with a truck. I don't remember asking them to come. Just as we had moved everything from Alton to Minnesota, we would move whatever we could fit in the truck and take ourselves and our few belongings to Menominee, Michigan, where the kids and I would live with my parents again. I had a chance to go back to the refinery to work, but I refused it. It seemed like going backwards, and I had given up that life to go back to school to improve myself. I was much worse off now than when I had started school. I would have to start all over, again.

My high wore off completely, and the world was drab and plain again. I plunged into the depths of The Black Dog, The Beast, The Pit, The Hole, Hell, or whatever you want to call the place where everything is hopeless and you are filled with an endless despair. I told my mother I might as well kill myself. I had failed at school, at marriage, at parenting, at everything I had loved and worked for. I thought the best thing I could do for all of the family was to just end it all. I had taken the cats to the humane society. The kids would be taken care of by my parents. I would make a clean getaway from Minnesota and my failures there. I could kill myself in Michigan, where the kids would be surrounded by woods and water and baby deer and supportive, stable grandparents.

Starting Over, Again

We drove to Michigan and moved our things into my parent's garage. This wasn't the first or even the second time we had moved back in with mother and dad. I felt not like the prodigal daughter returning to open arms but like a little kid coming home after running away for the afternoon.

They were as accepting as they could be, though, and Dad paid all my hospital and credit card bills. At that time, he was doing very well as the manager of a small paper company. He was a big man around town, a large frog in a small pond. He was happy and at the peak of his powers. He had no conception of what had happened to his golden girl. My mother was ill, as usual, and spent most of her time in bed or on the couch in front of the TV sewing. She had pretty much given up socializing, and she hated being so far outside of town.

It was fall and time for school to start. A small rural town was not going to provide the kind of education we were used to back in St. Paul. I might have never left Minnesota had I realized what a shock the new school system was going to be to Kassie and Donne.

We lived sixteen miles out of town on Green Bay, and the kids had to catch a bus to school out on the highway. We were used to life in the North by now, so the freezing rain and gray dreary days were not new to us. Maybe life would not be so bad here. Donne started football and seemed to enjoy it. Kassie joined the basketball team. Both kids hung out with the fringes of their school society, the interesting troublemakers.

Kassie developed a crush on one of Donne's football teammates, but he did not like her back. I shouldn't have been all that surprised when she took a razor blade and scraped a huge hunk of skin off her upper arm, leaving a six-inch scar. She claimed all the kids were doing it that year. I sent her to a therapist but she refused to go after the first time. I had never seen her depressed before. She had seen me acting out all those years in Minnesota. She was unable to express how unhappy she was with the move to a backwards hick town after the sophistication of St. Paul, and I think she felt too guilty to complain. It was the first and last time she ever took her depression out on herself. Later she would take it out on other people.

Over the next year, the kids developed lives they did not share with me. They both got caught throwing firecrackers at trucks out on the highway. The state police came and gave them a lecture, and they were forced to pay for a cracked windshield. Kassie's math teacher said she was the best math student he had ever had, and many of Donne's teachers fell in love with him. Kassie found a boyfriend who lived on the poor side of town and who hung all over her when they were together.

I slept all day, I wrote, I examined the new Macintosh computer dad had bought. It made no sense to me. I couldn't read. I watched endless movies with mom in the

TV room. I paid quality attention to the kids. Finally in the spring I began to feel better, and I tried out for a part in a play presented by the community theater group. I got a singing and dancing part, which pleased me highly. I went to church and I sang in the choir. I used Nautilus equipment, lost weight and got into shape. I went to my dad's company parties with him. I befriended a gay man who lived down the road. I thought I was getting along just fine until one night when the kids were watching TV and I was sitting on the couch uncharacteristically doing some needlework that mom had convinced me would be a good activity for me.

Head-Butting Dad

I've always been close to my dad. He is my kindred spirit. He has always treated me like a boy, like someone who is to be free of typically female jobs like cooking, doing the dishes, and taking care of the kids. I was supposed to be his little engineer. It wasn't surprising that I would rebel from his expectations.

I knew a fight was coming after I had struggled so hard for years to live up to his expectations and failed so miserably. Amazingly, I was not drunk at the time. In fact, I was attending AA meetings and hadn't had a drink in quite a while. Of course, I was taking psychotropic medications, and they made me sleepy and passive, not emotional or angry or distraught. This was the first time I ever crossed my father. It started so innocently.

Menotony, MI

It all started in the whirlpool. I was enjoying a leisurely morning after the kids had gone to school. I had run two miles and done a little weight training. I was headed for the steam room, where I liked to breathe in the damp air for a few minutes before I got into the whirlpool. I was joined by a woman I knew only vaguely. Her name was Joan, and I was introduced to her by my brother Derek. Derek was madly in love with her.

We began our conversation by talking about our psychiatrists. She hinted at problems in her marriage, and I thought, "Oh Derek, if only you could be here right now. I'm talking to your dream woman, and she's naked and telling me what a bastard her husband is." We had a few things in common, at least.

Then Joan mentioned some problems she was having with her pets. It seemed that one of her cats was getting beaten up by her two larger dogs and by her other two cats. I immediately felt sorry for the poor kitty. After all, I had lost all my cats in between moving and freaking out. I wanted to take her poor kitty home with me.

The kids and I had always adored cats. We've owned at least a dozen of them. In Michigan we were forced to be cat-less. I really couldn't face the fact that my parents hated cats with a passion and always would.

When I told Joan I would take her cat home with me, I suppose I knew what I was doing: disturbing the balance of the household. I couldn't live with the repression I had grown up with any more. I decided it was my job to shake my family out of their safe tree dwelling.

I could surely keep a cat upstairs in my room. What would be the harm in that? Besides, there were little brown Mickey-mice in my room, and I needed a good mouser to get rid of them.

I had set up the household for a big blowup as surely as if I had planted a bomb. I really wanted that bomb to go off and break through that shell of phoniness in my family.

I promised Joan I would take the cat out of its misery, and I went home to prepare the family for its new addition. The kids were delighted, of course, but my parents reacted as expected. They refused to allow the cat in the house; that was final. It wasn't my house, and they still made the rules, just like when I was a kid. By treating me like a child, they got a childish reaction.

The evening passed slowly. Dad and I and the kids were watching *The Amazing Mr. Limpole*, with Don Knotts. It was a silly movie, but the kids were enjoying it. Dad got up to get a beer from the kitchen. The kids doodled with a game on the floor as they watched TV. All of a sudden, I started to feel really sorry for myself. I was a grownup adult with rights and needs. Who were my parents to tell me whether or not I could keep a cat if I wanted to?

Then the sobs burst from me in a torrent and I was crying in front of my family, something I had never done in my life, even as a kid. I couldn't let anyone see me this way. I jumped up from the couch to flee to my bedroom, where I could hide my tears in peace. With my head down, I attempted to go through the narrow doorway to the kitchen. Dad's 325-pound, six-foot-one frame was blocking the doorway. He didn't get out of my way fast enough to suit my mood. I wanted to go have a serious crying jag out of the sight of my family. I didn't want him to see that I was upset. But then I was chanting to myself, "No one cares, no one cares, no one thinks of my happiness, no one loves me, I'm all alone."

I butted into my father's big belly with my down-turned head. I could smell the beer on his breath. I wanted him out of my way, and knocking him over seemed to me to be the easiest means to accomplish that. All the while, I was yelling, "Get out of my way, you're in my way."

Dad has a terrible Norwegian stubborn streak to match my own, and the more I rammed against him, the firmer he dug in. When I realized he wasn't going to move, I started to pound on his chest with my fists. "You motherfucker, get out of my fucking way, goddamn son of a bitching whore." I was screaming obscenities at him and pounding as hard as I could on his bulky body. The volume of my shouting turned up a notch, and he grabbed me around the waist. With my head hanging down at his knee level, he dragged me upside down to the dark living room.

I kicked and punched with the great but undirected strength of someone completely out of control. He grabbed my arms with one iron grip and then pinned me to the floor with his knee on my chest. It hurt and I screamed even louder, "You cock-sucking bastard, get off of me, I'm going to kill you, Goddamn it, I hate you." I kept up the yelling while he pressed his knee harder into my chest.

Then I couldn't breathe, though I kept struggling against him with some adrenaline-induced strength. I had no sense that I was crazy. My outburst seemed perfectly normal; I had no idea where it came from but it was real, and it came from a hidden place in me. Consciously, I had never felt anything negative toward my father in my whole life. But god, it felt so good to be angry, to be in a fury, to be so mad I was high again, as high as when I was drinking or running or fucking, and I wanted to keep it going, for as long as I could.

I was so angry I wanted only to destroy something, anything. I wanted to break glass, I wanted to damage electronics parts, and I wanted the stereo to leave the house through the picture window, I wanted to rip my father's guts out and strew them about on the floor. I wanted to watch the life slowly blink out of his eyes. I got into the swing of screaming, flailing, cursing and wailing at a man who weighed a hundred fifty pounds more than I did. His greater bulk prevailed and I was not allowed to break anything, nor did I hurt him seriously, or even at all. I have to admit it; the passionate, angry high I experienced was a feeling drug addicts would kill for.

I don't know how long this would have lasted, but then mom and the kids joined in for the spectacle, good-naturedly, as though they were tuning in to a good TV show. After all, there were no scenes in our household, ever. When mom realized it was no joke, and that I was truly out of control and screaming obscenities, she herded the kids upstairs where they couldn't hear or see what was going on. As I listened to her trying to cover up the situation with banal explanations to the kids, I was filled with shame, a pure, deep horrible shame that I had exposed myself to all these people and that I had let them see the monstrous person living inside me.

Dad held me tightly on the living room floor and waited out the fit. Suddenly I didn't have the energy to move another muscle. My mother came in and told me she loved me. Dad said he knew he'd been a horrible father, and that it was one of the greatest regrets of his life. He would have done better if he had known how. He was sorry he had screwed up all his kids. Then he looked so sad but said he really had to get to the school board meeting. I went upstairs to my cat. The kids hugged me and gave me their sweet, innocent sympathy.

As the days went on I sank further into depression and thought about killing myself for a while every day, as though it were a sacred ritual. I went to see a psychiatrist, and he prescribed some anti-depressants that put me to sleep and didn't work to cheer me up anyway. I got to keep the cat. Winning that battle made life worthwhile, at least temporarily.

Down Then Up

After a few months of sleeping all day while the kids were at school and getting up only for dinner and then going back to bed, I decided it was time to get out of the house. I could kill myself later if I really wanted to. I decided to do some volunteer work at the local rape crisis center. I spent beautiful spring mornings talking to women with even lower self-esteem than I had. Most of them had no idea what they wanted to do in life, other than get away from some violent man.

On one such morning I got a call from my mother that someone had phoned me about a job offer. I had sent out dozens of resumes, to get only a handful of negative replies. I was ecstatic. A real job doing what I thought I wanted to do. I called the company president back immediately. Yes, there was a job for me, a great job; the only catch was the pay, which was only six dollars an hour, less than I thought I was worth, but certainly more than volunteering at a rape center. I accepted the job offer immediately and agreed to start the following Monday. My mood took a sharp swing upward and stayed that way for almost a year. I can do a lot of damage when I'm in a good mood.

A Great Job and a Married Boyfriend

My new job was at a company in Peshtigo, WI called Advanced Engineering Research Company (AERC) that built $4000 aircraft seats for use mostly on private jets. The owners were a trio of engineers who had left a nearby helicopter company to start their own business. Helicopter engineers think in their own unusual way. My job would be to write technical reports for the FAA. The seats had to be able to withstand forces that would turn people into jelly if the plane crashed.

I enjoyed working in a technical atmosphere. I was lucky enough by chance to get a desk near a window, so I was happy. I spent a certain amount of time gazing out to the fields outside the window, just as I had in elementary school. I was still a dreamer. The third month I was at AERC, one of the company owners moved to a workstation directly across the room from me. When I wasn't staring out the window, I stared at Hal.

Hal was a mechanical engineer who spent his days designing the parts used in the seats. He was an old-time draftsman, and he used pen and ink to make his beautiful drawings. As a spatial relations dropout, I admired his skill. One day I was writing about how to install a brake mechanism so it would lock up properly. I couldn't for the life of me understand how the damn thing worked. Hal had invented the mechanism, so I went to him for an explanation. He tried to explain but then gave up after he got his words tangled up, the way lots of engineers do.

"Follow me," he said. We went out into the shop, where he showed me a disassembled brake mechanism. "Now do what I tell you," he said. I knew I was going to make a total fool out of myself. He proceeded to show me exactly how to put the mechanism together and how to adjust it so the seat could move in any direction before the brake mechanism locked it down into the proper position. In that position it could withstand 12 g's of forward force. Once I had put the thing together with my own hands, I finally understood how to write about it.

Before long, Hal and I were spending at least an hour a day talking across our desks to each other. I found that his dry wit meshed well with my nonconforming mind. Before long, Hal and I were talking for hours each day, to the amusement of the other people in the room. Soon I knew all about his troubled marriage, his frigid wife, and his miserable existence. I was a good listener in those days; I was his shoulder to cry on.
Soon I knew more about Hal than I knew about my first husband. I was definitely more attracted to his mind than his body. He was just less than six feet tall with a big, round, reddish face. (I call it the high blood pressure look.) His eyes were a devilish combination of green with concentric rings of yellow and brown, and they were small and squinty. He was barrel-chested and

about 20 pounds too heavy, all of it in the belly. He had short, stubby legs. He would have been a football player in high school. His hair was a combination of brown and gray. He would celebrate his fortieth birthday in a few weeks.

I had begun dating another fellow from work, Andy, a laid-back man with two small children he was raising himself. I had slept with him on the second date, on the floor in my attic bedroom. He was a screamer. He couldn't have an orgasm in peace and quiet: he had to let the whole world know. So I didn't sleep with him at my house; my sex life in the last few years had been shameful and embarrassing enough. He wrote desperately awful poetry that I snobbishly looked down on. He was a dull child compared to Hal.

The company was sponsoring a hayride in July. I planned to go, mainly for the beer bash. The crew loved to drink beer, and they drank it by the keg every Friday night in the shop. After all, this was Wisconsin, practically the birthplace of beer in America. I was feeling good about work by now, and Hal and I were definitely attuned to each other. I teased him about coming to the hayride. He said his wife didn't want to come, and I urged him to come alone. After my experiences with men, I should have been more cautious with a married man.

We got on the wagon at 7:30 on a Friday night. Thirty people or so had showed up. There were only fifty people in the whole company, so that was a good turnout.

The kegs were right on the wagon, so we happily drove around the countryside, drinking beer and laughing. I caught Hal looking at me, then lowering his eyes. He was sitting three people away from me, but I could feel his consciousness in my sphere of awareness. I put my hand on the side of the wagon just inches away from his left arm. By the way he avoided looking at me I knew he was well aware of where my hand was and what I wanted to do with it.

We drank beer and rode around for three hours. When we got back, we decided to go out for pizza. I offered to drive, and about eight people piled into the car. Hal was one of them. We ate pizza and drank more beer. I don't know how many kegs of beer we finished that night but I was feeling brave and grandiose, two dangerous states for me to be in. We lingered at the restaurant as people started to leave. Soon there were only four of us left: me, Hal, Pat, and Pat's wife. I offered to take everyone back to the company, where our cars were parked. We drove back and then Pat and his wife were gone. Hal and I were left together in the dark parking lot.

"Let's take a walk," I suggested. We smoked together and talked like old friends as we walked down a trail behind the building. After I finished my cigarette, I grabbed his hand and said, "Let's run." I pulled him along behind me and laughed. I was living in the moment and enjoying every second. I was wonderfully, happily drunk. I know that when I feel sexy I become much more aggressive and self-confident. Hal made me feel desirable again. We came to a hillock on the path and he tripped. He sprawled forward and fell on his face. Then I was on the ground and we were rolling together down the hill, giggling. Our faces merged in the dark and I found his mouth. He wasn't a bad kisser. I lay back on the ground and felt sticks poking into my back. The bugs were humming around us in swarms.

I said, "Let's go back to the building. At least there are no mosquitoes there." I was itching from dozens of bites already. We followed the path back, and he rummaged through the trunk of his car until he found a flashlight. He unlocked the building door. There were no inside windows or lights, so I couldn't see where we were going. After he closed the door, he switched on the flashlight and we could see a narrow swath of light ahead of us. I grabbed his hand, and he led me to a small office next to the blueprint machine. It reminded me of the organ chamber and the night I was initiated into the coterie of the sexually active by Henri.

We entered a small room, furnished only with an old desk and chair set. I hopped up on the table as he turned on the overhead light. It was an inside office, so no one could see the light from the outside of the building. Hal said, "The cops drive by this building at night all the time to check for burglars. But I do have the right to be here--it's partly my company." He pulled down my shorts and panties, and I sat open-legged in the bright light on top of the desk.

As he wiggled his fingers around in my wet vagina, I realized that I was too drunk to feel much of anything. Once again, I was higher than high, and mostly numb to the experience of sexual stimulus. I wanted to oblige him and return the favor, so I pulled him in front of me on the desk and tugged down his jeans as best I could. I was thinking that the whole trick to sex is to somehow manipulate your body into a satisfying position, all while you are tangled up with someone else's limbs and clothes, trying not to hurt them or put them into a gymnastically impossible pose.

His jeans slipped down his legs and I was into his underwear with my hands, and out popped his lovely penis. "It's not very big, but it does the job," he reassured me. I jumped off the table and knelt in front of him. I sucked and played with him, and then he did the same for me. We were so polite with each other. It was certainly different than making love to Andy, the screamer. Andy had to fuck violently to get off. Hal was gentle, kind, and very good at cunnilingus. I knew this wouldn't be our last time together. We were at the start of a long, complicated relationship in which sex played a large part.

For the next year Hal and I were together all day at work, and every evening we would sneak out and meet. Everyone in the office knew we were having an affair. I didn't tell Andy we were through, but he figured it out himself and started dating another woman in the office. Two months later I found an apartment in town, and the children and I moved into a two bedroom apartment for $135 a month. Things were really cheap in small towns in those days. Hal moved into a small, dismal apartment, but he stayed with me with me almost every night, and we made love every day, at least once, for a year.

Problems

There were problems with our new living arrangements right away. First of all, Donne had to sleep in the living room, which he hated. He had no privacy. Kassie took a violent dislike to Hal, and they sparred with each other regularly. Finally, Hal and I started going to the bar after work most nights and coming home smashed. Our friends at work got used to seeing us together and accepted us as members of the crowd. We all drank too much. It was the Wisconsin way. Kassie hated it when I was drinking. She knew it led to behaviors that were out of control.

Hal was a much worse drunk than I was. In fact, when he started drinking, he couldn't stop until he was unconscious. He would drink twelve beers, then piss on the kitchen floor and start to cry. He missed his kids. He missed his shop. When could he get back to making helicopter models? It was such a shame that this genius couldn't do the work he was meant to do.

And his wife was being a bitch about the divorce. She locked the doors to their house and wouldn't let him in to get anything he had left behind. He had so much equipment that he filled almost half the house with every tool imaginable, some of it comprising big, heavy stuff like lathes and saws. He had every tool needed to make metal or wooden parts to any machine. Hal could fix anything mechanical. He was very handy to have around. But his wife had locked up all the tools and refused to give him access to them until the divorce was final.

My kids were well into their self-centered teen years. We attended Donne's football games and Kassie's basketball games. We drank with our friends from work. I got a raise. The FAA finally certified the company's aircraft seats.

I kept in touch with my parents--we weren't mad at each other anymore, and they finally had their house to themselves again. My mother began to get lonely since they were so far out of town, and she wasn't really a beach person. She began to draw up sketches of her dream house. There were some lots for sale next to the golf course in town, and she wanted to buy one and build a new house on it. My father's brother was an architect, and he helped her draw up the plans formally.

It was the most beautiful house I had ever seen a normal family live in, aside from multi-millionaires. I didn't realize it then, but my mother designed as an integral part of the house an apartment downstairs for me and the kids. She somehow knew I'd never make it for long with Hal.

After a violent dispute between Hal and Kassie one summer night the kids and I moved back into my parents' house. Hal took a job in Philadelphia and moved into a small apartment near The Boeing Helicopter Company. I was laid off from my job at AERC.

For a year I cried and moped and couldn't find a new job. After Hal sent me yellow roses on my birthday I caved in and left my kids and my parent's house and moved into Hal's apartment with him in Philadelphia. I just couldn't stay away from him.

Office Politics

I got the job at Airequip because the engineer who hired me, Teddy Howard, was an archeology buff. I had majored in anthropology a long time ago and didn't follow it much anymore, but we had a lot to talk about such as Lucy, the Leakys, and the bones of contention about how old the human race really is. I told Mr. Howard that I was a natural tech writer because I was a perfect cross between being left- and right-handed. My first grade teacher had forced me to write with my right hand instead of my natural left so I would fit in better with the majority of the human race. This had made me a wonderful ambidextrous person who could think both logically and creatively!

That was a lot of bull to put out there in a one-hour interview, but I strongly suspected I was going to be hired after such a stimulating and charming exchange. I had one more interview with the manager of the engineering office, Mr. Roy Kozlowski, who was impressed that I had actually made it through five years of engineering school, although he seemed somewhat disturbed that I hadn't finished my degree. This man, who was to be my immediate boss and the father of my youngest child, called me that evening to offer me the job as a Technical Writer for Airequip at $25,000 a year. I was thrilled. The company was a sub-contractor of all the major manufacturers of military jets and helicopters worldwide. It produced aircraft engine-failure sensors, among other small electronic and electro-mechanical devices for engine cleaning.

Mr. Kozlowski tested me on my first day with an assignment to draw a graph of something or other. It was very easy. I hadn't studied engineering for nothing. Best of all, I got a lot of attention from the men on that day. It had been a long time since men hovered over me simply because I was a semi-attractive woman. I had all the curves if nothing else.

The only other women in the office were the two secretaries, Norma and Rosy. Norma and I were to share an uneasy truce for most of my time at the company.

I worked at the company happily for two years. By that time it was clear that I needed more engineering classes if I was going to understand in depth the material I was writing about. I looked into attending night classes at Widener University, only a few miles from my house. The engineering department wouldn't transfer all my engineering credits from the University of Minnesota but I was prepared to accept a loss to get my degree, finally. I could see not accepting the D's, of which I had three, but I couldn't see why they wouldn't accept my chemistry and statistics classes. Even if they accepted most of my credits it would still take me two years to finish.

Sexy Babe

Norma lived to attract men. She often said she never let a day go by without eliciting a wolf whistle from at least one man. Norma's clothes were all a variation on one theme: a low-necked short cotton dress cinched at the waist with a wide belt to give her an hourglass shape, and fuck-me heels in various bright colors; red, purple, blue, and green rather the standard black, brown, or beige, as mine were. To me she looked like a little fireplug on stilts, but the men seemed to appreciate her look. She was very '50s, only with the hem above her knees. She flirted shamelessly and made each man feel as though he was her favorite. Many of the men begged her to have affairs with them, my immediate boss in particular.

"Hey, let's go to lunch today," Norma said one morning.

The only reason she wanted to eat with me was so she could brag about her latest conquests.

My weight was hanging in there at about 155 pounds, so I agreed to go. I knew I would have to forgo the fattening stuff I knew Norma was going to order.

At the restaurant she ordered a burger with everything, a large fries, and a strawberry shake.

"You know, Kris, I can eat anything I want and not gain weight. It's these yellow and black pills my doctor gives me. He switches the brands every so often so I don't get addicted."

And how is it that this woman gets to have amphetamines prescribed for her regularly like they were some kind of vitamin? Looking back I can see that Norma was classic ADHD but at the time I had never heard of attention deficit hyperactivity disorder. I figured she just wanted to eat like a pig and never get fat. And then lord it over all of us.

Actually I thought my figure was better than hers. She had little nut-shaped boobs and a sloppy stomach punctuated by a horrendous Caesarian scar. I wasn't jealous of her shape or the attention she got, but I was jealous of the pure joy she got out of life. She loved who she was. She had the confidence of a winner no matter what she tried. I had always banked on my brains, but in this company I was at best average compared to the engineers, who were from all over the world and who mostly possessed a PhD or a Master's degree in engineering.

So I thought maybe I ought to make a little more effort to improve my appearance. Hal never criticized the way I looked, but he was such a nerd himself that he appreciated any female attention. Same with husband number one. So I bought some makeup, new bras, and inexpensive three-inch heels. I wore tight sweaters a few times. One night I went out to a jazz club with a younger man and didn't come home till 1 a.m. I hinted to Norma that it had been a really hot date, which of course it wasn't. The guy was 16 years younger than I was and only slightly interested in me as a sexual object

"So who are you fucking now?" Hal greeted me as I walked in the door.

My so-called date was drinks with a friend after work and a trip to South Street, an area I loved for its hippy shops and jazz clubs. Sure, I could have made out with the youngster but thought better of it, especially after only one date.

Hal's face was purple the way it gets when he's really upset and his blood pressure skyrockets.

"I'm going to read for a while," was all I could come up with.

House by the Tracks

My problems with Hal were getting worse and worse. One of the guys at work was leaving his apartment to move in with a girlfriend. It was a perfect size for one person. I told Norma and a few others at work that I couldn't stand to live with Hal another minute. They all disliked him so we were in agreement. I would go and look at the apartment for rent.

The rent was $375 a month, including utilities. That was cheap enough even for me. I would be free and easy again. I was ready to take the apartment before I even looked at it.

Being hypomanic, or a little more than slightly hyper, is helpful in initiating sexual encounters. Since I had been on a mood stabilizer that actually worked I hadn't had a single inappropriate sexual encounter for a long time, excluding the 22-year-old since nothing happened. I had not been manic for two years, the lithium doing its intended job.

Norma was a rabble-rouser though, and with a little prodding I was always up for some serious play. Norma's amphetamine-fueled behavior was nothing compared to my bipolar mania once I started in on a roll. I think I deliberately pushed myself into a great upswing in mood out of boredom with the status-quo. Norma and I were ready for action.

She led me on to a volley of adventures that happened during the winter of 1988.

My immediate boss was Roy, an electrical engineer with a master's degree. He was tall and slender, with sparse silver-blond hair and a wiry, athletic build that was spoiled somewhat by a silly little paunch that made me laugh. He had high Polish cheekbones and a spade-shaped nose. He was 53-years-old, married, and childless. Perhaps his extreme shyness and quiet high-pitched voice made me see him somehow as a caricature of the classic technical nerd. Physically I found him repulsive, and his quiet voice and lack of affect turned me off even more. He was a good writer for a technical guy, though, and he was so picky about the documents I wrote for him that he often wouldn't sign off on them for months. I found that if I went out to lunch with him and encouraged him to drink several glasses of wine I could sometimes slip a document past him.

Roy took prospective employees out for long lunches--particularly the women. He tried for a long time to find a woman engineer but with no luck. I found out his wife was a dumpy, unhappy, conventional woman who certainly wouldn't have approved of the way he sniffed after women like an unfixed dog. He claimed once in a rare burst of conversational honesty that his wife was going through the change and she had told him to Get It Elsewhere. Why I was privy to that bit of information I don't know, but I'm sure he was drunk at the time.

Roy trailed after Norma like she'd been drenched in pure pheromones. You could even say he was obsessed with her. For some reason she was his perfect woman. He wanted to fuck her so badly he didn't care who noticed his attentions to her. He begged her to go out to dinner with him. He gave her expensive jewelry, candy, flowers, homemade wine. She accepted all his gifts then laughed at him behind his back. She led him on unmercifully, another in her long line of conquests.

A man in heat is not a pretty sight, especially in an engineering office. I found out later that the reason he was so frantic for her was that she had given him a blow job in the back seat of his car one night after work. What the heck she was thinking I have no idea. From that night forward his one goal in life was to get her back in his clutches so he could have her all to himself.

Roy liked me alright but he treated me more like a man. That was fine with me.

My place in the company was on the fringes of the engineering department. I was the Technical Writer and Editor. My job was to work with the engineers and come up with documents for the FAA that showed how the company's engine parts conformed to military specifications. My work would have been pleasant had it not been for Roy's constant criticism and lack of cooperation. He was much more demanding than the feds.

My job involved interviewing the engineers about how the company product, called the quantitative debris monitor (QDM), worked and translating this information into language that could be understood by the assembly workers. I worked with lab testers, assembly-line workers, electrical and mechanical engineers, salesmen, accountants, managers, and secretaries.

In those days we didn't type up our own documents, so we were always sending various stages of drafts to the secretaries, who would type them up and give them back to us for editing and correcting. The documents had to be perfect. Perfection takes a long time and many drafts, depending on Norma's mood and where in the queue your document stood. This was just before the days of PCs and Word, so the documents had to be typed up on a typewriter, and corrections would often require the whole document to be retyped. If Norma liked you, your documents would be placed on top of her inbox. Rosy got the overflow, and if you got her as your typist you were out of luck. She was functionally illiterate and god knows where she had learned to type. You might as well type the document yourself as wait for her to do it. Everyone felt sorry for her because she had been dumped by her husband, who turned out to be gay.

Rosy loped in every morning like a greyhound coming out of the gate. She was always running behind time. Most mornings she was at least a half hour late and usually more like an hour. She didn't drive so she walked to work every day. All the walking kept her in great shape. Her attire comprised skirts up to her ass and tight sweaters mostly in pink that emphasized her huge boobs. When she sat down the men tried not to look like they were peeking up her skirt, but of course they were. She wore tennis shoes for her walk into work but changed into heels even higher than Norma's for the office. She had a size four body with a size 32 DD bust. She wore bright green contact lenses that emphasized huge eyes in a pale, freckled face. She wore her shoulder-length, strawberry-blond hair in a sassy ponytail or piled on top of her head. She looked like a teenager with crow's feet. I know she sounds cute and charming, but a 40-year-old woman trying to act like her 18-year-old daughter is more pathetic than anything.

Rosy tried hard to please everyone but she simply didn't have the educational background to keep up with a bunch of rude, perfectionist technical guys. Her grammar and spelling were horrible. Not only that but she had a disastrous personal problem, very similar to the one suffered by my first husband. She stank. Her smell was not just the odor of a cheap perfume. It was a down-and-out assault on the senses. She carried around with her the eye-stinging odor of unchanged cat litter. You couldn't really stand to be near her for long without coughing, sneezing, or gagging. I tried to breathe through my mouth when she was near but you could almost taste her smell, like someone had just spilled a bottle of ammonia in front of you. She would occasionally develop a crush on one of the young engineers in the office but as far as anyone knew, her only companions were her cats.

Teddy warned her again and again to take more showers and clean her clothes but to no avail. Rosy was what she was, and Teddy, with his soft heart, didn't have the guts to fire her. I tried not to be too critical of her but sometimes it was hard. She'd cry if you criticized her work but she never would improve. Some concepts she didn't get no matter how many times you explained them to her. She was the opposite of Norma, who never made the same mistake twice. Rosy was one of those people you put up with but secretly wanted to throttle.

It's no surprise that engineers in general are difficult to work for. The ones who worked at my company had no idea how to explain the difference between a transistor and a TV to another person who was not an engineer. That's where I came in. I understood engineering concepts and I understood how a normal person thinks. I was great at translating between the two extremes.

I was the one who got to write all the product proposals. We sent out two or three proposals every month. A proposal basically has to be perfect because it is a legal document once everyone signs off on it. We sent proposals out to all the big aerospace companies like Boeing, McDonnell-Douglas, Northrop, Aerospatiale, Sikorsky, Lockheed, Rockwell, Raytheon, Airbus, and any other fighter aircraft or helicopter manufacturer that was trying to horn in on big government military contracts. During the three years I was there, we were turned down only once.

Talk about the $10,000 toilet seat. That's nothing compared to what I saw every day. The QDM, one of many products made by my company, fit easily in my hand. It wasn't particularly complex. Its job was to capture and count the number of metal particles streaming past it in the engine oil and determine whether the number was normal or increasing. Past a certain rate of increase the monitor would send a signal to the pilot that the engine was failing and he should bail.

The device wasn't as simple as it sounds. In the proposal I had to tell exactly how the sensor would work and promise that it would always function as specified. Every part that goes into a military aircraft is required to pass dozens of environmental tests. Before any part was certified for use it had to withstand lab conditions of nuclear explosions, sand and dust, moisture, heat and cold, hurricanes, desert storms, lightning strikes, EMP, and any other natural disaster that might befall an airplane. I could never figure how any of the parts could withstand half the things they were subjected to. It was also my job to explain how to perform the tests as well as to record the results and send the customer the lab reports.

I spent about half my time on proposals. If a test report was late, the company could be fined up to $100,000 a day. The testing alone on any single part, which had to be paid for by the client, could be hundreds of thousands of dollars. I also had to set the prices for the tests, which involved bargaining with a lot of the test facilities. Obviously we couldn't reproduce lightning strikes, nuclear explosions, or hurricanes in our lab. At times I could get really stressed out, particularly when a deadline was approaching.

My job seemed to be important to the company, so I felt useful and valued. The things I wrote about were mostly interesting to me. While technical writing is about as dry as a Bond martini, I liked my job well enough. Besides, it was about the only technical job I could get without an engineering degree. No boss of mine ever seemed to value the five years I spent studying mechanical engineering. I might as well have taken home economics or farming. Still, in 1986 you didn't run into very many female engineers. The ones you did were harassed by the men and not given much credibility.

I was pretty happy until Roy pulled a fast one on me. He hired an engineer to oversee my work and sign off on it. I was furious. So not only could I not sign my own documents, but also if I did a good job, this other yahoo would get all the credit. First of all, he was an industrial engineer, which everyone knows is not as good as a mechanical or electrical one. Second, the man talked constantly, from when he came in at 8:30 until he left at 5. I couldn't figure out when exactly he did the important work of checking out my documents. That was it; that was his only job. What a slap in the face it was to me. After he had been working for a few months I could see that he was really not too bright. I couldn't see that he added a thing to my documents that would make Roy sign off on them any quicker. At my performance appraisal Roy told me I would have to go back and finish my engineering degree if I wanted to keep my job.

By the time I had been with the company for two and a half years I came to work every day seething, loathing the men who controlled me, and feeling an unusual lack of confidence. I was so happy I had broken up with Hal. He was just another control freak making my life miserable.

I had paid off all my engineering school loans. I was easily able to afford my little apartment. I bought flowery blue and orange rattan furniture, and the landlord replaced the old carpet with a toffee-colored shag rug that made me feel at home.

There were a few problems with the place. It had no heat controller, so most of the time the temperature hovered between 50 and 65 degrees, a little chilly for me even with my Norwegian genes. Also, the kitchen was the size of a small closet, with a half-sized oven and refrigerator. I could barely turn around. The walls were a greasy green, as though no one had ever bothered to wipe them down. It was a drab and depressing place to cook, so I didn't bother to do it much.

I figured an inadequate kitchen was a small price to pay for my freedom. I didn't give Hal my new address. Norma and I went to Weight Watchers and vowed to lose 20 pounds. I started to walk to work three or four days a week, which was six miles a day. I lost weight quickly and replenished my wardrobe in a smaller size. Still, I didn't buy anything tight or revealing.

One Friday afternoon I was working on an important proposal. The company had been working for months trying to perfect the QDM so it would pass FAA requirements for use on the V-22 Osprey made jointly by Boeing Rotorcraft Systems and Bell Helicopter in Texas. The engineers were having problems passing one of the electrical tests. I knew I was going to have to lie in the formal documents. The part just didn't pass the test. Not even close. I was finishing up final details and figuring out how to word the test requirements so that it didn't sound like we were lying to our contractors. Roy knew all about this and was being very helpful in trying to get the wording just so. I was under a lot of pressure: Fed Ex came at 4 p.m. The final draft would have to be done at least an hour before that so Roy and Teddy could read it over one last time and sign it. It was a typical last-minute effort.

I was depending on Norma to type up the final changes. In those days, as I mentioned before, there was no word processing. Everyone was still arguing over whether to use the Mac or a PC. Word didn't exist yet, and WordPerfect was just starting to be used widely. No one at our company knew how to use it. All document changes had to be made on the document itself. At the least it meant fiddling with whiteout. Also, for every change the boss had to reread the document to make sure the corrections were actually correct. My adrenaline was flowing freely that day, and I was as cranky as an old Model T.

By noon I was finished with my changes, and I took the document to Norma's desk. I figured she could easily have the corrections done by 2:00 p.m., which would give the bosses plenty of time to sign off by 3:00 p.m.

Norma wasn't at her desk. I figured she'd be back from lunch at minute now.

"Hey Rosy, you know where Norma is?" I asked.

She looked at me blankly and then said, "Oh yeh, she went out to lunch with Charlie. She left about half an hour ago."

God, why did she have to pick today to work her magic on another poor unsuspecting, horny engineer?

I ate lunch though I wasn't hungry and read the proposal over for the hundredth time. I tapped my fingers, went to the bathroom three times, and talked to my neighbor Ed the Greek. Still Norma did not appear. I watched the hands of the big wall clock move from 12:45 to 1:00 to 1:30. My blood pressure rose about 30 points. I sweated. I picked at a zit on my face.

She could have given him three blow jobs by now, I thought.

She waltzed in at 1:50 and boisterously plopped herself into her chair.

She glowed, like a woman who has just been laid gloriously.

"He's fantastic," she mouthed across the room to me.

I was so angry with her that I didn't even ask her for all the salacious details I knew she eventually would tell me.

"I've got to have that proposal done by 3:00," I accused her, trying to sound tough and like her boss, which in a way I was.

"Oh, that," she said airily. That'll just take a few minutes. She laughed and said, "What, are you worried?" like it was some preposterous thing.

I stood by her desk and waited for her to make the changes. She made a typing mistake and had to white it out, no doubt because I was standing over her shoulder. Then she had to wait for the white-out to dry. She typed the correction, and it smeared a little. "I don't care," I said. "Just give me the damn thing."

It was as done as it was going to be.

Roy read it over and found another typo. By 4:00 I was out of energy. I didn't care if the proposal went out with Fuck You typed on the front page. But there it was, signed by me and all my bosses, on its way to the Bell Helicopter Company.

I admired Norma's ability to juggle her professional and personal interests. When I fall for someone I get involved and wrapped up and can't think of anything else. I couldn't stay mad at her for long; she was extremely good at her job, and she was so good-natured, as long as she wasn't talking about men. She didn't see why anyone would care if she had a long lunch with one of her bosses.

"Where were you?" Teddy asked, pretending to be mad. She didn't tell Teddy that she had been at lunch with Charlie; she told him she had been at a dentist appointment. "Uh oh," I thought. This relationship must be more serious than a normal flirtation for her to lie about it.

That lunch was the first of many "appointments" over the next few months. Norma's relationship with Charlie soon progressed. They fucked on his desk and on the floor of his office: after hours, before hours, during hours, in the park, in his car, and in Baltimore for a smuggled weekend. He promised to buy her a new house. He bought clothes and underwear for her. He pledged undying love.

But of course, as we wiser women know, his love was not for Norma exclusively. She did not understand that at first. When word got back to her that Charlie had divorced his wife and moved in with Sugar, the manager of the accounting department, Norma was so surprised that she forgot to be mad, at least for a few seconds.

"I'll gouge her eyes out," she muttered. "I'll get him back." The next week she took up with a man she met at the bowling alley.

Roy never gave up trying to get Norma into a hotel room. He was downright weird about her. She had gotten into his blood, like a virus hanging out in his nerve endings, waiting to be activated by infection or low immunity. I think he figured that all he had to do was be persistent and she would eventually give in. After all, she had given in once before. Obsession is not uncommon among perfectionists.

In spite of all the attention Norma was getting, I couldn't see that she ever actually benefited from it in the long run, outside of a few bangles. She got good reviews about her work, but she never got promoted nor did she ever earn significantly more money than she deserved.

I had slept my way to the top in the small hick town I came from but I didn't think that would help me in the big city. The world of aircraft engineers represents a group of the most repressed and emotionally backward men anywhere. It never occurred to me to wear sexier clothing or act dumb on purpose. I have big boobs and was used to men speaking to me with their eyes fixed on my chest. When I worked in the factory, even dressed in my work uniform, the men around me acted as though I was the first woman they had ever seen. The engineers were a little sneakier but the idea was the same.

I was into my third year at the company, and I loved my newfound freedom. However, the office was becoming unbearable. I was a bit hypomanic, which means I wasn't totally out of control but that mania wasn't far off. I craved the excitement and adventure that were not to be found in our small part of the world. There were no new affairs to gossip about. Norma was tired of getting the same flowers and jewelry every holiday and birthday from the same old men, and she had settled in with a new guy. We were still in Weight Watchers, although now I laugh that I wanted to lose weight at 155 pounds.

Roy and I had been getting along pretty well in early 1988. When I could get him to talk about something besides work he showed something of a sense of humor. He was obviously one of the smarter men in a room full of smart men. When you could hear him he demonstrated verbal as well as engineering skills. Sometimes he even made me laugh. I hated his picky precision but I could see that it served him well in technical pursuits.

One day he appeared directly in front of my desk and hovered there while I worked, pretending to ignore him. When I finally looked up at him I could see him peering down at me through his silly granny glasses. He had a strange expression on his face; kind of a smug, decisive look, as though he had made his mind up about something and wasn't about to tolerate my usual sarcastic remarks. This behavior scared me a bit--it just wasn't like him. I figured I had learned to handle him pretty well in the last few years. This was a new look. I wondered what I had screwed up this time.

Without a word he tossed an envelope on my desk.

"See Norma about the details," he said casually and then headed back to his office.

I opened up the envelope and was stunned to find a round-trip airplane ticket to Dallas/Fort Worth, Texas. What the hell?

I bustled back to his office, entered, and quietly closed the door. There were no windows in the office, and the walls were quite substantial, so I felt I could be honest with him.

"What do you want?" I asked. I was a bit confrontational. I always got the feeling from Roy that he considered me second-rate in most ways--technically, physically, and emotionally.

"You're going to Bell Helicopter. We need you to write up the FAA documents for the V-22 when we're down there so they can sign off on the part when it's installed on the aircraft engine."

Roy had never indicated that I was worth much of anything to the department other than acting as a glorified secretary, and not even a sexy one.

Of course what he needed me for was exactly that--a glorified secretary. But I'd have to work quickly and accurately, and I'd have to understand exactly what was going on.

All in all, I was pleased, flattered, excited. I couldn't wait to tell Norma.

"You're going on a business trip with three men? Right," she said, with the kind of nasty leer on her face that only an oversexed woman can give to another woman.

Business Trip

"Right," I said. Business trips brought to my mind meetings with bigwigs, seafood and steak at fancy restaurants, margaritas, an early breakfast and well laid-out plans for the day, a soft bed and cable movies after dinner. I would wear a nice pants suit and a pair of flats to work so as to be comfortable in the lab setting but not too casual. I would have to find an IBM typewriter to type up the test results in the evenings after the workday was over.

I planned for everything except for what I really needed.

January 1988 was so warm that I was walking to work nearly every day. I had lost my weight watcher's goal of 20 pounds, so I weighed only five pounds more than in high school. I hadn't given Hal my new address, and I wouldn't answer his calls. All my student loans and charge cards were completely paid off. My medications were working. I lived in a cozy little tree house apartment and loved listening to the trains going by at night. I had never been so happy and free. I thought about joining a dating club.

I had found blessed solitude, at last. I hadn't realized how much I'd been wanting and needing it. Around other people I always gave in. The luxury of thinking without interruption or compromise during my free time set off a pure joy in my spirit that had been missing for a long time. I had no desire to leave the apartment after work, even to go to the grocery. I listened to the sound of the wind roaring through the tall trees outside my windows. I read science fiction and started my memoirs and even ironed my clothes. I was content, and contentment was enough.

This sated mood lasted for less time than it took me to have my address changed at the post office.

First of all, Hal found my apartment after walking around nearby neighborhoods looking for my car. He came to see me every evening, so my alone time was suddenly gone. I wrote less. I watched TV more. I cooked more. We watched dirty movies.

The day of my flight I gave Hal a blow job before he took me to the airport. I guess it was my way of thanking him for the ride and at the same time getting rid of him without a whole lot of conversation or involvement. I felt the way I had when mother and Karl dropped me off at college in the fall of 1967--relieved, energetic, looking very much forward to the brave new world of the Business Trip.

I had no idea just how brave I was going to have to be to face the future I was about to create for myself.

Hard at Work

I got to the airport nearly an hour early. For the trip I bought a Tor horror novel called *The Scream* by John Skipp and Craig Spector about a demon rock 'n roll band. It fit my mood, and after I was into it a few pages the rest of the world faded away. When I looked up forty-five minutes later I saw that two of the three other members of the Aerequip entourage had arrived. The men looked a lot more relaxed and human wearing jeans instead of their customary poorly-fitting brown suits. I told you earlier I was the only woman in the group. Eat your heart out, Norma.

I wondered where Roy was but while I was wishing that he would miss the flight he jogged up to the gate, slightly winded, and took off his sunglasses to see if we were all present. He was wearing a long, buttery-soft leather coat that must have cost him more than I made in a month and a pair of tight jeans. The sunglasses and the coat should have been enough to make him feel cool and sexy but the tight jeans with his little paunch hanging out in front like a kangaroo's pocket with a baby in it was plain ridiculous. Still, I had to admit this outfit was better than his normal brown polyester. I hoped to god he wouldn't be sitting next to me.

But of course he was. He had brought his briefcase so he could work on documents during the flight. I thanked the lords of fragrance that he was wearing

English Leather, one of my all-time favorites. That's the cologne my siblings and I bought for my father every year at Christmas. He smelled great. I breathed in his odor surreptitiously while avoiding his gaze.

He was broad and tall enough that he didn't fit well into the aircraft seat, so of course he spilled over into my personal space. He knees splayed outward and brushed my leg. I turned away from him and read my book, pretending to ignore his elbows poking into my side. I concentrated so hard on ignoring him and trying to read my silly book that we had arrived at the Dallas/Fort Worth International Airport before I knew it.

We disembarked and wandered around until we found the Hertz desk. Ron wanted a Lincoln but they were all out. He frowned and waved his hands around but the young man behind the counter assured him that there were other good cars besides Lincolns. We got stuck with some sort of generic Ford sedan. Who cares what kind of car you get when you're only going to drive it for a few days anyway? I certainly had no plans to drive in a strange city. Ron was his usual extremely annoying self. He climbed in behind the wheel and asked Terry, a stooped ex-basketball player, to navigate since no one knew where we were going. Good, I could continue to amuse myself with *The Scream*. We loaded our luggage and got into the non-snazzy car.

Between the airport and the car I had been shocked to feel little balls of ice bouncing off my uncovered arms. Sleet? It couldn't be sleet. I thought Texas was supposed to be warm and humid. I hadn't even thought to bring a long-sleeved shirt, much less a coat. I felt cheated. Philadelphia had been cold and rainy when we left and here, thousands of miles south of there, I was being subjected to the same miserable winter weather.

Roy screeched out of the parking lot. Freezing rain or not he streaked out onto the nearest Dallas/Fort Worth freeway, accelerating to 70 mph in the first minute.

"God, can't you slow DOWN?" I yelled.

I was too busy hanging onto the seat and hiding my eyes to read my book.

Tom directed Roy to an exit that supposedly would take us to the hotel we had booked for the next three days. The back wheels of the car slid back and forth, and we finally veered onto the ramp. We drove for a good half hour before someone noticed we were going the wrong way.

I was cold, I was pissed, and I wanted to get out of the car, which by now felt to me like it was skating all over the icy freeway.

"Where did you learn to drive, anyway?"

"Hey, I used to drive race cars. Not to worry."

I spent an hour-and-a-half biting my nails and praying for a peaceful end in between cursing Ron for his macho driving. We would be staying at one of the new Marriott Inns that featured rooms with suites. We walked into a warm, humid atmosphere filled with the scents of tropical flowers. The central area of the first floor was a lush garden complete with palm trees that grew all the way up to the fourth story balcony. I saw orchids, hibiscus, lilies, and hundreds of other blooming flowers I couldn't identify. Gushing fountains created a soothing background noise. The tables stationed throughout the first floor would be great for evening drinks and early morning breakfast buffet. I kept saying "wow!"

We checked in, got our keys, and the other three men, indifferent to the surroundings, went straight to their rooms. I wanted to look around before changing for dinner. I asked at the front desk for an ironing board and a typewriter, which were both available. At least I would be able to get my work done, assuming I could figure out how to use an IBM Selectric, a novelty to me. I still used an old Olivetti I had gotten for a Christmas present many years earlier (even then I had dreams of becoming a writer).

I loved my "suite." There was a living room with work table, couch, and several chairs, all upholstered in light blue and beige. The small kitchen was replete with refrigerator, microwave, and breakfast nook. In the bedroom there were two queen-sized beds and the usual TV, radio, and alarm clock. The place was actually about the same size as my apartment. It was a bargain at $120 a night (which sounded profligate to me at the time).

I changed into a beige pants suit and met the men for dinner. Ron wanted to go to a restaurant he had discovered on a previous trip. After putting up with his driving again, I was ready for a Margarita by the time we arrived at a place called the San Francisco Steak House. Strange name for a steakhouse in Fort Worth, I thought.

I was even more surprised when the evening's entertainment began a few minutes after we were seated at our table. Roy looked up and folded his arms across his chest. As I followed his gaze, I saw a woman climb out from a little platform onto a swing attached to the ceiling. What, were we going to see a trapeze act?

She took off in an arc across the room and began to pump higher and higher, the way kids do on a backyard swing set. She was dressed in a skimpy red velvet dress like a saloon girl in an old western movie, only with a very short skirt. Every time she swung toward us we got a very good view of what she was wearing underneath it, which wasn't much of anything.

As the men watched entranced I finally got the point. I suppose I could have gotten up and walked out but instead I just drank a lot, three Margaritas to be exact, and that was before dinner. I tried not to think about the woman's crotch hanging out over my meal as I ate. I'm sure the steak was delicious, but by then my taste buds were pretty well numbed by salt, lime juice, and tequila.

We skipped desert and ordered more Margaritas at the bar. The pornographic meal no longer bothered me. The men wanted to continue drinking, but I protested that I had absolutely reached my limit.

Roy said, "It must be time to switch to wine."

He ordered a bottle of nice Cabernet and I managed to down two glasses. The other men were looking a little wrung out by now, but Ron and I were laughing hysterically at anything and everything.

"I'm going to turn in," said Tom. "Me too," said Kevin, and they more or less wove their way unsteadily to the elevator. I noticed that their rooms were on a different floor from mine. That should have sent out a warning, but when Roy suggested we take a bottle to his room I rolled with the punches and followed him. His room was on my floor.

For some reason I felt like I had to not only keep up with him on the drinking but also outdo him, like Karen Allen in the first scene of *Raiders of the Lost Ark*. I followed him into his room (his bedroom, idiot) gamely, somehow knowing what was to come but wanting to somehow better Norma in the game of who got to go on the business trip with three men. Why not have one more drink with the boss? What possible harm could come from it?

I was obviously drunk off my butt and in no shape to be making important decisions (like whether to follow my boss into his bedroom). I walked through the doorway after him and turned to shut the door. When I turned back towards him he had already peeled out of his shirt. By the time I had taken two steps into the room, he had more or less ripped my shirt off. He undid my bra without a fumble.

"You must have some experience with bra unhooking," I exclaimed breathlessly. "You're the first man I've ever met who knew how to do what you just did."

"I practically invented the bra," he said.

I was horrified to find that my heart was pounding and I was as excited as a teenage girl experiencing her first make-out session. I could only recall one time when I had been ravished. That was with Sammy Black back in Chicago in 1970. I knew by now that a manic expectation of sex is usually much better than actually doing it.

"I have special skills," he crooned in my ear. I didn't have the willpower to resist.

Hastily we tore off the rest of our clothes. I heard a button pop as my pants slid to the floor. Damn, I'd have to fix that before tomorrow. Then we fell onto the bed.

I wondered how I could possibly have let myself get so desperate that I would have sex with someone I had never in my wildest dreams considered as a candidate for my affections. I had been separated from Hal for less than a month, and masturbation kept the edge off. So I thought.

Roy was a much better kisser than I would have predicted. He wasn't a cold fish at all. He was warm and gentle and passionate without being sloppy.

So this is what tension in the workplace leads to. At work I felt like I was dealing with a stubborn three-year-old. Now I couldn't keep my hands off a man I didn't even think I liked. So much for logic and more to the point, so much for lithium.

I suddenly felt a little less guilty about sleeping with my bosses. It didn't seem like such a sin. This was my second affair with a married man, and even though the first one turned out to be a disaster that didn't mean this one would. There were definitely advantages to having causal and meaningless sex. I was so turned on that my teeth were tingling. I wanted Roy to penetrate me and drive his penis all the way through my body and up into my throat. I wanted him to fuck me for all he was worth and leave me spent, like a raggedy doll.

Even after all the alcohol I had absorbed, my senses were sharp and clear. Normally I would be totally numb by this time but Roy was doing a world-class job on me. I could see that up to this point my lovers except for Henri had all pretty much been amateurs. I had never been taken by such a master at awakening my senses. Or perhaps I was speeding forward into a really manic break.

"No ties," he said. "Nothing comes from this except our pleasure." I agreed and encouraged him to get on with it.

I briefly noted in my impaired mind that it was approximately the middle of my menstrual cycle but after all, Hal and I had been screwing happily for years without using birth control. Obviously I was no longer fertile. I didn't give birth control another thought.

Roy gently put my glasses on the table next to the bed (what happened to my contacts, I wondered) and the room appeared before me as a blurry underwater playground. He began to lick me on the belly and as he moved lower I worried that I would come too soon. Isn't that what the man is supposed to worry about?

"Let's go slow," he said. "What do you think of my body?" He stood up at the foot of the bed and turned so I could see front and back. He was surprisingly slender for a man of his age. I said, "Wow, you have the body of a 25-year-old." Which was a slight exaggeration but I was drunk, and I naturally try to say what people want to hear, so I didn't see that telling him a little white lie would hurt anything. I didn't want to spoil his pleasure by adding, "except for your Poo-Bear belly."

Roy had a strangely effective love-making style. He was hung like a horse, as we women say with smacked lips, though I can't recall ever seeing a horse's dick to know whether or not it is really large. I knew that if he had plunged in right away at full staff, I would have gotten sore pretty darn fast. But since he was as drunk as I was, he wasn't exactly rock hard. I figured he wasn't all that turned on by me but it turned out to be the fault of all the booze we had imbibed. He was inflated half or three quarters of the way for most of the night. We made love for hours. I came a couple of times, though I was as drunk as he was. For once I was not numb during impulsive, manic sex. I'm not sure what the difference was, except that he was a master of foreplay.

We got tired finally shortly before dawn. He gave it one last big effort and then came with a wonderful warm whoosh, part of which slid satisfyingly down the crack of my ass. The rest of course stayed in me, doing the job it was designed for.

I was smiling like Scarlett O'Hara the night after Rhett finally satisfied her in bed, but I didn't hum. I had no idea why this particular sexual congress had worked so well for me. It was as though I finally found someone who fit me in all the right ways. No insult to my previous lovers but this was really the way sex was supposed to be. I had briefly felt this way with John, the arrowhead maker, but he used sex to manipulate me and turned everything sour. I wasn't about to let that happen with Roy; at the worst it would be me who did the manipulating. What I wanted from him was a mystery hidden deep in my unconscious. I knew I was not done with him. Not just yet.

I fell asleep wrapped happily around his body.

When we woke a few hours later I knew I was in for a most trying day. I put my clothes on, breathed a quick goodbye, and sneaked out the door. What if one of the other guys spotted me? I rushed to my room, finally feeling the guilt that had been so absent the night before. What in god's name had I gotten myself into? I wouldn't have been human if I hadn't felt somewhat ashamed of my behavior, even though I had totally enjoyed myself. Mostly what I felt though was sore; so sore I couldn't walk with my legs together. And on top of the soreness I felt again that infinite desire to be filled up from snatch to brain that is called, in common terms, having your brains fucked out. I felt that my sexual needs had become unquenchable. Was my biological clock ticking? Maybe. Was it unbridled lust? Probably. More likely it was manic over-sexuality, but without my normal numbness.

Mania galloped up to me like a playful pony inviting me to jump on and let him take me for a gentle trot. His call was deceptive and Faustian, and I knew this beast was not a friendly pet but my childhood giraffe man, who had plagued me with his mysterious demands when I was a little girl. I didn't know where he would take me but wherever it was it would be exciting and intense and a challenge to my heightened senses. I hopped on running, and the beast took off with a breath-taking, rump-slapped gallop. I breathed in deeply and held on for dear life.

The Morning After

I was too sick for a good breakfast but I forced down a few bites of scrambled eggs and toast. The hotel coffee tasted like warm bathwater, so I drank a half glass of grapefruit juice instead. My stomach was filled with a mix of so many sour and bitter liquids that I doubted whether I could make it through the day without a violent eruption from some orifice.

I had taken a shower when I got back to my room, but I couldn't face hairdressing or contact lenses. I looked like myself in eighth grade, before I had gotten cool. I figured that looking like a geek might serve me well as the only woman in the test facilities at Bell Helicopter. You never knew. If you looked good the men would figure you for an airhead. If you looked bad they said you were unfeminine. You couldn't win. I wore jeans and my favorite vest over a short-sleeved shirt that day. My loose and baggy clothes were the farthest thing you could get from sexy and alluring. I looked like the tomboy I was underneath it all.

The four of us from Airequip gathered in the lobby at 8:00 a.m. Ron led the way out to the car, and I followed. Just as I was walking through the door, the wind caught it and slammed it in my face. I pushed through it to the sidewalk and within seconds I was so cold I felt like the lonely little matchbook-girl that froze to death on Christmas night. I might as well have worn a bikini for how well my thin vest kept me warm. I wanted to be folded into Ron's big wide warm embrace, and I was horrified at myself for wanting it. How could I look at him all day and not think of his half-hard prick and how it felt stuffed up into me?

Business went surprisingly well that day. My biggest problem was finding a woman's bathroom. There wasn't one in the testing lab. I had to walk down endless halls to the reception area to find one. What the hell, next time I would use the men's.

Roy performed test after test with the Airequip sensor mounted on the V-22 engine. When the engine was turned on, I could feel every molecule of my body vibrating. The big earmuffs I wore softened the noise but made me feel detached as if I was in a cold gray world where big machines ran noisily all day long but didn't ever go anywhere.

I recorded data in my small notebook and tried to look like I belonged there and not like a high school cheerleader urging her team on and definitely not like I had just screwed the hell out of my boss a few hours before.

I have no idea what Roy was doing all day long, but whatever it was I hoped the part would work properly, as a culmination of the months I had spent stressing over each word in the contract. By the end of the day he finally got test readings that satisfied the Bell engineers. That was the problem with my technical knowledge--when something finally functioned as it was supposed to I saw it as magic rather than good engineering.

I scribbled a first draft stating that the sensor satisfied all FAA requirements, and I typed it up in a nearby office. Roy and the Bell witnesses signed the document, and we were out of there by about 7:00 p.m.

We went out for ribs. You have to eat ribs when you are in Texas. The restaurant was in a charming area next to a stockyard where horses and bulls that had performed in rodeos once pranced and pawed and bucked in rodeos that were no longer. The stalls and fields were all empty, gone with the barren oil wells. It seemed that every other house we passed on the road was boarded up. I wondered what manufactured products were keeping the Texas economy afloat, if any.

I drank ginger ale before dinner and found that I was starving. When I get truly manic I don't need sleep and I either eat nothing at all or everything in sight. That night I ate a rack of ribs about two feet long, fries, and a huge salad. I was glad to see that there were no ladies on swings over our heads. After dinner no one suggested drinks at the bar, and when we got back to the hotel we all departed to our own rooms.

I sat on the bed in my room and wondered. What was the protocol for illicit liaisons during business trips? Did he come to my room? Did I go to his? Were we just going to skip it for tonight? Perhaps I should see what was on cable.

The phone rang, and I snatched it up as though it was going to disappear if I didn't answer it right away. I was stone cold sober. Could I face Roy without a belly full of alcohol? With my teeth I pulled a hangnail from my bird finger while I listened to his polite invitation. I would be going to his room.

That night he managed a pretty standard hard-on, and I enjoyed sex with him for most of the night again. He fell asleep at around 4 a.m. I wasn't sleepy at all, of course. I dressed, quietly opened the door, and went back to my room. I needed some down time to gather my senses. I felt like I had jumped off a cliff and was falling, without an end in sight.

Sex at the Thunderbird

The four of us spent the first half of the second day of our trip in meetings with Bell executives. I daydreamed, jotted notes, and thought about sex. At lunchtime Roy dismissed the other two engineers, and they left to get on a plane back to Philly. His excuse for having me stay was that I needed to type up the notes from the morning meetings. I typed all afternoon, trying to get the swing of the Selectric and making a lot of errors. It had built-in correcting tape but that was not very useful for me, as I tended to make errors whole sentences long, or I later decided to move whole paragraphs. I was an amateur typist in spite of all my years of practice. Desktop publishing saved me later, but that didn't happen in my field for another year or so.

The last night of the trip I think was meant to be romantic dinner. I ate calamari and lobster, both for the first time. The calamari took a little getting used to but I plunged into it like a new adventure. I was grossed out by the green part of the lobster, but when I found the good part and drenched it in butter I decided that it was probably the best thing I had ever eaten. We had a huge salad with gobs of blue cheese dressing after the main course, European style. In addition to three pieces of homemade sourdough bread spread with butter, we completed the meal with mud pie for dessert. I weighed at the most 140 pounds, which is pretty good for a large-boned, 5'7", 38-year-old woman. I'd gain a hundred pounds in one day if I ate like that now (and later on, I came close to doing just that).

After dinner we talked by candlelight as we finished a bottle of nice chardonnay (white with seafood).

I learned about Roy's early membership in a sex club while he was in college. No dorms for the football players, but furnished apartments. He didn't talk about his marriage but he assured me he had a woman in every port. I guess he counted me as the home-port woman, since so far Norma had largely rebuffed his approaches.

Over coffee we discussed other important events of our lives. I told him about the threesome that ended my first marriage. I guess he assumed I had the same open-minded approach to sex that he had. What he didn't realize and probably what even I didn't was that having sex while manic is reckless and impulsive, not just an open-minded activity for mature, consenting adults. He assumed I had birth control taken care of, and I assumed that I mysteriously could not get pregnant. I was like a teenager who believed herself invulnerable.

We checked out of the Marriot and went to a cheaper motel that night called the Thunderbird Inn. There were Indian rugs on the walls and rugs and pots decorated with earth-toned geometric designs on the floors. It was still cold and rainy and I was out of clean clothes. All I wanted to do that night was to fall into bed and hide under the covers. Roy joined me and we made love briefly and sweetly for the last time. All my inner knots unwound, and I felt at peace. My biological clock stopped ticking and a different kind started up.

A month later I noticed that my breasts had become extremely sensitive to the touch. I broke out in unusual rashes on my hands and body. I had a very light period; only a smear, unlike my usual crimson tide. I gained a few pounds. I continued to take my lithium, figuring that the mania I experienced on the trip would level out if I continued. I went back to Weight Watchers and continued to walk to work several times a week.

Another month went by, and I began to feel a pervasive dread, as though there was a large animal in my psyche waiting to ambush me. I ripped off hangnails on most of my fingers. I bought jewelry and makeup out of catalogs.

I refused to think about what all these little signs might mean.

Four more weeks went by, and my period didn't show any signs of appearing.

Roy stopped by my desk one day and very quietly asked, "You don't have any diseases or anything do you? Because my dick is so sore it feels like it's going to fall off and the skin is red and raw." That didn't sound good, but it didn't really surprise me. I've had recurring problems with yeast infections ever since I started having sex. Usually a run of Monostat would take care of it for me. I assured Roy that it was probably a yeast problem and he should get treated for it.

As he turned around to head back to his desk I said nonchalantly, "Oh, I have to get some Midol after work. I get really severe cramps." I was being manipulative, I knew that, but I wanted to assure him that I was cool with what had happened.

He told me later in the week that his doctor had diagnosed him with ketosis, which was not surprising because he had been on a low carbohydrate diet in an attempt to lose his little belly. He said the ketosis made his body so acidic that everything peeled. I was relieved that his condition wasn't my fault, but I was also grateful that he hadn't accused me of anything. His attitude also conveyed a distance from me. Well, that was fine. I didn't foresee any business trips in the future.

Anyhow, I had a good excuse to make an appointment with the gynecologist, since I did feel some itching and burning in the vulvar area, and I also felt bladder pressure like when you have a UTI. I couldn't get an appointment for three more weeks. The doctor I saw was a kind and caring guy, and by the way, movie-star handsome. He had big blue eyes that looked right into your soul, the way you wanted your husband to look at you.

Test Results

After the doctor told me the pregnancy test results were positive I jumped up from my chair and whipped the magazine I was holding across the room. The chair tipped over and knocked against the end table. The lamp on the table fell to the ground, and the bulb shattered into a thousand pieces as I waved my arms like an autistic child.

No, no, no, it can't be; that's impossible. I knew it was true deep down, but I had to put on a show to declare how disturbing and unfair the whole situation was.

Ignoring the damage I had just wrought, the doctor calmly and sweetly said he could run the test again. He was good at calming down hysterical women. I know this wasn't the first time he had gotten a reaction like mine.

I thought "Not this man. He's ugly. He's old. He's Polish. He's not the daddy I would have chosen for a child of mine. He's totally unacceptable. His kid will be a freak of nature. I have a child seventeen years older than this one."

The doctor must have read the rapid expressions flickering across my face: shock, dismay, fear. Not a positive one in the bunch.

He said "I want you to go home and think this over through the weekend. Come back on Monday and we can discuss your options. Because you are so far along we'll have to act right away if you decide to terminate the pregnancy. It's a safe procedure that we do in the hospital. Your insurance will probably even cover it."

I had to go back to work after hearing that I was almost three months pregnant by a man I detested (although on occasion I appreciated his sense of humor). I did not think he would find my news amusing at all. I wasn't sure I would even tell him the baby was his.

The doctor said, "I'll run the test again."

It came out the same.

Easter and Abortions

It was Easter weekend of 1988. I flew from the Philly airport to St. Louis and arrived to a bright shiny spring. My sister had a new house: yellow, cheerful, but not quite big enough for her growing family. Her youngest child was five months old, unremarkable. My sister had a disconcerting habit of leaving him wrapped up in a blanket on the floor in the middle of whatever room she happened to be in. She and her husband had just bought a video camera. That trip was the last time I ever saw it work. She took movies of everyone. I felt very self-conscious. I wondered if my pregnancy was showing in any way yet. I didn't think so but maybe I couldn't see myself the way others did.

My sister made me hold her baby. I didn't want to but I held the baby for hours as I rocked in the wooden rocker by the living room window.

On the flight home I burst into those primal tears that you know you don't stand a chance of holding back. Lousy father or no father at all, I knew I could never go through with an abortion.

As soon as I decided to have the baby my whole mood changed. I became so giddy and happy that it seemed mania was imminent or even had already arrived. Of course I had to go off the lithium right away. It was bad enough that I had already been taking it for the last three months. I briefly remembered scare stories about babies born with deformities when the mothers were taking lithium during pregnancy. My doctor assured me that those studies were never documented and that there was no proof at all of lithium causing deformed babies. I was so happy about the pregnancy by then that I didn't worry about a mutant baby for another minute of my almost-ten-month term.

Pregnant and Happy

What else could I do except move back in with Hal? I was so happy I figured I could put up with anything. After all, I had told him the baby was his, and he deserved to share the experience with me, so I thought. I knew that my small apartment would be too cold for a baby in the winter.

We rented a larger apartment and prepared for the new baby. We were married in July 1988 before a Justice of the Peace, and we didn't tell any family members until after the modest ceremony. I bought a three-toned gold ring that made my ring finger itch and peel.

I was high and happy for the whole pregnancy. My work people gave me a baby shower, and I got all the things I would need. I grew so big that finally one of the engineers refused to let me sit in the "good" engineering chairs for fear that my water would break and leak out all over it. I happily worked until the last two weeks before the baby came.

Once again, my labor did not go smoothly. I didn't flinch when the anesthesiologist gave me the epidural but the anesthetic went straight into my left leg instead of where it was supposed to go. I screamed bloody murder for the last three hours of labor.

The baby was huge, probably because of my gestational diabetes. He was perfect, though, just as

Kassie had been. He didn't look a whit like Hal. Of course he didn't.

Hal was in the labor room with me the whole time, and he seemed to enjoy the experience. We took the baby home two days later, and I was ecstatic. I took six weeks off from work to breastfeed and get into the swing of being a mother again.

Nick was everything you wanted in a baby except that he was always hungry, and he didn't sleep all night, ever, until he was over two years old. Maybe he never slept through the night. He was always awake when I went to sleep and awake when I got up. It was exhausting. He had an ear infection every month of his first year—antibiotics just didn't seem to work very well for him until we discovered Augmentum, and that gave him uncontrollable diarrhea. Even through the pain he was so bright and alert I couldn't believe it. He took his first independent step when he was seven months old, and started primitive speech when he was just over a year.

Hal and I were deliriously happy for about a year, and then reality set in.

My meds weren't working very well and when Nick was two, I went headlong into a deep depression. That was inevitable considering that I had been either manic or hypomanic for almost three years. I knew I was headed for a hospital stay. I felt controlled, stifled, and unhappy in my new role as a working mother. Work was going very well, but I began to be bored with writing the same old documents year after year. I knew I would have to go back to school to update my skills.

Then Hal and I weren't happy together anymore. We decided a change was in order. We quit our jobs and moved to Norfolk, Virginia, where I would stay at home and be a mother, and Hal would start an exciting new job designing small helicopters for military contracts. We were grasping at straws in an effort to save our disintegrating marriage. We moved in the summer of 1989 just before Nick turned one.

Playing with Matches

I have always had a vivid imagination. In 1990 when Nick was two I began to imagine horrible things happening to my family, mostly at my own hand. My psychiatrist told me I had obsessive-compulsive disorder because I was imagining the same horrible scenarios over and over. This was the worst of all:

I saw myself cross the room, impassive, without concern or anger. I reached over to him and pulled the matches from the pocket of his worn red and black checked flannel shirt. He didn't move or blink when I struck the match, but when I set fire to the flammable cotton of his shirttail, his eyes opened wide in surprise and shock. As the flames grew, I watched him through the smoke and realized that soon the screams would begin... but not mine.

It was dinner time. How sick I was of casseroles at five. I warmed the baby's milk, watched a movie I didn't like next to a dozing husband, and then listlessly dumped the dirty dishes into the sink. I hadn't bathed in days, maybe weeks. My greasy hair flopped onto my greasier forehead, and I saw the world through strings of despair. When we moved into the house, I loved most the first real kitchen I'd had in years; the blue tile floors, the matching mosaic pattern along the edge of the counters, the large window looking out onto the back yard.

Now I was interested only in the contents of the liquor cabinet. I peeked in and saw that it contained a few bottles, mostly less than half full: J & B, Absolut, and Bacardi Gold. How much better I would feel if I allowed myself to drink and drink until lovely oblivion. I would wait until the household was asleep. Next to the kitchen the bathroom medicine chest beckoned with its dozens of bottles of medications that didn't work, prescribed by a well-meaning but totally clueless psychiatrist. She was the one whose nose ran and who sniffled continuously throughout our 45-minute sessions. She seemed to be too sick herself to really help anyone else. She was from the Philippines. She had a lovely name, Estrellita, and she was my age. Like me, she was married to an engineer. I wondered what her story was.

As I roamed the kitchen, I saw the mousetraps set out behind the toaster, baited with a pretty poison named Warfarin; sounded like a traveler on the seas. Take the blue powder and drop a pinch in the baby's bottle. No more dinners, no child wakeful through the nights.

. . .

I never told Hal exactly what my visions were about, but he knew I was in bad shape. He sent me to the hospital with four changes of clothing, a toothbrush, shampoo, makeup and lipstick, and a sewing kit filled with pins, hundreds of hurtful points. I could use them to let out the steam of my anger. Then I was forced to make a contract with the orderly: no violence to self or others. He took away the pins and a compact with a glass mirror.

What did they know about how deep, how essential to the windings of my coiled personality my anger was?

Group therapy happened in a tasteful room furnished with puffed up chairs and roomy sofas. A large glass window was on one side. Was it there so they could see in, or that we could see out? I imagined myself taking the graceful wooden chair I was supposed to sit on and slamming it through the clear pane. Shards would fly like vicious birds through a stormy sky. The glass-cracking sound would be so satisfying, the sound of circus noise. I started to raise the chair to continue this fantasy of carnival glee. Eleanor, who was even larger than I am, grabbed me from behind. I screamed at her to take her hands off me. Through the heavy air, I heard the screams of others, more victims of my rage.

Medication was the only really important aspect of life on a psych ward. The nurses watched me swallow the pills. How easy it would be to slip them under my tongue and fertilize the plants with them later. Balanced meals were served at the same time every day, and comprised better food than I served at home. We played games at night. They weren't much fun; no one knew bridge, and I beat everyone at Scrabble. Our first assignment in group therapy was to write a letter to mom or dad and tell them how you were feeling. I listened to the trite phrases and grade-school prose. The other patients cried during this exercise but I did not. Such sentiments were beneath me, the "I love you," the "I can't forgive myself," and the "why did he leave me?" This wasn't the kind of therapy I needed. I called my daughter and told her not to let the family know I was in a psychiatric facility.

Then I was dizzy and queasy. I was convinced that the doctors had poisoned me with their evil cocktails. I felt like I was in a weathered boat on wavering seas. The sickness worsened as the day waned. By sundown I curled into a fetal roll to minimize the gut cramps that struck with the tiniest of movements. The yoga cat-stretch position worked better than the balled-up one. My cheek pressed into the musty carpet, and my knees curled against my rollicking stomach. I smelled years of screaming, fearful, sweating inmates. The waves rose to storm height and I took the brunt of all the force in my digestive system.

My stomach and bowels finally shot their contents in equal and opposite vectors, canceling the progress of my boat body, leaving me in the cross wake of conflicting currents. I wished to jump ship and swim to safe ground. The waves came faster and more furiously. I sucked in air before certain submergence.

I was in a vertiginous, liquid black storm of moving pain. I heard voices over me and felt the needle jab. There was no immediate relief. I hyperventilated, and they made me breathe into a bag. What a funny cure for this sickening vertigo. I broke out in pretty red lumps on my chest and boobs. More pills. Endlessly later the seas abated. I slept fitfully, invaded by cruel forces. The next morning while making my bed I found a pack of cigarettes and a book of matches under the mattress.

The match,
A mighty little flame,
Spot checks the tender skin,
Cotton gown ablaze,
A cozy campfire fueled by flesh.
Red burns oozing,
The pain of my losing.

Now I screamed, but the burns didn't really hurt that much.

Cheating

When I got home from the hospital after Thanksgiving, life didn't get any better. I was still searching endlessly for the right drug that would do the right thing (mainly, make me feel high, creative, energetic, and productive) with bearable side effects. My psychiatrist didn't know what to do with me. She opted for a psychotropic solution rather than therapy, and we settled on a combination of lithium and imipramine, both medications that had been around for a long time and at least caused predictable side effects. I began dieting and exercising regularly and for a while, my mood improved. In spite of my moodiness, the baby was happy and so intelligent I was busy all day long trying to challenge him and keep him amused.

My psychological state never stood still, though. The lithium by now had affected my thyroid, and I began seeing an endocrinologist regularly. For a year I alternated between hyper- and hypo-thyroid states. The imipramine caused dry mouth, and my teeth began to rot out slowly. In the next year I needed five root canals. The gastrointestinal disturbances from the lithium started out as an annoyance and then turned into a constant distraction that anyone would surely find unbearable. On my own, I found a group to attend every week where people with diagnosed mental illnesses talked about their problems. I liked the group, but I didn't tell anyone why I was really angry.

At least I wasn't having visions of killing my family members any more. I began to feel better, better enough to get in trouble again.

One quiet Sunday afternoon in February, I was restless and bored. It was too cold for a walk, and I didn't feel like calling any relatives. It was the year after the Persian Gulf War, which had provided so many hours of TV entertainment. I was using a small word processor to record some early memories, and I was pleased with the results of my writing.

While my husband was out working in the garage and my baby was entranced with Legos and miniature cars on the living room floor, I picked up the phone in the den. After four or five aborted attempts, I dialed information for the Cincinnati white pages. I easily found the number I was seeking, the number connecting me to my unhappy past, and I dialed.

He recognized my voice immediately. After I said, "Hello Karl, will you talk to me?" he paused for a long time before consenting to speak. I knew that calling him was the wrong thing to do, but I couldn't stop myself once I decided I wanted to talk to him. I had brought him misery before; the promise of fixing it all, like reweaving a torn fabric, appealed to him, and we continued. A thread of possibility wound through the conversation; several hours later, a brocade of promise glinted of a future meeting. I knew he would call me again; the call of our passionate past was too strong to ignore.

Calls lasting hours and well-written but increasingly clichéd love letters followed. The weight I worked so hard to lose returned, even with increased exercise. I was a mountain now, stony frozen, the lava of my volcanic activity prehistoric as dinosaurs. I acted out the expected passion. It must be true what they say: people who talk constantly about sex never actually do much of it. When Karl and I finally met, I made sure that I couldn't actually feel sexual passion for this man by taking Prozac, which kills my ability to have an orgasm. I'm not exactly sure why I did that, but I wanted to be in control when I finally met him again. Prozac can give you a deep feeling of well-being and good cheer, and I was counting on that. I figured I could work around the sexual side effects.

When I got Karl alone in the bedroom, I lifted my skirt and encouraged him to plunge in. He wasn't ready. He couldn't get an erection after all the flirting and talking on the phone and the professed eternal love. Our romance was as doomed as his wilted prick. He gave excuses. I was genuinely appalled, but realized that I had affected the outcome by my mountainous expectations and grandiosity. He blamed me, I blamed him, and we agreed to meet again.

The second time went somewhat better, but we ended with a spat. I grew increasingly irritable. Everything he did rubbed me the wrong way. We seemed to need on a bad note, if only to stop this compulsive coming together and splitting apart. We hung on to our tenuous relationship, parasites dug into the meat of muscle and sinew. I thought that pulling apart could cause real damage that would take years to heal, new scars over the old ones, made from past skirmishes.

I enjoyed pretending I was in love with Karl. My poems and letters could be inspired when the possibility of true love lay before me.

The end with Karl came soon enough. I returned to a job, a child, and a preoccupied husband. I was not strongly attached to two of the three; raising the child was my only meaningful activity in life. I felt shallow and deceptive. I fought with my new boss, abandoned my child to long daycare hours, and contemptuously ignored my husband.

Our blowup came three months after my return to the family fold. I had been a boat and a mountain; now it seemed that I was required to suffer for my strength and perfidy. Large as I was, I still couldn't get a physical advantage over a larger man. I was not well-trained in fisticuffs. After a verbal battle one Sunday afternoon, I finally snapped and flung an impulsive "Fuck you," at him, and you would have thought I'd killed his precious dog. He came after me for all he was worth. I swung at the crazed bull in front of me, his mouth flecked with specs of chewed-up Tums, saviors of his stomach lining. All his pent-up rage at my infidelity came out through his fists. He pounded my head, to pound sense into it,

I thought. He split my lip, blackened my left eye. I bled at the knee and elbow, yet I didn't land a blow on his bloated body. I determined to take some karate lessons. The child heard scuffling noises behind a locked door; he screamed, knowing the sounds of animosity. After the battle was over, the man begged forgiveness when he saw my bloody wounds. "Hug, me, touch me, and love me, even though I'm bad. I didn't mean to…"

I held him in contempt and lay down with the quivering child. I moved into the spare bedroom. Under the handmade quilt my mother gave me for a wedding present, I felt peace and control, waiting for the time to leave.

NASA Langley Research Center

I had cheated on Hal, and he had beaten me up. It seemed like an even trade, even to me.

Neither of us felt we had gotten the better or the worse end of the deal. In any case, I had returned to him after my affair with Karl, feeling that no matter what had happened we still belonged together. Hal feared that I had somehow contracted AIDS or some horrible disease from Karl, and I thought that he would beat me up again with little provocation. It seemed like a standoff. Then he did one thing that redeemed him in my eyes before I moved back into our bedroom.

What he did was pretty extraordinary. I had been trying to get hired by NASA as a Technical Editor ever since we had moved to Virginia two years before. I never even got a rejection letter from them, which I couldn't understand since I had six years' experience as a Technical Writer in the field of aerospace engineering. I applied again in the spring of 1992. This time I got a real rejection letter, and I gave up trying to convince them to hire me. I was crushed, and I figured that I would never work as a Technical Writer again.

After we started having sex again, Hal accepted the fact that I probably didn't have AIDS, and he wanted to get on my good side, if only to keep our bedroom activities alive. So he called the Manager of the Technical Editing Department at NASA Langley Research Center, a woman named Nancy McDonnell. I hated all women named Nancy after my experience in Massachusetts that ended my first marriage. I had refused to call her to plead my case as the person she most needed to hire for her Technical Editing Department. Somehow Hal talked her into giving me an interview. He told her that all I wanted in life was to work at NASA, or something to that effect. She agreed, and the interview was set for the following day. I was in a panic. What could I wear? What samples could I show her? Would she hate it that I had a small child? Was I qualified to work as a Technical Editor for a group of sophisticated aerospace engineers and physicists?

I went to the interview wearing a conservative but flattering navy blue dress with a white belt and a miniature red rose corsage affixed to the collar. I was so nervous I wondered if I would be able to speak at all when the time came for me to plead my case.

The interview went so well Nancy hired me on the spot to be her Formal Reports Editor. I would start the following Monday. I was in heaven, and suddenly all was well with my world again.

How Could Work Possibly Be More Boring?

My work comprised editing engineering reports for men who wrote possibly the most boring documents in the history of technical writing. There were no women aerospace engineers, physicists, or mathematicians at Langley. The men were arrogant, detached, and totally immersed in their work. They lacked social graces and the smallest remnants of introspection. They wrote for other experts, and they didn't want anyone to fuck with their precious reports. My problem was that I had been told to render their technical papers into writing at an 8th grade level so that real people could understand what they were trying to convey.

The way I accomplished this miracle was to edit the documents and then set up interviews for reviewing the "suggested changes." We were allowed a month to edit one document. I pored over these reports and usually rewrote them entirely. Once I even found a mistake in an equation a physicist had written.

Most of the editors were English majors who did not have a clue about what they were reading. There were reports on space physics, wind tunnel data, and mechanical engineering experiments. I had trained as an engineer so I understood most of it. I was not intimidated by these men, as I had grown up around engineers and had even been married to two of them. I had my tricks for how to flatter them while at the same time telling them their writing was horrible.

My methods worked with all but the crustiest of them. They loved my re-writes that made them sound brilliant but understandable to the common man. I was so proud of myself at my success with them. Many of them asked for me as their personal editor, which wasn't really allowed in a department where the assignments were handed out randomly.

I should have been the happiest editor in the world.

I wasn't. Editing came so easily to me that I found it hard to stay busy. I began looking for extra projects to do, and there were very few of those available to me. I did some time studies and some budgeting work for Nancy. Then the trouble began.

First of all, our offices were extremely small, and three editors were packed into each room. Only one person could be up walking around at a time. I would sometimes put my phone on the desk of the person sitting next to me if I had a lot of papers to work on at one time.

Worse than the space problems was the fact that Nancy micromanaged our work so heavily that she would often edit our edits. Not only did we have to negotiate with the engineers about our changes but we also had to justify our changes to the boss.

I began to feel that big brother was watching me. Nancy started picking at me in small ways at first.

One day she screamed at me to get my phone off my neighbor's desk. Right as she might have been, I resented her embarrassing me in front of everyone. She would check my desk at 7 a.m. to make sure I got there on time, which was something of a problem since I had to drop the baby off to daycare before work. She told me I was over-editing, even though not one engineer had complained about me. She didn't like the way I edited figures and photographs. I felt that she was criticizing me at every turn.

And my medications were giving me problems. Because of severe diarrhea from the lithium, I felt like I was spending half my time in the bathroom.

My car battery regularly died in the parking lot after work, and I didn't seem to be able to find the time to get it replaced. I had two flat tires. My alternator went out.

At the end of my year at NASA the fight with Hal happened, and I appeared at work with a face that looked like I had participated in a Fight Club bash. I said I had been in a car crash, but even to me that sounded like a lie.

Super-Conducting Supercollider

To top it all off, I rekindled my relationship with my first husband Kevin, who by now was managing the Computer Department at the Texas Super-Conducting Supercollider. We wrote endless emails to each other on the NASA Intranet, which was connected to all the other research facilities in the US. In other words, we wrote love letters on company time and equipment. I knew that my behavior was unacceptable, but I didn't stop writing. I was rapidly heading into mania.

Late on the night before the 4th of July long weekend in 1992, I packed up the car and the baby, picked up Kevin from Norfolk International Airport, and drove across the country from Norfolk, Virginia to Palo Alto, California. I didn't tell Hal I was going, but I did leave him a goodbye note.

The note lay face down on the top of my dresser, mixed in with a dozen books and magazines, a rumpled shirt, and a set of Legos. It read:

Dear Hal,

By the time you read this note, Nick and I will be on the road to California. I have decided to return to Kevin, who promises to love and cherish me and be a good father to Nick. Kevin has flown here to drive west with me.

Kevin and I have been corresponding by e-mail for the last three months. As you know, we met last spring after a nineteen-year separation at Kassie's college graduation. We hit it off very well, although we were both a little nervous about seeing each other after such a bitter breakup. In our correspondence we have worked out the problems that destroyed our marriage. Of course, e-mail is a natural platform for a computer geek and an isolated bookworm like me.

We did not intend to plot this reunion behind your back, but after you beat the crap out of me, I didn't feel that I could come to you with my feelings of alienation. When you suggested we get drunk and watch some movies this holiday weekend, all I could see was you flying into a rage over nothing and beating me up again, or worse yet, taking it out on Nick.

You've been such a jerk. I tried to love you, against advice from family and friends. I supported you and defended you for eight years. I've put up with your paranoia, depression, and negative view of the world. I'm the only person who knows that underneath your bearlike exterior, you are just a hurt little boy who wants love and recognition for the wonderful things that you create with your hands and brain. You're one of the most creative people I've ever met, but I can't stand to be around you anymore. You used to help me and support me. Now you only want to tear me down and control my every move. I think you're becoming more and more dangerous.

I'm afraid for myself and the child you seemed to be so thrilled with.

I know the basis of your anger with me is not my unfaithfulness, but that I lied to you about Nick's paternity. I am sorry I lied. I wanted to be pregnant and nothing happened between us in five years of not using birth control. I did something stupid, and then I deceived you. We were so happy there for a while, when Nick was a baby, before you knew. You loved that baby as much as I did. How could you stop loving him just because he doesn't have your blood in him? Now I realize that you will resent us both forever. I even lied to myself about what happened, but now I am ready to face what I did. I will just be facing it with Kevin instead of you.

I know you will be relieved to be rid of us. Work is the thing you care most about. Now all your time will be your own. I wish the best for you. I hope you can believe that.

Do not make any attempts to find us. We do not wish to see you for a long while. If Nick wants to see you in the future, we will try to work something out. As it stands now, within a few days there will be a whole continent in between us, and that's the way I want it. Don't bother my family; they know nothing about us leaving you.

Have a good life; I intend to.

Kris

The drive west with Kevin and Nick took almost a week.

Kristy in the Valley

I don't know why I always return to old husbands and lovers. I guess because the problems with them are so familiar, like bad habits. I know things will never work out any better than before. I always think I have learned from my mistakes and can forgive and forget; in truth, I don't learn, I can't forgive, and I never forget a thing.

To get myself to California in secret with a four-year-old child required a mania of huge proportions. I was a mess when I got there and was in even worse shape when I left. It helped that Kevin joined me on the drive west, but not much.

I found myself living in a household of men. Very quickly I got sick of cleaning toilet lids and the areas thereabouts. Donne joined us in September, making it a household of three men and one woman. Donne started bringing home women to sleep with right away, but I don't count them as roommates since they were there only for a night.

In California I felt like I was living on a different planet than the one I grew up on. The sun was always in my eyes and on my skin. I couldn't wear my contacts because my eyes burned and watered as soon as I went out. Even though I smeared tons of level 30 sun block lotion on all the exposed parts of my body I still got sunburned. The first person I met was a lady in the park who proudly showed me the skin cancer on her neck. It was a black, blue, and green festering sore that she says she got only two years after moving to California.

The trip west had threatened my manic good mood. We had visited my old friend Freddie and his wife April in Chicago. April asked Kevin questions about our plans, and he just looked at her blankly, as if to say, "I do not deign to answer any questions from you inferior humans." I kept asking myself "What have I done? Is this the man I want to spend the rest of my life with?"

Also, there was another problem with Kevin: he reeked. The smell was like fermented, concentrated cat pee. He didn't shower all that often, and his clothes didn't get washed unless I was in the mood to do it. The odor clung to him like clematis on a fence. Sometimes days went by when he neither showered nor changed his clothes. I acted like I didn't care but inside I was alarmed, and I wondered if he had some horrible disease he wasn't telling me about.

Donne called me a stick floating on the river of life. He said things like,"You go where the current takes you." He didn't mean that in a complimentary way. My sense was that California was not the place for me. I wasn't sure I loved Kevin anymore but I wanted him to be reunited with his kids, and I was the bridge to any reconciliation.

Soon my mania dropped away, and I fell into my fall depression. The day my furniture arrived from Virginia, my mood dipped even further. It signaled the end of my marriage to Hal, and I wasn't prepared to find that I had strong feelings of sadness at leaving him.

I was unhappy about the house layout. It had no front door. To get in, I had to squeeze through a narrow path in between a bunch of old cars in the garage. All the overhead lights were burned out so I could not see where I was going at night. I was almost knocked off my feet with fright when the 1 a.m. train went through not 25 feet from the back porch at intervals of fifteen minutes during the day. "Great," I thought. "It's like living in Chicago next to the El."

I had been looking forward to all the beautiful flowers in California, but when I looked out the front window all I could see were half a dozen very old cars parked on the dirt strip that was the front yard. Rusting, junky vehicles were not appreciated in a neighborhood of million-dollar homes.

The place looked like a used car lot. I wanted flowers, blooming shrubs, orange trees, and a few rose bushes. I hadn't bargained for all this rusting metal in the front yard.

I knew Kevin was no housekeeper, but I wasn't prepared for the house to be such a slum. After all, the damn place was worth hundreds of thousands of dollars, because it was smack dab in the center of Silicon Valley. In northern Wisconsin, you couldn't get rid of it for $40,000. The windows didn't shut. There was no heat in half the rooms. It was a tar box. The kitchen was the size of a small closet. I felt like I was camping out. This style of house was called an Eichler, which was supposed to be a big deal architecturally in California. I didn't see anything great about it.

The house was filthy from bottom to top. Obviously no conventional woman had lived there for a long time. There were layers and layers of heavy dirt all over everything, thanks to the endless stream of trains. Donne complained of spiders crawling over his face in the night. The spider webs draped the walls and corners like decorative fishnets.

When I got truly discouraged, I went outside to work in the yard. The property, which was the size of my old living room, was covered with masses of hideous weeds and sticker grass. California was more than just a garden for beautiful flowers; the weeds grew here just as fervently. I started clearing out the weeds. Most of the California weeds seemed to have vicious thorns that left burning scratches all over my skin. "I ought to just take a match to them and let the whole mass burn to the bare ground," I thought. Lots of people did just that to get rid of the weeds in their yards.

I planted some red and pink impatiens in pots, and I hung baskets of lush fuchsias from the porch eaves. The plants did cheer me up. I wouldn't be happy until I could look out on a whole yard full of exotic blooming plants.

In hopes of finally straightening myself out and learning to avoid the disasters caused by bad judgment in the past, I found a local shrink and a psychotherapist.

I'm Not Bipolar, I'm an Astral Traveler

The therapist was a chubby, rather disgusting man who picked his nose while I talked and sometimes dozed off in the middle of a session. Still, when he did have something to say, it was usually perceptive and to-the-point. His first advice to me and Kevin was to discuss our views on money. That turned out to be good advice. Kevin forced me to make a budget, though in the end, all we agreed on was that he would pay my charge card every month. He didn't have a word to say about where all his money was going, nor did he share his own budget with me.

The psychiatrist was an Ecuadorian woman who was about my age. I felt a competitive edge to our relationship. I was able to con her fairly easily, and I didn't tell her about my real fears or problems.

In Silicon Valley it felt to me like everyone else was in on some big secret that they knew but I didn't. They all acted like they were smarter and more educated than I was. Kevin's friends worked at Stanford and SLAC and cutting-edge computer firms. Many of them had started their own computer companies. When Kevin introduced me, he said only that "Kris is the mother of my children," and "Kris's parents went to Stanford." My sensitivity read into those statements that he felt I was not really equal to him or his crowd, no matter that I was wild and crazy and fun and original.

I also felt that I was unemployable in California. I got my courage up and went on a job interview to NASA at Moffet Field. After all, I had worked at NASA Langley for six months and was very successful. The woman who interviewed me was extremely kind, but basically laughed me out of there since my experience was so scanty.

As time went on and I didn't work or go to school, I got bored. Kevin wasn't home much, as he was trying to make a lot of money working for $85/hour, which was a lot of money at the time. Donne was around but had gotten a good job and was busy. Besides, he was upset with me a lot of the time and wouldn't speak to me. He told me I was an unfit mother. Most of the time, I agreed with him.

After a year in California I was in trouble with Kevin. I had been inviting my mentally ill friends over for meals, and Kevin didn't like them. They all talked a blue streak, were open and honest about their feelings, were philosophical and original, and on top of that, they were fun. They amused me. They read fiction and philosophy. They cried openly. Kevin's friends only read computer manuals or machine language, which was unintelligible to me.

So I just shut up and smiled around his friends, like some kind of grinning idiot. They were all computer geeks who couldn't carry on a reasonable conversation if they tried (which they didn't). They talked about their work or their machines. I couldn't stand to be with them. Kevin made me invite them for dinner. I felt just as imposed on as he did. I wished he knew some normal people. He wished the same of me. In March 1995 I got a job at a very hip bookstore, just like I had always dreamed. It didn't pay well, but I got 35 percent off on all the books I bought. I could find a real job if I needed to. I thought, "I might as well do what I love as long as I have a choice."

My dream world was shattered in April 1995. I received some shocking news, and I acted with remarkable equanimity. I didn't engage in screaming fits or hysteria.

True, I had suspected what was coming. Hearing the dreadful words plop through the air like shit coming from a dog's butt startled me into a realization of my situation: Kevin was dumping me.

I was now a woman used and discarded twice by the same man. The passionate thrills from my renewed relationship with Kevin had evolved so quickly into an ordinary, practical, dreary routine. One day flowed into the next with what was to me a comforting and safe predictability. After a roller coaster life, I was finally ready to settle down with my sweet and gentle man, even if life was not perfect. Now I would be uprooted again.

The intrusive words formed a catalytic lump in my brain jelly around which other thoughts orbited sluggishly, then scattered to some far perimeter. I skewed off into a land of disbelief and pain.

Kevin said, "I'm going on a cruise with Lara."

I'm

I'm going

On a cruise

On a cruise with Lara

With Lara, with Lara, with Lara...

When had he ever taken me and Nick on a vacation? The last trip we took was to his father's funeral.

He had never had one good thing to say about Lara, his ex-wife. And now he was going to go back to her? How unbelievable that was to me, even though I had done exactly the same thing when I had returned to not one, but two exhusbands. All I could think was that he wanted to prove to her that he wasn't impotent any more, that he really was a manly man and not gay. I felt as if the whole situation was my fault. How weird it was to think that she would even want him back when they had never consummated their marriage in three years of being together 30 years ago.

I knew his thoughts were transporting him to a boat on the Caribbean, a boat rocking, rocking, rocked by the waves, rocked by the waves of fucking, fucking with another woman on a million dollar yacht, in a million-dollar blue sea, in the Car-i-fucking-be-an.

I went into action. I wanted to do some honest-togoodness physical labor, work up a sweat, and sweep away the anger from my system in a spring-cleaning fury. Otherwise, I'd have to hit someone, maybe even someone not guilty. Most satisfying, I imagined bashing the guilty one and burning his house. I had wanted to love someone from the tip of my toes to the top of my frizzy head and receive the same in return. Finally I had learned the value of plain ordinary life, and I was being discarded for my trouble.

I felt so foolish. And then I thought, "What the hell am I gonna do next?"

Moving Back Home

Nick and I rather happily moved back into my parent's house. My father's career had taken off again in his 72nd year when he formed a company to build a huge paper recycling plant on the Menominee River. Somehow $250,000,000 became available for the project from loans by various banks and state programs. It was an incredible venture for an old deaf guy. Too bad that he hadn't included a good money man or woman with his four partners.

The company was sold a year after its construction due to an unfortunate engineering mistake made by the waste treatment contractor and by the fact that the value of paper dropped to less than half its value over the course of the year. I don't understand bonds but I gathered that the company defaulted on its bond payments, and another company bought it out. As dad so nonchalantly put it to me, "There goes your inheritance." He was crushed, though he tried not to show it.

Meanwhile I took a few contract tech writing jobs, but ultimately I was laid off and sitting around the house looking for something to do in addition to helping my mother through her last illness. At that time, my father's brother had moved into the house due to extremely declining health, and then Donne decided to move back into the basement to start an Internet business at home. We were a household of two invalids, a healthy but depressed old man, a teenager, a young man, and me. Fortunately the house was large and roomy enough for everyone to survive without feeling cramped, though my mother complained about having to share the TV. My father fixed that problem by buying TVs for every room so that everyone could watch their own channel.

I decided to enter nursing school rather than take a bad job. I had already worked in enough factories and department stores. I was as thrilled as ever to be going back to school. I had always loved learning better than actually doing anything. Going to school is a great activity for a hypomanic or even a manic person. As long as I could keep my mania somewhat under control I was usually the smartest person in my classes. In the past I had simply dropped out when I crashed into depression rather than face failing grades.

Donne, Nick, and I took over the basement area, which included two bedrooms, a huge living room, and a good-sized workshop. We all enjoyed each other's company, and Donne and I took turns home-schooling Nick, who had not attended school regularly since eighth grade. It was an ideal setup for a bunch of unconventional bums, as we really were. Donne couldn't stay employed, Nick couldn't stay in school, and we all wanted to act like teenagers.

Trouble started slowly but inexorably as everyone in the household moved toward personal crises late in the year. Dad lost his paper company, Nick became depressed and ended up on a psych ward, Donne declared bankruptcy, my mother died, Uncle Bill entered a nursing home, and I ramped upward toward one of my worst manic episodes ever. My family has never been boring. The only saving grace was that there was plenty of family money to support the whole menagerie. That started to dwindle quickly, though, as time went on and no one had a job.

The parties started at about the time I entered nursing school.

Sex, Drugs, and Rock-'n-Roll, Again

Dad's house was so large and so well set up that Nick began to be popular among a certain set of kids his age: the cast-offs, the weirdoes, the unpopular, the drop-outs, and mostly, the musicians. I was so busy succeeding at school that I failed to notice the drug and alcohol usage at first. Most of the kids did not attend school, so soon there were people in the basement apartment at all times of the day and night. Dad ignored them and kept to himself upstairs, in mourning after his wife's death.

I loved the kids. They were bright, talented, funny, and irreverent. They thumbed their noses at most forms of authority, so I became a friend rather than a parent. I was no authority figure. I didn't know that before long I would become one of them. When the partying got out of control I attempted to set some house rules, though very few of them were ever obeyed.

Psychiatrists—Bah!

Before I discovered the medications that turned me into a healthy, happy, high functioning adult, I went through some hard times with psychiatrists. I wrote the following poem to express my feelings about psychiatry as it was offered in our small, isolated part of the country, the Upper Peninsula of Michigan. Later, I found a doll of a psychiatrist close to home, and he turned me onto the path I am traveling today. There were some bad years, though. For several years I saw a psychiatrist who just about did me in. He gave me all the feel-good drugs I could ever want, and soon I was hooked on large dosages of Adderall to wake up and all the Klonopin I wanted to go to sleep. On that regime I became very cavalier about my illness. Who cared if I was sick when I could feel this good!

In Need of Giving to the Psychiatric Till

Give this drug to the dissidents
And that one to the sexually bents.
You blunt their skills,
By giving them pills.
Why not relieve them where they hurt,
Not throw them in your psychic dirt?

Kris Rock

You separate and scrutinize them,
Put them where their pains don't cease.
With your diagnostic labels,
They're mixed into your jails and psychic Babels.

You don't love to smoke,
YOU'RE ADDICTED.
You're not unmotivated,
YOU'RE EVICTED
You're not tipsy,
YOU'RE INEBRIATED.
You're not tired,
YOU'RE NARCOLEPTIC.
You're not thin,
YOU'RE ANOREXIC.
You're not sad,
YOU'RE CHRONICALLY DEPRESSED.
You're not worried,
YOU'RE HYPERVIGILANT.
You're not shy,
YOU HAVE GENERALIZED ANXIETY
You're not having a heart attack,
YOU'RE HAVING A PANIC ATTACK.
You're not tidy,
YOU'RE OBSESSIVE-COMPULSIVE.
You're not busy,
YOU'RE ADHD.
You're not energetic,
YOU'RE HYPO-MANIC.

I'm Not Bipolar, I'm an Astral Traveler

You're not creative,
YOU'RE HALLUCINATING.

You'll never call us mostly normal,
But give us a name that's medically formal.
You think we all are seriously ill
And in need of giving to the psychiatric till.
When we turn in brave-new-world directions,
We'll get rid of those with control predilections.

Cornucopia

One day I looked into the medicine cabinet and assessed its rainbow contents:

- Metformin-Cigar-sized pill for lowering blood sugar
- Lithium-Pink cigar-shaped capsules for balance and calm
- Lamictal-Big white tabs for mood stabilization
- Klonopin-White tablets for anxiety and sleep
- Dexedrine-Yellow jackets for energy and organization
- Adderall-Orange tabs for zip
- Seroquel-Small white tablets for la la land
- Wellbutrin-Big purple tablets for depression
- Advil, aspirin, Excedrin, Tylenol, and Naproxin for minor pain
- Vicodin, Percocet, and Ultram for major pain
- Vitamins of all letters
- Risperdal-Dissolving white tabs for delusions
- Anafranil-Pink tabs for OCD
- Levothyroxin-Small beige tabs for thyroid
- Inderal-Tiny white tabs for stage fright, test anxiety, and blood pressure
- Contac-Red tabs for allergies
- Simvastatin-Medium-sized orange tabs for cholesterol
- PeptoBismol-Pink liquid for diarrhea

- Cymbalta-Blue and yellow capsules for fibromyalgia

And those changed with the years as new drugs came on the market, supposedly new and improved; often just new. I would have to add Amaryl for my Type 2 Diabetes and Abilify when lithium no longer worked. Of course I didn't take them all every day, but I had taken all of them at one time or another.

One day I took the white tablets and the yellow jackets from the places on their shelves. The pills were there to make me feel better. These two made me feel the best of all. A spoon and a small plate were easily accessible from the kitchen, and I had at least one dollar bill.

I took my drugs and paraphernalia into the den and wondered what the proper technique for snorting powder was.

"Let me show you how to do that," someone said.

By midnight all I wanted was more drugs. I checked all the medicine cabinets in the house and found more. This went on for some time.

All the while I got straight A's in both undergraduate nursing school and in my following master's program in business. I loved school, and the 60-90 mg/day of Adderall I took helped me to maintain the energy I required to function at a manic level.

Hallucinogens were bound to come into play in my life eventually, and somehow I discovered salvia, the drug Miley Cyrus got into trouble with on her viral internet video. Salvia was a wonderful drug that allowed you to trip balls for about twenty minutes and then come back to reality with no after-effects. For most people, it is extremely dangerous and can cause you to freak out in a big way. I don't recommend it, but I can't deny that I smoked it many times and loved it. I wrote about it after the last time I took it.

S. Divinorum

"Help!" John and Marie looked at each other. "What do we do?" Marie whispered.

"Help!"

"I don't know. Should we try to bring her out of it somehow?" John answered.

"Help!"

"But how?"

"I never saw anyone freak out like this. Most people just sit and laugh their asses off."

"Maybe it's got toxins in it or something."

"It's an herb, retard. It grows in the garden."

"Help!" This cry was more urgent.

"I'm not doing that shit. No fucking way." Marie grabbed a cigarette. "Hey, dude, where's my lighter?"

He fumbled in his pockets and pulled out a cheap pink Bic lighter that he tossed to her. "Sorry. I must have picked it up by accident."

Marie gave him a scathing glance and lit up. "Yeh, right," she said, blowing smoke in his face. He ignored her and turned toward the woman who needed help.

Eyes closed, she was sitting in the corner of the room in a raggedy, overstuffed chair in front of a desktop computer. She held her arm up as though she were sinking under water for the third time. "Help, please help!"

"I can't stand this anymore," John said as he rushed over to the helpless woman. He grabbed her upraised arm and pulled her up out of the chair, which had a large wet spot on it.

"Geez, that's kinda disgusting," he said, indicating the wet seat cushion.

Awareness returned to the woman's eyes, and she coughed as she looked around. "Oh, I'm back," she said. Seeing concern on the faces of her two comrades, she said, "What's the matter? It was fine. I had a lot of fun."

"You just screamed "help" for ten minutes straight. You sounded like you were being tortured." said John.

"I was in a room with no doors or windows. The walls, ceiling, and floor were made of small tiles, like alternately green and white bathroom tiles. The whole room looked like an Irish checkerboard."

Drops of sweat rolled down the sides of her face. She was flushed, and her hands were shaking. There was a smoky smell in the room like a combination of burning tobacco, weed, and catnip. The fresh urine didn't smell yet.

"Can we open a window? I am burning up," the woman requested. John struggled with the window behind her and yanked it halfway open, letting the freezing January air into the room.

"Ah, that's much better," the woman said. "I'll explain what was so scary."

She continued, "All the surfaces of the room were undulating, like, well, uhmmm, like an unfurled

American flag blowing in the wind. No, maybe more like rolling waves. Yeh. Anyway, the walls were rolling like waves around the room in a clockwise motion horizontal to the floor. It was like being in the eye of a storm, with waves made of green and white tiles circling in regular pulses all around me. Every time the waves made a complete circle around the room, it got a little smaller. Then the room was closing in on me, and I sensed I was in a parallel universe where I had always lived and would go on living forever. But there was something terrifying about being trapped in that world. I knew I had to get out fast, or I would never have another chance to escape. The room was dynamic: it was shrinking and curling and rolling and whirling and squeezing, faster and faster, and there was only one way out: through a small opening I could see in the far right corner of the ceiling. But the hole was getting smaller and smaller by the second, and it was nearly all the way closed. I knew I had to get out through the rapidly closing hole. I was terrified at what I might find on the other side of the mysterious exit from the checkerboard world. I jammed my arm in the last little passageway, blocking the ceiling tiles from closing up all the way and trapping me inside the room. That's why I raised my arm and called help once or twice there at the end. I was desperate for someone to pull me up through the hole, and you see, someone did. I squeezed out just in time. Thank you, John. It felt so good to be rescued. I don't know what would have happened to me in that little green and white room. If I had been trapped there, I felt as though I would have disappeared from here. Kind of weird, huh?"

She looked at her friends thoughtfully and said, "I think I know what that trip was all about. I believe I have just been reborn."

John and Marie looked at each other once again, in silent agreement that this woman was truly nuts.

"Yeh, whatever," sighed John.
"Hey, that was totally awesome. Marie, aren't you next? Funny the affects you can get from smoking a weed commonly found in people's gardens. What is it called again? Salvadoria, or something like that, right? I find it far superior to mushrooms. How did you know that plant was hallucinogenic?"

"I must have read about it somewhere on the Internet. I think I'm going to pass on it this time. Tripping is not really my thing. I'll stick to the kind of weed I'm used to," Marie answered. She looked a little green about the gills.

Little Yellow House

Things got so out of control Nick and I finally had to move out of dad's house, and we got a place of our own. It was a little yellow house right across from Nick's school. I earned my MBA, but I never did graduate from nursing school. I stopped taking Adderal and Klonipin, and I fell into a burned-out depression. All I did during that time was watch movies and read and write a few poems. I began hanging around with a few retired veterans I saw every day and with whom I got into no trouble at all. They bugged the crap out of me, but they were adult friends who were boring but also dysfunctional like I was. I hung out with them for about a year until I couldn't stand what I was becoming: a loser, burnout, depressed slug. Maybe they didn't care, but I very much did.

Coming Down

The depression was a long one: I slept for a year, and I thought everything was wrong with me except what was really wrong. After all, I'd been taking medication for bipolar disorder for the last 30 years. It shouldn't have surprised me that I was depressed again, particularly since I had just come off three years of taking uppers and downers on top of my normal bipolar meds. Yes, I had managed to go to school and get fantastic grades. But I had also totaled one of the cars by falling asleep at the wheel after being up for three days writing papers. Wasn't it obvious that I had just plain burned myself out, finally and for good? I wasn't sure I'd ever be able to get up again.

So I slept 14-18 hours a day. I took a job but was fired four months later. I was fed up with being labeled with a horrible chronic illness; I refused to be bipolar anymore. I just didn't have the energy for it. My Scientologist-leaning son Donne was right. Psychiatrists were devils, and psychotropic medications were poison, designed by the drug companies to get us addicted and then happily take our money for the rest of our lives.

I had gained weight on the amphetamines; that was the world playing a bad joke on me. Who gained weight on speed? After my three years of being too high or too low I weighed as much as most linebackers, not the balletic quarterbacks and tight ends. I weighed more than I had when I was nine months pregnant. I felt like a huge discontented cow.

I looked up symptoms for all the auto-immune diseases. I was convinced I was suffering from chronic fatigue syndrome, rheumatoid arthritis, fibromyalgia, or maybe lupus. My doctor wouldn't go along with any of those except for the fibromyalgia, and I discovered that my blood sugar level was way too high. However, even severe, untreated diabetes wasn't going to cause me to sleep 18 hours a day for a year. I refused to face the simple truth: I was depressed again, as I had been dozens of times before.

This bout of depression was different from all my previous ones. I felt like I had already died, not just that I wanted to. Because my body wasn't moving much, my mental energy started to increase in weird ways. I had vivid dreams that I thought were messages from the universe. I believed I could heal people with my hands. I thought a lot of things, but very few of them were based on reality.

Inevitably, I sought various kinds of homeopathic treatments for my ennui. I went to the health food store and bought quantities of vitamins, herbs, trace elements, acids. I swallowed green liquids that tasted awful and purple ones that tasted great. I drank fish oil by the tablespoonful. I saw chiropractors and acupuncturists. I saw hypnotists. I switched psychiatrists four times and my family doctor three. I read my nursing and anatomy and physiology books until I was familiar with just about every disease there is, and I was convinced I was suffering from most of them. I quit smoking and then started again. Throughout it all I took my prescribed medicines faithfully. Still I couldn't rouse myself from bed except for a few hours a day, and that was to pay attention to my son and or to go out for cigarettes, beer, Taco Bell, and ice cream. I also watched several movies every day, but they didn't take my mind off how awful I felt.

Something had to give. With bipolar illness, something always does.

Up till then, lithium had always been the most trustworthy medicine for me. I have tried most of the psychotropic meds out there, and I always ended up back on lithium. When I started taking Metformin for my high blood sugar, I began having god awful stomachaches and even worse diarrhea. Lithium and Metformin didn't mix well for me. I stood it as long as I could, and then my doctor and I started looking for a new mood stabilizer. I had big problems with all of them. So I did what any self-respecting manic-depressive would do: I stopped taking all my psychotropic meds.

Within days I began to feel better. I was awake at least half of the day. I had enough energy to get out and about. I cleaned the house. Within a week, I was feeling fantastic, then really fantastic, and then I started writing flirtatious letters to my ex, exercising, sending poetry out to contests, being friendly to my family, keeping a journal, trying to get a partner to go into business with me, and getting in touch with old friends I hadn't seen in 20 years; in short, I was ramping up into hypomania and getting ready to go on a manic spree.

I went straight from a brief constructive and friendly hypomania to an irritable, violent bad-girl mania.

When I got to the point that my head felt like it was going to explode with the over-energy of constant speeding thoughts, I finally admitted to my doctor that perhaps it was time to find a new mood stabilizer.

I did that, and then I was able to be awake most of the day. I ate normally, mostly acted normally, exercised regularly, and best of all, I was able to write several days a week with at least a small measure of coherence. I was tired at the end of the day, and I still took naps, but the new routine was a great improvement over the previous year. I made a vow that I would not dwell too much on the past. I made a good start on that vow by saying goodbye permanently to some people who had damaged me and whom I had not been able to get out of my life. I flushed them down my mental toilet and felt much better now that they were gone. I welcomed my biggest problem: I had no friends left because I had flushed all the old ones away. It was time to make new ones.

This task was not so daunting. After all my moves and jobs and careers, I was used to getting to know new people quickly. I couldn't let myself get too distracted by the fact that if I didn't make good choices I would be in the same quandry as before. I vowed not drink, use illicit drugs, or hang out with people who were no good for me.

Since I was feeling so much better, I decided it was time for me and Nick to go on a road trip.

An Aluminum-Head's Journey to Ozzfest 2007

I had been anticipating the 2007 Ozzfest concert for over a year, ever since I learned that Ozzie Osbourne was giving out free tickets for the shows. I couldn't wait to hear that unique blend of thundering drums and ridiculously odd syncopations that made my body thrum with seductive rhythms and my heart feel like it was speeding down a train track to hell. I anticipated guitars that whispered, screamed, whined, moaned, groaned, begged, pleaded, dared, angered, overwhelmed, invited, laughed, excited, dismayed, and scared. Their melodies could be sweet as little girls at a tea party, sulky as teens who hated all adults, and angry as dispossessed hornets. I awaited singers who were in turn sassy and growly, cynical and honest, depressed and manic, and who all seemed in desperate need of validation and approval.

My daughter Kassie dropped us off at Coors Amphitheater near the Denver Tech Center at 3 p.m. on a Saturday in late July 2007. Nick and I had driven 1200 miles to Denver from the Upper Peninsula of Michigan to see the concert and visit my daughter.

I'd be lying if I said the day was pleasant. The temperature wavered between 90 and 100 degrees, and, strangely for Denver, it had begun to drizzle. We might as well have been spending an afternoon sipping mint juleps in Savannah, Georgia where the humidity is so heavy you feel you are one with the air. I expected a thunderstorm that never came.

We got a late start on the day because we had stayed up all night partying. The evening concert would take place in the Fiddler's Green Amphitheater. I was all set to see Ozzie at 9:30 p.m. in the VIP seats. Nick and a friend would sit on the grass and smoke grass. The afternoon bands were playing in the amphitheater parking lot. The space was jammed with young men outfitted in black band T-shirts, with an occasional gothed-out girl mixed in for good measure. I was garbed in the closest thing I could come to metal cool: a simple black T-shirt and black jean shorts frayed around the hem. Yes, I was old, wrinkly, and fat, but I had paid my money, and I really wanted to be there. In a funny way I didn't feel out of place. I didn't have nearly enough piercings or tattoos, but I could only stand so much pain for the sake of conformity to the fads of youngsters.

Along the sides of the parking lot were trucks bearing goods to attract the young metal heads: T-shirts, hats, gothic jewelry, and long black coats. I was interested only in finding a beer truck. After a dizzying trip through the crowd I found only one vehicle selling beer; that was, of course, a Coors truck. A single 16-inch cup of Coors Light was $8.00. This was getting to be a not-so-free concert. I gave up the idea of beer and instead waited in line for the free energy drink, which went down extremely well. Go Monster!

By the time four or five heavy metal bands had played my legs were getting wobbly, so I sat down on the heavily-graveled ground. I had brought a book to read, so I read for a while and tried not to think about how hot and dirty I felt and how much the gravel was cutting into my butt. The music was superb. People give metal music a bad rap because of the dark lyrics but in truth I couldn't understand any of them anyway. A good metal guitarist could give Itzak Perlman a run for the money.

I came to metal music by way of a long and winding road, as The Beatles so aptly put it. By the end of the sixties I looked and acted like a typical hippie. Inside I felt like a total fake. I was uncomfortable around people with names like Sunshine. I was terrified of cops. Marijuana made me intensely sleepy and paranoid. In short, during the late sixties and early seventies I felt not exhilaration but a deep, depressed, morbid fear of the world and what was happening. Learning to love metal music and the philosophy behind it at the age of 58 was my real rebellion. I had spent most of my rebelling years either freaked out or as a young mother.

I came up with the name "aluminum-heads" for us older metal fans for a reason so obvious you will smack your head in amazement that you didn't think of it first. The latest evidence on Alzheimer's disease indicates that one of its suspected causes is aluminum that gathers in your brain and causes the all sorts of brain deformities.

Many of my peers will suffer from Alzheimer's before we die, so you might as well call us aluminum-heads for all the metal that is wrecking our brains slowly but inexorably. After all, I'm not going to stop wearing deodorant.

For several months I studied metal bands from morning to night to find out what music I had missed and what bands were on tour. This music might have represented my own depression and dark thoughts, but it provided for me transference from inside my horribly troubled mind to an outer world I could handle.

Who, man or woman, could be unmoved at the sight of many large, hunky men, diamonds in the rough, who were running, pacing, gyrating, teasing, communing, and performing all manner of hi-jinx on the stage while at the same time singing and playing stringed instruments in ways rarely heard before on this earth?

Most mesmerizing of all to me was the way these men threw their hair about. When I was a teenager, I washed my long hair almost every day and then ironed it to make it look good enough for me to appear in school. I can't even imagine what these musicians do to keep their hair so exquisitely coiffed and groomed. They must travel with their own personal hairdressers. During the Lamb of God concert, I was standing right in front of Willy Adler, and I found myself transfixed at the sight of the surprisingly clean and wavy brown hair that he flung, twirled, shook, twisted, hurled back and forth, and subjected to many other innovative actions. I don't quite understand how he managed to do all that without ending up with his head bouncing on the floor or at least getting seriously dizzy, but he did. True, some of the band members I saw at the concert looked ratty, but most of the featured performers had obviously taken pains with their appearance.

While head banging, hair tossing, and skipping across the stage, these amazing multi-tasking musicians at the same time managed to sing or play an instrument or both (!) in a style so technically complex and with fingers flying so quickly that I wonder if any other musician in the world could keep up with them. The notes come so quickly that the ear could not pick up all the sounds. ...When my son was practicing shred-metal songs he learned from Joe Stump at the Berklee College of Music, he was playing 32nd notes. That's very fast.

Ozzie was wonderful, as I knew he would be. Zak Wilde appeared, wearing a kilt. Together they performed all of their old hits and a few new ones. Zak played the guitar behind his back and with his tongue. Ozzie brought his granddaughter to the stage, and she head-banged along with him. The air was heavy with the smells of marijuana and leather. I was in metal heaven. Even after Lamb of God I felt uplifted and energized while chanting lyrics about death and pointless wars. When Ozzie sang "Mama I'm Coming Home" I cried, and when he sang "Paranoid" I sang along with the other kids who knew the words by heart.

Joints were being passed fast and furiously down the line of seats, and no one was left out. I smoked as much as I could and lay back in my comfortable chair, mellow and lazy. The temperature had dropped 20 degrees, and the cool air ruffled my short hair. I looked around me. Large clumps of grass were flying through the air and landing on people's heads. It looked dangerous to me, but everyone seemed to take it as good fun. The concert ended at about 12:30 a.m., and we strolled out, happy and stoned to the gills, to where Kassie was waiting to take us home.

Feeling Better and Back on Meds

When I got back home from the Ozzfest, my depression began to stabilize. Soon I was acting like an adult again. Strange to think that it took the dark, pounding, growling sounds of heavy metal music to bring me around. I think metal was the sound of my soul. I often long for the smoky concerts in large dark halls, where every part of my body vibrates to deep rhythms and primal screams coming from the bands, where crowds of stoned kids sway and lurch violently in mosh pits, where I don't notice the condescending and disbelieving looks from black-clothed youngsters, and where I am in a place that allows me to lose myself for a few blessed hours. This immersion into my dark side illuminated my shadow and integrated its energy into my being. I suppose this is one way of dealing with a mind that revels in extremes.

I wasn't to get manic again for a long time, and that was because of a medication change. Maybe I never will again. In a way, that would be a blessed relief. I leave you with a poem I wrote about how I feel when manic.

I Hate Being Manic Because:

I hear voices coming from the walls
   that accuse me
   of extremely unacceptable
   and indecent behavior.
Those in power take my children and animals away,
   claiming I am an unfit guardian of the lives of others,
   much less my own.
I get dizzy from watching sidewalks that slip smoothly
   under my feet like strips of film.
The characters on the TV talk back to me.
Patterns on my clothes spin and swirl.
People's faces turn into snarling animal heads.

I run into the same shady stranger no matter where I go,
   and that person has an evil intent.
I spend all my money,
Borrow from others,
And max out my charge cards.
I bounce checks, dozens of them.
Sighing relatives and spouses bail me out
And give me sage advice I don't take.

I eat the same thing every day.
I forget what I once loved.
I look for instruments of torture to use on myself.
I sleep with anyone who offers
And sometimes with more than one person at a time.

Kris Rock

There are ants crawling under my skin.
Random speeding thoughts fuel a rage in me
    like oil wells set on fire.
In another second my head is going to explode
    and flood its venom on everyone around me!
I wish the aliens would take me to another world:
I'm not bipolar; I'm an astral traveler!

Milton Keynes UK
Ingram Content Group UK Ltd.
UKHW051042250324
439991UK00002B/377